Disability, Handicap and Life Chances Series

Challenging Prejudice through Education

The Story of a Mental Handicap Awareness Curriculum Project

John Quicke, Karen Beasley and Caroline Morrison

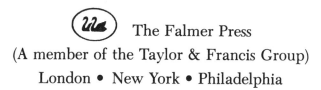 The Falmer Press
(A member of the Taylor & Francis Group)
London • New York • Philadelphia

UK   The Falmer Press, Rankine Road, Basingstoke, RG24 0PR

USA   The Falmer Press, Taylor & Francis Inc., 1900 Frost Road, Suite 101, Bristol, PA 19007

First published 1990

British Library Cataloguing in Publication Data available on request

ISBN 1-85000-692-X
ISBN 1-85000-693-8

Jacket design by Caroline Archer

Typeset in 10½/13 California by
Chapterhouse, The Cloisters, Formby L37 3PX
Printed and bound in Great Britain by
Redwood Press Limited, Melksham, Wiltshire

Challenging Prejudice
through Education

Disability, Handicap and Life Chances

Series Editor: Len Barton

The Politics of Caring
Susan Foster

The Politics of Special Educational Needs
Edited by Len Barton

Disabling Policies? A Comparative Approach to Education Policy and Disability
Gillian Fulcher

Integration: Myth or Reality?
Edited by Len Barton

Disability and Dependency
Edited by Len Barton

Challenging Prejudice through Education. The Story of a Mental Handicap
Awareness Curriculum Project
John Quicke, Karen Beasley and Caroline Morrison

Contents

Acknowledgments   vii

List of Abbreviations   viii

Series Editor's Preface   ix

Introduction   1

Chapter 1   Education, Prejudice and Change   5

Chapter 2   Mental Handicap: A Story of Progress?   21

Chapter 3   The Project: An Introduction   39

Chapter 4   School A: Inter-group Contact in a Changing
             Curriculum   55

Chapter 5   School B: A Child-centred Approach — the 'Ripple
             Effect'   69

Chapter 6   School C: A Module within Humanities   81

Chapter 7   Three Views of the Research Process   89

Chapter 8   Judging Pupils' Progress   105

Chapter 9   Pupils' Cultural Meanings   127

Chapter 10   Teacher Commitment   145

Chapter 11   Summary and Evaluation   161

Chapter 12   A New ERA of Prejudice?   175

References   183

Index   191

Acknowledgments

We should like to offer our thanks to the Mental Health Foundation and MENCAP City Foundation for their generous funding of the project. Thanks are also due to all the teachers who committed themselves to doing a 'good professional job' in difficult circumstances. We would also like to acknowledge the contributions of many individual members of various agencies and the local community and in particular Pauline Hughes who brought joy and hope into the classroom and Roland Sugars and Janet Williams from MENCAP who willingly gave of their time when we required it. The project could not, of course, have taken place without the interest and cooperation of the pupils and for this we thank them. Finally, we are grateful to Sheffield LEA and the Headteachers who welcomed us into their schools.

List of Abbreviations

DES	Department of Education and Science
DOE	Department of Employment
ERA	Education Reform Act
GCSE	General Certificate of Secondary Education
HMI	Her Majesty's Inspectorate
LAPP	Lower Attaining Pupils' Project
LEA	Local Education Authority
MENCAP	Royal Society for Mental Handicapped Children and Adults
MHF	Mental Health Foundation
MSC	Manpower Services Commission
NC	National Curriculum
NCC	National Curriculum Council
PE	Physical Education
PSE	Personal and Social Education
PTA	Parent Teacher Association
SAT	Standard Assessment Task
SCI	Sheffield Curriculum Initiative
SFS	School Focused Secondment
TA	Teacher Assessment
TES	Times Educational Supplement
TGAT	Task Group on Assessment and Testing
TRIST	TVEI-related In-service Training
TVEI	Technical and Vocational Education Initiative

Series Editor's Preface

The analysis offered in this book raises some important questions about the purpose of education, how schools work and how change can be pursued through working, within and upon, existing structures and relationships. Particular consideration is given to the significance of the curriculum, teacher attitudes and teaching styles in relation to how schools can combat prejudice.

Examination of the question of special educational needs is set within the context of education for all. Thus, meeting special needs must be seen as the responsibility of all teachers, and by addressing the issue within an equal opportunities framework, the authors are able to offer a serious challenge to deficit views of 'disabled' people.

In their endeavour to explore the ways in which teachers can be committed to creating an enabling environment, one in which disabling images can be contested, the authors analyse the nature of such crucial issues as equality of respect and collaborative group work. The centrality of whole-school policies as an essential prerequisite for effective change within schools, is also a significant element of the general perspective offered in this book.

The authors are quite open about their commitment to improving pupils' knowledge and understanding of disabled people, so an innovatory feature of the account of their work is the serious consideration they give to the identification and understanding of pupil perspectives. The focus of the analysis includes pupil images of people with 'mental handicaps', the impact of gender on such perspectives and the question of integration. Insights are drawn from an examination of material gained from observations, interviews and questionnaires. A further interesting aspect of the book is the account of the research project undertaken in schools. The authors discuss the nature of the research process, the difficulties and possibilities of this form of investigation and, in particular, the involvement of a small research team. Finally, consideration is given to the question of current changes in legislation and the impact on schools, and how this may possibly affect the opportunities of children with special educational needs. This includes the crucial issue of integration.

In seeking to understand the ways in which disabling images develop and are constantly being reconstituted in the everyday practices of pupils' lives, the book has provided some essential material through which we can begin to identify and explain the complex factors involved. Studies of this nature help to build up our insights into the social construction of disability.

The book is very readable and informative, and provides challenging ideas for reflection, debate and possibilities for further research. It should appeal to students and professionals.

Len Barton
Bristol 1990

Introduction

The argument of this book is based on the assumption that a serious challenge to prejudice in society can be mounted by radically reforming the curricula of schools. Such reform needs to be concerned with all features of shool life — the structure and organization of teaching and learning, the content of the curriculum, the mediating social processes and 'cultural climate' and relations with the community. 'Radical' clearly implies more than just tinkering with the existing set up, but it does not necessarily mean the changes required have to be totally discontinuous with the past. Indeed we would argue the kinds of reform required are derived from a view of education which has always existed as an ideal in our education system. The ideal has been described in various ways but usually it is referred to as liberal progressive education, and it is through this form of education that we feel prejudice can be effectively challenged.

Programmes which attempt to tackle prejudice in schools by reforming curricula face many difficulties. Some of these stem from the material constraints within which schools have to work, others from the conservative ideologies of teachers, administrators and those who run the education system. Others derive from outside schools, in society at large, where various stereotypes are continually being reinforced by the media and the 'common sense' view of communities in which pupils live. Prevailing political and economic conditions also play a part. The prospect of challenging prejudice in schools is therefore daunting. There is no guarantee that the outcome of even the most well thought out and adequately funded programme will be successful. So many things can go wrong since there is so much that is outside the control of programme developers.

The chances of success, however, are improved if the task is approached in a way which takes account of how schools work and how the proposed programme might fit in with the existing curricular and pedagogical arrangements. It is too often the case that anti-prejudice programmes are 'bolted on' and wither almost immediately because they are not rooted in anything the school has done, is currently doing or intends to do. In recent years there has been an increasing focus on 'whole school' approaches to challenging prejudice and it is the principles and practice of this approach which inform our thinking in this book.

The authors have a particular interest in disability and especially mental handicap which they feel has been a neglected area of curriculum development. People with disabilities are oppressed in similar ways to other groups in society like blacks and women, and yet compared to multiculturalism/anti-racism and anti-sexism there has been an absence of programmes dealing with prejudice and discrimination against disability. A policy of 'equal opportunities for all' as the Fish Report (1986) suggests, implies that schools look critically at existing perceptions and interpretations of disability as well as those of race, gender and class.

Teaching about disability and handicap clearly demands as much careful planning as any other sensitive issue and criteria for good and bad practice need to be established. Practice in this area is particularly prone to the 'sentimental' approach, which reinforces pupils' stereotypes rather than weakens them and encourages patronizing attitudes whilst undermining attempts to foster compassion and critical understanding.

This book is based on an account of a curriculum project entitled 'Teaching About Mental Handicap in Secondary Schools' (henceforth referred to as the Project), which aimed to avoid all the pitfalls of a sentimental and 'bolted on' approach. It took place in the comprehensive schools of a northern city between 1985 and 1987. A University-based research team, consisting of the Project Director and one part-time Research Worker in each year of the two-year Project, worked with teachers to develop curricula designed to improve pupils' knowledge and critical understanding of mental handicap. In each school an attempt was made to integrate the project into ongoing curriculum development plans and relate the research to teachers' current professional concerns and personal commitments. In this way it was hoped that the Project would make a lasting impact on the curriculum. In School A a cross curricular module was prepared which involved contact with pupils from a special school, in School B a more child-centred approach was tried and in School C a module was developed within the humanities department.

The first two chapters are introductory and give an overview of the ideas which constitute the background thinking and rationale of the Project. In Chapter 1, we felt it was important to explicate our perspective on the relationship between challenging prejudice and reforming education, prior to discussing 'whole school' approaches to change and the relevance of certain social, cultural and political features of school life. In Chapter 2 the focus is specifically on mental handicap. We locate the Project in a particular tradition of moral argument and historical discourse, explore continuities between past and present and examine attitudes and perspectives in contemporary society, particularly in relation to pupils, teachers and the school context. At the end of this chapter a specific link is made between the Project and integration policies for special needs pupils.

Chapter 3 consists of an introduction to the Project itself and contains a description of the local authority and school context in which it was located together with a brief discussion of the role of the Research Team and some examples of teaching and learning strategies used. Chapters 4, 5 and 6 are case studies which focus mainly on how the Project was taken up in schools. The aim is to provide a straightforward account of 'what happened' in order to give the reader an impression of the particularities of the Project's development in each school. The next chapter is written in the same vein. Each of the university researchers provides a personal account of 'what it was like' to be involved in the Project.

The next three chapters are intended to be more analytical. Chapter 8 contains the results and interpretations of a questionnaire study. It gives a detailed account of pupils' knowledge and understanding of mental handicap and discusses the criteria according to which judgments were made about pupils' progress. Pupils' moral reasoning was highlighted in the introductory chapters as a key concern and in this chapter examples are provided of this reasoning in relation to the issue of integration. The research methods employed here were a mix of quantitative and qualitative approaches, and the data provide evidence on the 'effectiveness' of the Project in one school. Likewise, data produced by the purely qualitative method described in the next chapter, Chapter 9, also contribute towards the overall evaluation of the Project. In this chapter the understandings and interpretations of one particularly interesting class of pupils are explored, with a view to finding out what kind of impact the Project was making on the social world of the pupil. This tied in with a theoretical interest briefly referred to in Chapters 1 and 2 which anticipated that pupils' cultural concerns would be crucial influences on their attitudes to handicap. In the same way, our analysis in the introductory chapters of the nature of teacher interests anticipates the focus in Chapter 10 on teacher commitment. The aim of this chapter is to illuminate the features of teacher motivation which sustained their commitment to the Project, at a time when it clearly didn't have top priority for them.

In Chapter 11 in an attempt to provide a summative evaluation much of the material in the previous chapters is pulled together by commenting on a number of criticisms of the Project. Several important themes are touched upon — teacher 'ownership', the role of inter-group contact and child-centred approaches, the relationship between the Project and the rest of the curriculum, pupils' attitudes, etc. — and brief comparisons are made between the three schools. Finally, in Chapter 12 we look to the future and the changing scene brought about by the Education Reform Act (1988). We discuss the possible impact of the National Curriculum and its associated assessment system on the progressive reform of education and assess whether prejudice is to be further challenged or consolidated by the new system.

Chapter 1

Education, Prejudice and Change

The aim of this chapter is to provide a brief explication of the philosophical and sociological orientation which was a major influence on our thinking about the Project. We clarify the link between challenging prejudice and 'good' education and go on to suggest that the main determinant of prejudice in school contexts is the traditional curriculum, which fails to facilitate the development of moral communities or establish genuinely educational environments. Radical reform of this curriculum is an essential prerequisite for challenging prejudice in schools. The discussion then focuses on a rationale for policies which are most likely to bring about the kind of reform that is required. Lasting reform requires 'whole school' policies and teacher ownership of change. We argue that these ideas have to be grounded in an understanding of the micro-politics of the school and the nature of teacher and pupil commitment.

Education and Prejudice

From the outset, our intervention was guided by certain principles about how prejudice should be challenged in schools. Programmes which sought to reduce prejudice (and it matters little what the 'object' of the prejudice is: people with disabilities, black people, a minority religious group, etc.) should be compatible with what is generally regarded as 'good education'. Thus the aim of such programmes should be to encourage children 'to give reasons in support of a point of view, show respect for evidence, be open minded, act with empathy and humanitarianism and explore fundamental questions relating to social justice, equality and the exercise of power' (see Carrington and Short, 1989, p. 230).

Education has clearly inherent within it an antagonism to pre-judgment. In an area where prejudice exists, an approach which defines the world from an educational perspective would inevitably highlight the necessity of challenging this prejudice as an anti-educational form of thought. Fundamentally the approach required is one that appeals to pupils' judgments, and progress should be assessed by examining the quality of these judgments.

The role of the teacher is to prepare pupils to become moral agents who make judgments based on ethically informed rational argument. The process will inevitably involve critical reflection upon concepts and experiences and the most appropriate teaching strategy would appear to be one which eschewed didacticism and encouraged pupils to think through issues for themselves. We agree with Lynch (1987) that 'forced value injection is doomed to failure'. An interactive style is required which values the experiences of pupils and establishes the conditions whereby pupils feel confident enough to discuss these experiences in the classroom. Much development work on strategies has been concerned with racial prejudice but many of these teaching approaches are equally applicable to the exploration of prejudice against people with mental handicaps. Page and Thomas (1984) demonstrate and discuss various experimental gaming approaches and Twitchen and Demuth (1985) outline attempts to explore pupils' and teachers' feelings about institutional racism. Klein (1982) and Quicke (1985) have discussed the advantages of approaching the topic through fiction.

In methods making extensive use of discussion there is a constant need for good 'value dilemma' material (see Jeffcoate, 1979; Rudduck, 1979). One fruitful way of generating this is for pupils to become involved in social and community action projects, like the Project described in this book, which not only function as a proving ground for discourse skills (see Newman and Rutter, 1983) but are also likely to provide experience of a whole range of 'new' moral conflicts. However, we cannot assume that awareness of value dilemmas will necessarily emerge as a result of such experience. In order to structure critical reflection, it may be necessary to develop strategies of pre-preparation of the kind described by Stephan (1985) and Cohen (1980) and to establish guidelines for principle testing outlined by Kehoe (1984).

Most experiential and 'active learning' techniques — drama, role play, group discussion, etc. — are eminently suitable for these purposes. Usually, it is necessary to establish some basic rules of the game, such as that no one is allowed to express views which are intimidatory or offensive and that the process has to be democratic and rational involving turn-taking, giving a person a chance to speak, honesty and due consideration of evidence. A rule of thumb is that persons are allowed to express views freely provided that this does not prevent other persons from so doing; or, what amounts to the same thing, that this does not stifle others' willingness to communicate their experiences. However, in teaching and learning approaches of this kind there are bound to be views expressed which are unpalatable to some people.

Such teaching strategies will be familiar enough to those teachers who aim to adopt a child-centred approach to their teaching, and who oppose illiberal and authoritarian attempts to coerce children into a 'correct' consciousness. They would be morally opposed to practices which merely substituted new prejudices for old. They would believe that in an educational context — if not in certain other extreme contexts involving matters of life and death — the ends do not justify the means, and if the goal is that pupils should learn to respect the rights of others, then they themselves should be treated with respect. Treating pupils with respect means more than refraining from making sarcastic remarks or 'belittling children who cannot retort in kind' (see Entwistle, 1970, p. 206) or attributing failure to the pupils' stupidity and lack of intelligence. Crucially it means being optimistic, almost incurably so, about pupils' potentialities to achieve moral autonomy, and to participate fully in educational communities.

But this is not to say, of course, that the teacher can assume that pupils will be 'naturally' aware of the parameters of the debate within an area of concern. They may have some knowledge of these, often more than the teacher expects (particularly a teacher working with a deficit model of her charges), but it is unlikely that all pupils will be familiar with all the issues involved and without such knowledge, pupils' rational argument and moral decision-making will not be sufficiently informed. They have to be familiarized with the 'story' of the tradition of debate so that they can engage in the arguments about the best way forward for that tradition and 'grasp those future possibilities which the past has made available to the present' (MacIntyre, 1981). Inevitably, a certain amount of induction is required so that pupils can become acquainted not only with the 'facts' but also with the moral dilemmas and social and political issues which drive the narrative of that tradition.

It may be thought that such an inductive process contradicts the child-centred approach advocated earlier — a point worth mentioning because according to certain definitions of the latter any form of learning which is not child-initiated is not real learning; a pupil has the 'right to design and engineer his own education' (see Entwistle, 1970, p. 266). But in our opinion it is a point which is self-evidently false. Understanding a tradition of debate is similar to joining a moral community. If pupils, or adults for that matter, are to participate in moral communities they must

7

acquire some knowledge of the values, rules and practices of those communities, even if they eventually decide that they would like to ignore or change them. For some children, those who have reached a stage where they could be said to be autonomous learners, this induction process is self-conducted; that is, they themselves decide when, where and how they will be introduced or introduce themselves to the historically determined issues in the area of concern. However, it is clear that many children and even many adults would not see the necessity of going through this procedure in a systematic way. The tendency is for most people to rely on their own experience of human relationships as a basis for their arguments and expressions of viewpoint and indeed up to a point this is what one would expect of learners who were striving to be morally autonomous. But the exploration of moral issues goes beyond personal experience and requires consideration of the legacy of human experience to date.

In this situation the teacher's responsibility is to make sure that the historical 'facts' and issues are given a full airing. According to MacIntyre (1981) one would expect moral issues to abound if the tradition was still 'alive' as an 'historically extended, socially embodied argument'. The hope is that pupils thinking critically within the discourse of the tradition will be able to 'transcend through criticism and invention the limitations of what had hitherto been reasoned in that tradition' (p. 222). In so doing they would be active participants in an ongoing debate rather than passive recipients of a dead tradition. Thus for us 'active learning' means moral reasoning within an historically defined practice. The teaching methods employed would be characterized by a focus on rational discussion of issues and permeated by a democratic ethos where all participants were encouraged to contribute in an historically determined moral setting.

It is in the light of these considerations that we felt that challenging prejudice should involve a teaching component rather than merely relying on what can be 'caught' informally in day to day relationships in school. Thus the title of our Project — 'Teaching About Mental Handicap in Secondary Schools' — is intended to draw attention to the aim of encouraging teachers to incorporate a planned element on this topic in their curricula (see Chapter 3). However, we were aware that it was insufficient just to focus on the formal curriculum content and on interactions in formal teaching contexts. There is plenty of evidence (see Lynch, 1987) to suggest that successful strategies have to involve changes in the overall social climate of the institution concerned and have to be part of 'whole school' policies for combating prejudice (Banks, 1985). Respect for pupils' views and appeals to their judgments must imbue all interactions both formal and informal and be reflected in the process, structure and organization of the school. If this does not happen then, as one of us has pointed out elsewhere (Quicke, 1987), teaching about mental handicap may contain elements which, to say the least, will seem paradoxical to pupils. On the one hand the teacher might be encouraging critical engagement with ideas and practices revolving around issues to do with prejudice, discrimination and respect for persons, whilst on the other the very same teachers might be identified with a school system which fosters teaching styles and structures disrespectful of pupils. A classic example would be a situation where teachers discussed the labelling process in relation to mental handicap, without recognizing that pupils, particularly in a streamed school, might themselves be feeling the effects of this process and be disadvantaged by it.

Thus an important aspect of the teaching approach will be the ongoing critical examination of the hidden curriculum, described by Hargreaves (1982) as exerting 'on many pupils . . . a destruction of dignity which is so massive and pervasive that few subsequently recover from it' (p. 17). Innovations that fail to make an impact on these deep-rooted features of school life are usually difficult to sustain, particularly if these features are constantly working against the very values, like respect for persons, which the innovation is seeking to establish and which underpin its rationale.

The alienation of pupils resulting from such contradictory practices is an aspect of a general feeling of malaise experienced by both pupils and teachers. It stems from the basic lack of proper concern, the lack of trust and mutual caring which seems endemic to much of our institutional life. Without an improvement in the quality of relationships in school settings, it is difficult to see how the kind of intimacy required for the development of pupils' moral sensitivities can ever be established as a regular, taken-for-granted form of pupil–pupil and teacher–pupil contact. Moral education, according to Kleinig (1982) is only partly achievable through teaching even though, as we argue above, a formal component is necessary. It is 'a matter of becoming a certain kind of person . . . of coming to care in certain kinds of ways' and developing a sensitivity which only arises 'through immersion in and reflection upon relationships of an intimate kind' (p. 253) not typically found in schools, where people tend to relate through roles rather than personal relationships.

Moral sensitivity is a slippery concept but we use it to refer to the often poorly articulated and inadequately expressed concern for others which we see even in young children. Without such 'social feeling', children would grow up with no motivation to engage in moral reasoning. This basic feeling or sense is logically prior to rational decision-making and provides the moral setting for the teaching activities discussed above. It is capable of being refined by what Kleinig (*op. cit.*) refers to as education in the virtues which are the familiar ones of 'love, honesty, fidelity, kindness, justice, sympathy, respect for others, humility, self-control, courage' which 'in various ways mark out disposition of character — ways of caring' (p. 250). Schools have difficulty in fostering the virtues because relationships between teachers and pupils are often not pitched at a sufficiently intimate level of mutual care and understanding.

It is the 'traditional curriculum' defined broadly to include both the formal and informal or 'hidden' curriculum which has been responsible for the souring of human relationships in schools. At the formal level the main problem is that school knowledge is still, after decades of 'reform' (see Hargreaves, 1989) hierarchically organized and located in cultural forms which make high status knowledge inaccessible to the majority of pupils, particularly those from working-class backgrounds, whose opportunities are even further restricted if they are female, black or 'handicapped'. Whatever the 'good' intentions of such a curriculum it inevitably produces a divided school and thus creates a breeding ground for prejudice.

It is not the form of intellectual activity which is alienating for many pupils, but the content and the mediating social processes. Subject teachers' preoccupation with the internal coherence and 'dignity' of their subjects leads to a blinkered view of the relationship between their knowledge and the 'outside world', resulting in largely irrelevant subject matter being foisted on pupils whose social and cultural backgrounds do not enable them to communicate on the same wavelength as their teachers.

Moreover, this subject-based, hierarchically structured formal curriculum has to be delivered in schools which are under-resourced, and poorly designed and organized. This combination of factors creates a teaching/learning environment where the only teaching methods that 'work' tend to be the most didactic and least respectful of pupils, where knowledge is packaged in a way which is indigestible for most pupils, and where the most efficient assessment methods are group-administered and norm-referenced. The whole edifice is buttressed by a legitimating ideology which attributes the causes of 'failure' to the pupils' intellectual weaknesses and deficiencies in their social backgrounds. Rather than a moral or educational community the features briefly outlined here produce a social environment which fosters competitive individualism and alienation.

Change

It is clearly essential for the traditional curriculum to be radically reformed if 'education for all' is to be achieved, and an innovation which seriously aimed to challenge prejudice would have to be an integral part of this wider process of reform rather than a separate intervention. In their exhaustive overview of the literature, Balch and Paulsen (1979) conclude that it is unlikely that short-term interventions based on a single strategy will be as successful as those which are more long-term and integrated into the continuous process of the school. A similar point is made by Stenhouse, Verma and Wild (1982) who conclude that for changes to be permanent they have to be contextualized in the broader policies of the school and the community. These authors are concerned mainly with racial prejudice, but the principles can clearly be applied to strategies for reducing any form of prejudice.

In short, policies should aim to be 'whole school'. While initially the focus of reform may be in a particular area, changes have to occur on a much broader front if the policy concerned is to take root and permanently alter the social/educational environment. Banks (1981) divides the school into eleven areas in all of which at some stage reforms need to take place. These are the culture of the school and the hidden curriculum, as well as more formal aspects like assessment strategies, teaching and learning styles, instructional materials and teaching content. Most writers in this field make similar points. Above all, it is felt that an appropriate school climate is a crucial factor. This is difficult to define precisely but it involves an ethos where open and caring human relationships flourish and where the norms, expectations and routine practices of the school create a framework which has an in-built intolerance of prejudice.

This harmonious environment is one which is worth striving for, but not at the cost of reducing teachers and pupils to passive conformity. We eschewed what Holt (1987) describes as the 'technocratic' view of change; that is, a view that change results from the application of 'scientific' principles and procedures by experts and managers. Changing the curriculum is not a procedural matter but one which involves practical judgment and thus moral questions will always be at the heart of the change process. Such questions cannot be decided beforehand in relation to any particular set of circumstances. This is not to say that an innovation should not have 'aims' but these must perforce be only general guidelines. In the classroom not only do new goals emerge but on-the-spot decisions have to be made about existing goals which may be in conflict with each other. Intentions are subject to moment-to-moment changes and issues arise which are essentially unpredictable. Practical decisions have to be based on intimate knowledge of the setting, an understanding of its complexities and an awareness that there is usually no simple conflict-free solution.

It is for these reasons that teachers have to feel they 'own' an innovation. They have to perceive themselves and be perceived as moral agents whose judgments will be respected. The alternative — teachers' activities determined by procedures and teacher-proof packages — is not viable because we cannot see how such a model could produce the autonomy required for the development of judgment. This is not a recipe for teachers 'doing their own thing.' We would expect their deliberations to take into account the reflections and perspectives of others in the school, the local community and nationally, and we would anticipate that this would take them beyond self study to the framing of policies requiring reflection not just on 'ways and means' but upon education as a whole (see Schwab, 1978).

We were also critical of the sociological counterpart of the technocratic view of teaching and change — the systems model, allegedly derived from the findings of organizational science. This model often appeals to advocates of 'whole school' policies because it is founded on a view of schools as 'whole systems' with separate sectors which are functionally interrelated. It also appeals to those who want to change schools by manipulation from above because it enables them to present many aspects of their policies as neutral, value-free and thus uncontroversial, since they are said to be derived from a rational 'scientific' view of how schools operate as systems.

Although in practice the systems approach is often only one of a pot-pourri of approaches which busy managers of change will employ, analyses of curriculum innovation in the recent past (see Holt, 1987) suggest that, even in a watered down form, it is still a very dominant and powerful influence on policy conception and implementation. Essentially the approach is positivist. It treats the school as an organic whole with sub-systems which have to be integrated and rationalized if the system is to survive, and change is largely expected to take place in ways which ensure the survival of the school as an entity. There is a tendency for participants or members of the system to be conceived as blank sheets to be 'filled' in functionally appropriate ways, as 'programmed role players' or as 'personalities' imported into but not created by the system.

Moreover the model de-emphasizes the role of conflict and thus according to Ball (1987) fails to recognize the importance and significance of the micro-politics of school life. The stress on functional unity leads to a misrecognition of the unique aspects of schools as organizations. The system of control in schools, for example, is described only in the abstract by a systems analysis, which examines (and also prescribes) the formal role and function of participants, the boundaries of staff responsibilities, the structure of decision-making, etc. But what form of control is actually accomplished will depend on the outcome of a multiplicity of interactions between very different and often competing interest groups in the school, each with its own aspirations and perspectives.

Teacher Interests

However, whilst recognizing that conflict is endemic to school life, it seems to us to vitally important to distinguish between types of conflict. We see qualitatively different conflicts arising from different teacher interests. Sociological researchers recognize several kinds of interests, but for our purposes the crucial distinction is between what Ball (1987) describes as ideological interests on the one hand and material/vested interests on the other. This is similar to the distinction made between 'paradigmatic' and 'pragmatic' concerns (see Hammersley, 1977). 'Ideological' in this context refers to the 'educational perspectives and commitments of teachers; views about classroom practice, teacher–pupil relationships and pupils' learning which often rest upon more fundamental beliefs and ideas about social justice and human rights and the purposes of education in society' (see Ball, *op. cit.*, p. 281). Material and vested interests refer to concerns 'about working conditions: rewards from work, career and promotion...' (*op. cit.*, p. 17). A third category, self-interest referring to 'the sense of self or identity claimed or aspired to by the teacher, the sort of teacher a person believes themselves to be or wants to be' (*op. cit.*, p. 17) seems to us to derive from teachers' basic values and therefore to collapse into the ideological.

Conflicts which are a reflection of different ideological interests are the very stuff of genuine educational debate. Education is a 'practice'; that is, 'an action directed towards the achievement of some end, [an end which] is not to produce an object or artefact but to realize some morally worthwhile "good"... practice is what we would call informed or morally committed action' (Carr, 1987). In any concrete setting it will not always be obvious what actions are required to realize such 'goods' or indeed which 'goods' should have priority given they usually cannot all be realized at once. Inevitably, the choices which have to be made involve teachers coming to terms with moral conflicts and dilemmas, and making judgments which sometimes appear diametrically opposed to those of their colleagues. This form of conflict may lead to intense discussion, even heated argument, but it is 'healthy' in that it is a celebration and perpetuation of education as a practice rather than a technical activity, and thus is a form of conflict which is and, one would argue, should continue to be endemic to school life.

Unfortunately, conflicts in school do not only stem from different ideological interests but also from vested interests and more often than not the two are conjoined. Thus meetings called by the head to discuss, say, a new 'whole school' assessment policy become a site for yet another power struggle between the English and Maths departments. Arguments may be couched in educational terms but the hidden agenda relates to vested interests.

Are vested interests avoidable? For MacIntyre (1981) institutions inevitably have a potential 'corrupting' power because they are concerned with 'structuring in terms of power and status and the distribution of money, power and status' (p. 194). They have to do this otherwise they could not sustain themselves in a society like ours, where resources are scarce and all claims for a larger share of the cake seem to be equally reasonable. Nevertheless, though perhaps an inevitable part of social life, these material concerns or vested interests are from the individual's point of view inward-looking, concerned primarily with the welfare of the self as the main goal, and are thus basically 'selfish'; and when they are the prime motivation in institutional settings can be corrupting of the practices of those institutions.

The most important question from our point of view is what in any particular circumstance is the relationship between ideological interests and vested interests. Do the latter completely take over and subsume the former in this instance or do the ideological concerns hold their own in the motivational dynamic? Our understanding of this was crucial, because as we indicate later one of our main criteria for continued involvement with the Project and for evaluating the whole process was the degree to which we felt the teachers' commitment was genuine.

Although our strategy relied on alliances with progressive forces and although we were at one with these forces at the level of rhetoric, and thus took up a definite position in the ideological debate, we were constantly aware that self-styled progressives and self-confessed 'reactionaries' were not always what they seemed. A teacher may seem enthusiastic about reform and may be able to articulate progressive arguments but may be primarily motivated not by ideology or even a mix of interests but by vested interests alone. Likewise, a teacher who claims to be purely concerned with 'self' and is not willing to support proposed reforms may be fundamentally a values-driven person and committed to genuine educational reform. In the current circumstances, he or she may not trust the motivation of reformists and may judge that action taken in the name of reform is likely to be counterproductive. The concern with 'self' comes about because the teacher does not wish to 'sacrifice' his or her own peace of mind and maybe even his or her status and working conditions for an energy-sapping attempt at reform which, at best, is likely to be only partially successful. Clearly, there are also teachers who use just such an argument as an excuse for taking no action at all and in doing so are *primarily* thinking in terms of their material interests. Superficially the perspectives are similar, but they are qualitatively different.

Throughout the Project the basic distinction to which we held fast was between, to put it bluntly, teachers who genuinely cared and those who didn't. By care we meant concern with establishing positive human relationships and 'good' educational environments, not because it happened to fit with their vested interests but because that for them was the 'way of virtue', to use Kleinig's phrase. Thus in Chapter 10 we attempt to explicate the nature of teacher commitment, since it is vitally important for the achievement of long-term, radical reform that such commitment is sustained.

We felt that what teachers had in common in the form of commitment was more significant than the differences between them derived from subject sub-cultures, the pastoral/academic split, age, gender and other identities. At the same time, we were aware that groupings based on these identities might relate to ideological positions as well as material concerns. Thus, it could well be that the young teachers we encountered were typical of the 'novitiates' described by Riseborough (1986) and Poppleton (1988) as tending to display 'a resilient identity built on their recent history of educational success, moral investment and voluntaristic position regarding change'. Such teachers might have been more likely to participate in innovations for ideological reasons than the 'veterans' who were more pessimistic and cynical in their outlook. Likewise it was possible that female teachers might have been more receptive and supportive of the changes we were proposing than male teachers; some subject sub-cultures keener on collaborative work than others, and pastoral and special needs teachers more supportive than subject teachers.

In the final analysis, we felt that commitment derived from basic features of teachers' 'personalities' and would be sustained if those participating in the innovation felt as if they 'owned' it. Such feelings of 'ownership' come about when teachers have a say in decision-making, are involved in negotiations about how the project will be interpreted and taken up in their schools, and recognize that these discussions are genuinely about educational issues and not a vehicle for the advancement of vested interests. From the point of view of the person or persons introducing the innovation (in this instance the Research Team) the key word is negotiation. If such negotiation is genuine, then participants feel they can expose their own ignorance and recognize that others may have more knowledge about the topic than they do without surrendering ownership to the 'experts'.

Pupil Interests

Earlier we referred to the lack of mutual respect and trust which characterized relationships not only between teachers and pupils but also between teachers and teachers and between pupils and pupils. Pupils react to this in various ways and their perspectives, cultures and strategies are part of the social context which has to be considered when introducing, monitoring and evaluating an innovatory project.

We can begin by dividing pupils' reactions into two broad categories in a similar way to our analysis of teacher interests. First, pupils' behaviour may be motivated by ideological concerns. For instance, some pupils act as moral critics of the traditional curriculum and derive their criticisms from values such as equality, justice and respect for persons. These criticisms can be voiced by any pupil whatever his or her school constructed identity in terms of ability and/or behaviour. They are deploying 'respect for persons' when they object to teachers not being 'human'. Specifically, such teachers are felt to lack an understanding of a young person's perspective (see Marsh, Rosser and Harré, 1978), which is a serious fault because not only does it lead to insensitive behaviour towards pupils but it also does not encourage pupils to respect their teachers. If teachers act as if they were never young themselves, then they appear to have no sense of their own history and therefore no self love. According to Fromm (1949) self love is the basis of love for others and the opposite of selfishness and self interest.

Such teachers are often seen as inconsistent, irrational, superior in their attitudes, too formal, inflexible in their demands for obedience to rules. They are given to making sarcastic remarks, putting pupils down, and picking on pupils. By contrast the human teacher is one who will 'have a laugh' with pupils but is firm and fair when it comes to disciplining them and making them work. In short, pupils evaluate teachers in terms of the quality of relationships they establish with pupils. Even pupils who are 'deviant' use similar moral criteria to assess a teacher's worth (see Tattum, 1982).

Second, pupils whatever their moral criticisms of schooling might also act in ways which are strategic. They will manipulate the social environment in a way which maximizes benefits for themselves — in other words rather than a universalistic concern with values or virtues, they are primarily motivated in this instance strictly by 'looking after number one'. As with teachers, it matters a great deal if strategic action is carried out against a background of pupil as moral critic or pupil as amoral or immoral, but the behaviour nevertheless has similar features at a superficial level for all pupils who indulge in it.

In the present study it is particularly important that the two main perspectives — the pupil as moral critic and the pupil as strategic actor — are analyzed in relation to each other. To examine one without the other tells us nothing about the dynamics of pupil motivation. Thus, some pupils resist school because they see it as basically unfair. They rebel or 'get by' because they do not want to be associated with and thus help legitimate the prevailing ideology of the formal and hidden curriculum. Other pupils resist teacher authority purely because it interferes with their own material interests and immediate wants and they may have little or no interest in the fairness or otherwise of 'school'. For others no one interest or group of interests is clearly dominant — their orientation will vary from time to time and even from place to place in the same school and may change several times during their careers.

Of course, pupils may also resist progressive reforms for a variety of reasons and many of the divisions which create competing, non-communicating groups of pupils are supported and reinforced by the pupils themselves. We should remember that the traditional curriculum is constituted by a variety of interactions and attitudes in school including those amongst pupils as well as amongst teachers. Pupils are divided along age, ability, grade, race and class lines and any innovation which seeks to create a more integrated social and cultural setting may come up against pupil as well as teacher resistance. Such an innovation may be resisted by a pro-school group because it threatens their hard won status. On the other hand it also may be resisted by those on a 'lower rung of the ladder' because of their blanket opposition to anything that the teachers want them to do. Or they may accept their 'lot in life' as defined by the traditional system, and internalize the definition of themselves imposed upon them by the school.

External Factors

Another significant feature of the context of our intervention were the external factors and social and political forces in the environment outside the school. As we shall explicate more fully in a later chapter we ourselves were construed as an influence from 'outside'. But at this point we merely want to indicate our awareness of several possible factors. Schools do not exist in splended isolation. It is widely acknowledged that the autonomy often claimed for schools and the teachers within them is only relative; that is to say, their freedom is limited by the pressures exerted upon them by outside forces and the constraints of the environment in which they are located. There are broad parameters within which all schools have to work and in recent years, as Dale (1979) points out, the national state seems to want to shift from a situation of 'licenced autonomy' to one of 'regulated autonomy', the latter implying more control over the curriculum and teachers' working conditions, whilst at the same time paying lip service to the importance of teachers' professional judgments and 'ownership' of change. This development reached its pinnacle with the passing of the Education Reform Act (ERA) in 1988.

In addition to the national state, there are two other factors of importance in this context, parents and Local Education Authorities (LEAs). Parents are and always have been potentially an influential force, but one that has been difficult to activate in any unified way because of the practical difficulties of securing their involvement *en masse*. Occasionally, particularly in largely middle-class catchment areas, parents can act as an effective pressure group. Hatton (1989) describes how a steering group of active high-status parents exerted considerable influence on the way their local school was run, even managing successfully to oppose innovations with which they disagreed. The increase in parental choice allegedly facilitated under ERA may enable a wider range of parents to exert their power as consumers.

This factor was salient from our point of view because we intended the Project to be one that involved the 'community'. It derived from the principle of respect for pupils' backgrounds and previous experiences, and from the idea that a genuinely open school would welcome the involvement of non-teacher adults as well as parents from the community in a project of this nature. We supported the notion of a school that actively engaged with its community and opened itself up to influences from that community, even if this meant introducing further pressures on staff.

We were particularly encouraged by the fact that our Project seemed to fit philosophically with the kinds of initiatives currently supported by the LEA. We shall have more to say about this later (see Chapter 3) but for now we merely want to note that these initiatives are part of a trend in recent years for LEAs to become more interventionist. The framework set up in the mid 1980s (see Bennett, 1984) gave LEAs the role of constructing guidelines for governing bodies for overall curriculum aims within frameworks set by national state policies.

However, there is something of a paradox here. On the one hand LEAs have been encouraged to take initiatives which have aimed to help teachers experiment with new ways of working, but on the other they have been implicated in policies involving more control of teachers' work and reduced funding. The situation in the area where we were working was turbulent, to say the least, with innovations being introduced at a rapid pace, so that teachers were experiencing 'overload' or intensification (see Apple, 1983). As the workload increases teachers find they are doing more administrative work, are attending more meetings, and working longer hours, but still have the same amount of contact time with pupils. However, teaching pupils seems to be relegated to a lower position in terms of everyone's priorities — a fact which many teachers bitterly complain about.

Of course, not all these forces are acting in unison. In some authorities the LEA is constantly attempting to redefine and reinterpret national policy in a way which suits them (see Chapter 3) and schools are doing the same. This brings us back to the micro-politics of the school. New initiatives involve more resources and the changes they aim for may require a school to rethink its priorities, its curriculum and internal organization. Inevitably, all this will be a new area for struggle for the various interest groups in the school, who will want to make sure they don't lose out. Individual teachers may find that being involved with an initiative gives their career a permanent boost by, for instance, creating new types of posts which they are in good position to fill. Others may find their days of glory are temporary, as the 'old guard' takes over the initiative when the dust has settled and manages to reinterpret it according to its own interests. Thus an initiative will be mediated via the internal micro-political processes and in fact may become a constituent part of these processes, perhaps being nullified by existing structures but potentially capable of restructuring the political relations of the school.

Concluding Comment

In the second half of this chapter we have attempted to provide an overview of the features of school life which have to be taken into account if the Project is to succeed in making an impact on the school curriculum and if the nature of that impact is to be fully understood. In particular, we have focused on teacher and pupil interests and have tried to tease out two strands which seem to us to be of vital importance — these are the ideological or moral aspect on the one hand and the strategic or vested interest aspect on the other. In relation to individuals, of course, such descriptors do not give a complete picture of teacher or pupil psychology, but they do provide a framework for analyzing patterns of motivation and commitment in the social and cultural setting of the school. They thus enable us to clarify criteria against which to judge pupils' progress (Chapters 8 and 9) and evaluate teacher commitment (Chapter 10).

Chapter 2

Mental Handicap: A Story of Progress?

Although we perceived the Project as part of a wider reform of schools our specific concern was with challenging prejudice against people with mental handicap and we were determined that this should not be lost sight of. As stated in the introduction, strategies for dealing with such prejudice have not been given the same amount of consideration as multicultural/anti-racist and anti-sexist programmes, and there has been a great deal less debate about the issue generally. There may be several reasons for this but no doubt the lowly status of people with mental handicaps in our society is a major contributory factor.

In this chapter we want to explore the tradition of debate concerning society's treatment of such people and to examine the moral and cultural underpinnings of our present day attitudes with particular reference to the school context. The aim is to provide a thorough contextualization of the Project by introducing the reader to our interpretation of the historical discourse on mental handicap, a discourse which will be illuminated by examining the continuities between attitudes and policies of the mid and late nineteenth century and those of more recent times. Just as in the previous era a period of reform was followed by one of regression, so a similar pattern seems to be occurring in the second half of the twentieth century. Of course, the story is not finished yet and we shall have further comments to make on it in the final chapter.

The Tradition: Humanitarianism and Social Interests

The tradition of moral argument in which we are interested is 'humanitarianism' which as a coherent influence on social policy can be traced back to the reform movements of the nineteenth century. The humanitarian tradition can be contrasted with that with which it was in contention; namely, the tradition dominant in the seventeenth and eighteenth centuries that people called idiots were incapable of morality and functioned at the level of animals, and could therefore with some justification be treated in the same way as, at that time, people treated animals, i.e. with a heavy emphasis on fear and coercion. For the reformers these 'beings' were not beasts but essentially human, even if they lacked certain qualities. Inspired by the work of Itard and Seguin, the first asylums were based on an educational philosophy which assumed the moral nature of idiots, and used treatment methods where the emphasis was on patience and firmness rather than force. The concern was for moral treatment; it was a question of harnessing the will of the patient and inducing him or her 'to regulate his or her behaviour more harmoniously' (*op. cit.*, p. 95). For Seguin, 'The will of the teacher is important to commanding the weaker will of the child.' These asylums gave idiots an experience of social life of which they were deprived when locked away at home by their parents.

The debate within the humanitarian tradition has been focused not on the appropriateness of regarding idiots as human, but rather on just *how* like us, the rest of humanity, they are. More recently, as we shall see, the debate has taken a different form, but the basic questions remain. Social policy was influenced by the answers to these questions. The more interpretations favoured the 'common humanity' idea that the more idiots and other 'deviants' like lunatics were thought to be reformable or, in present day terms, educable.

However, there is another side to the story which cannot be ignored. Moral discourse has never existed in a social vacuum and the moral force of an argument is usually only one determinant of social policy. All kinds of other factors help to determine policy creation and policy outcomes, and not least of these are the various social, economic and political interests which influence the course of events through a variety of channels, e.g. public figures, the media, pressure groups. According to Tomlinson (1982) in her analysis of the growth of special education, such interest groups attempt to structure debates in ways which are helpful to themselves. A contemporary example would be 'the way special school teachers would like to structure the debate in terms of the difficulties inherent in the integration of handicapped children into ordinary school life if this would eventually lose them clients' (p. 58). The subsequent fate of reforms in the late nineteenth century cannot be understood without recognizing this dimension.

By the late nineteenth century it is evident that reform had failed.

Many idiots were still found in workhouses and lunatic asylums, despite the fact that it was acknowledged that the workhouse was not the place for the non-able-bodied who were incapable of managing their own affairs. Even more than the eighteenth century the nineteenth century saw strains put on families by the industrial reorganization of work and also witnessed the move towards large scale public provision to cater for the old, sick, insane, criminal and young who could no longer be handled in families. The specialist asylums for idiots were built to relieve the workhouse of an element which disrupted the process of disciplining the able-bodied work force. Attitudes to mental handicap were derived from views about how to deal with the 'dangerous classes', the submerged 10 per cent. According to Ryan and Thomas (1980) the Victorian bourgeoisie viewed the asylum and all large public institutions as 'prototypes of a new social order'; healthy, rational and disciplined unlike the 'wretched conditions of working class life'.

In 1886 the Idiots Act separated idiots and imbeciles from lunatics, but whilst most idiots were clearly not recognized as able to fend for themselves the emphasis in the specialist asylums was still on the work ethic and cheap provision, particularly for the 'higher grade' idiot who was considered to be capable of benefiting from instruction. The regime in these asylums was repressive. This was partly due to their size — all were grossly overcrowded — and partly due to the late nineteenth-century interpretation of moral treatment as rigid discipline. However, the institutional solution served its purpose. It kept the idiots off the streets, out of the workhouse, out of sight and out of mind and the poor were glad to rid themselves of an intolerable burden.

Of course once asylums became established they created an increased demand for their own services. People recognized that troublesome relatives could be locked away and taken off their hands. The medical profession was on hand to provide 'expert' opinion and enhance its reputation by claiming knowledge and responsibility for the care and control of the mentally defective in a similar manner to the way it had operated in the field of lunacy (see Scull, 1979). As industrialization got under way and factories had to become even more efficient and productive it was more and more difficult to integrate even the 'high grade' idiot into the work situation. The factory owner had no financial interest in training idiots and the speed of production meant that relatives working nearby could be of no assistance. All the family had to work so the older child could not be left at home to look after the sibling with a mental handicap.

With the introduction of compulsory schooling came a widened definition of 'idiocy'. The passing of Forster's Education Act, 1870, and later Acts which made education compulsory meant that a variety of needs which previously had remained hidden became increasingly visible. Sutherland (1981) comments on the fact that the London School Board Committee in 1889 estimated that one child in eight was underfed and suffering from malnutrition, diseases and various disabilities. It was soon recognized that many of these children were not benefiting from normal schooling or, at least, from schooling under the constraints of the Revised Code. Such children were identified not as idiots or imbeciles but as 'feebleminded' — a much larger category. Intervention was required in order to ensure the smooth running of the system. As Tomlinson (1982) acknowledges there was also an economic motive involved in that it was thought that if such children remained uneducated they would swell the ranks of the poor. The Egerton Commission (1889) recommended that 'feebleminded' children should be given separate instruction and that 'imbeciles' should be given residential training. There were fears that there were more 'feebleminded' than had been supposed and medical 'experts' claimed to have discovered a large layer of them amongst the dangerous classes.

The 'feebleminded' were a particularly worrying group because it was thought by some that if they were allowed to breed it would result in an increase in degeneracy. Such attitudes were reinforced and given scientific status by the growing acceptance of Social Darwinism. As these ideas began to become more popular, idiots were increasingly dehumanized. The blame for this widespread social evil was placed squarely on the shoulders of the parents who were themselves degenerate and passed this on through inheritance to their offspring. According to degeneracy theory, the hereditary trait of degeneracy was polymorphous, i.e. the degenerate tendency expressed itself in different ways. Thus alcoholism and idiocy were both expressions of the same tendency. Moreover, traits that were acquired through 'the sins of the father' could be transmitted to the offspring. When this was coupled with Social Darwinism, it lead to the view that people with mental handicaps were not so much unfortunate victims as members of an inferior breed who should be allowed to die out.

These ideas were influential in the eugenics movement which became established in the late nineteenth century and was a dominant force until the 1930s. Various pressure groups supported by this movement came to the fore to argue for policies requiring the life time segregation of defectives. In 1896, for example, the National Association for the Care and Control of the Feebleminded was established. This powerful pressure group pushed for segregation and the prevention of sexuality and reproduction. All this must also be seen in the context of growing fears about the deterioration of the 'race'. Widespread physical disability amongst the working class had been revealed by medical surveys of soldiers recruited for the Boer War. The decline in the quality of the racial stock was thought to have resulted from the high birth rate of the disreputable, degenerate classes relative to that of the respectable working class and the middle and upper classes.

These views were widespread and held by people of a variety of different political persuasions. Thus eugenics' solutions were advocated by Fabian as well as Conservative politicians, although it should be pointed out that the former tended to favour positive eugenics (e.g. encouraging respectable working-class people to have larger families) and later became more concerned with environmental explanations for poverty. It is difficult to determine whether or not these views penetrated into the consciousness of the majority of ordinary men and women. Certainly at that time racial stereotypes were popular.Idiots were sometimes seen as they had been in a previous era as primitive forms of man or as 'animals' whose nature was essentially uncivilizable. Shearer (1981) reports that a mental retardation worker in 1884 characterized one of his charges like this: 'With great, soft, jet eyes, he reminds one of a seal' (p. 82).

The high point of this movement was the Mental Deficiency Act 1913 which established a separate service, excluding people labelled as mentally defective from education, welfare and other social agencies. Wide powers were provided for the identification and segregation of people officially diagnosed as mentally defective. The following categories were established by the Act: idiots, imbeciles, the feebleminded and moral defectives. A Central Board of Control required County and County Borough Councils to ascertain the number of mental defectives in their areas and to provide institutions to 'care' for them, and LEAs were required to report all children over 7 years who were ineducable. When the diagnosis (which had to be carried out by two doctors) was complete the mentally defective person could be detained indefinitely subject to periodic review.

Past and Present: Continuities

The story presented thus far is one of humanitarian reforms bedevilled by 'practical realities' and a policy agenda shaped by the vested interests of powerful groups in society. Reforms were underfunded and implemented in a manner which was counterproductive. The clock was put back.

Legitimating ideologies which dehumanized 'deviants' became influential and experts were on hand to make a flawed system work.

Since the Second World War the idea that people with mental handicaps were a biological threat to society has waned and progressive ideas have once again come to the fore. The 1960s and 1970s saw some radical changes in declared public policy in the treatment of people with mental handicaps. The White Paper *Better Services for the Mentally Handicapped* (1971) emphasized the aim of developing comprehensive community-based services which would enable people so labelled not only to be located in 'normal' communities but to become integrated into them. For as many of them as possible life was to be 'normalized'. They were to be discharged from hospitals and there was to be a shift to community care.

A parallel movement developed in the field of education. In 1971 following the Education Act (1970) local education authorities assumed responsibility for the education of children with mental handicaps. Junior Training Centres, previously under health authorities, were transferred to the education service. In the wider area of special needs, there was increasing support for integration into the mainstream. The Warnock Report (1978) recommended that statutory categories of handicap be abolished and recognized the counterproductive nature of 'labelling'. Although there was a great deal of fudging on the issue of integration in this Report, it was widely perceived as pro-integrationist and set the parameters for the Education Act 1981. The Act was not as progressive as some integrationists had hoped but in relation to integration the duties of LEAs were made clear. Section 2 of the Act stated that:

> Where a local education authority arranges special educational provision for a child for whom they maintain a statement, it shall be the duty of the authority if the conditions mentioned below are satisfied to secure that *he is educated in an ordinary school*.

There are clearly continuities here with the humanitarian concerns of the early and mid nineteenth century when efforts were made to make lunatics, idiots and other 'deviants' genuine participants in human society. However, in subsequent attempts to implement these policies there are ominous parallels with what happened in the late nineteenth century. In relation to community care reforms have not been as successful as was hoped by the optimists of the 1960s and 1970s. As Scull (1977) has argued, in practice community care has often meant disabled people being left on their own in poor conditions in run-down welfare hostels. Even if reasonably well-resourced, such hostels can become mini-hospitals and replicate all the faults of the system they are supposed to have replaced.

Another option has been for them to live at home with the back-up from the support services. But if the provision of the latter is not adequate, which is frequently the case, this merely results in them becoming a burden on their families and usually on one member of the family in particular, the mother. Moreover, as Bayley's (1973) study has shown, they can be just as isolated living at home as in a run-down hostel. Community care has in fact in its present form become a cheap alternative to institutionalization and appeals to those who are under pressure to cut public expenditure (Oliver, 1985). If proper support services were provided and genuine attempts were made to develop the community infrastructure, community care would be a far more expensive policy than 'warehousing'. The shift in policy has not even meant a shift in resources from hospitals to local communities but a change in the type of labour employed to care for people with mental handicaps — from paid, trained professional to the unpaid and untrained.

As for the integration of pupils with special needs into the mainstream it seems that the loopholes in the Act, mainly to do with the 'conditions' referred to above in Section 2, have been fully exploited by LEAs. In a recent analysis of data from the DES, Will Swann (1989) showed that there had been very little progress in integration between 1982 and 1989 (defined in terms of the percentages of pupils still in special schools). Overall there has been a drop of only 7.8 per cent in the total number of pupils attending special schools, this in a five year period following a major piece of legislation which was heralded as pro-integrationist. A minority of LEAs — eleven altogether — had actually increased their levels of segregation during this period and in twenty-six authorities more than 10 per cent of children placed in special schools were not statemented, thus foregoing the protection offered under the Act and denying their parents the right of involvement and appeal.

The majority of children with special needs are, of course, already in the mainstream. For them, integration usually means a move from being partly integrated in a functional sense to being fully integrated. The meaning of integration is controversial and we shall argue later in this chapter that even some of the most up to date 'whole school' policies are flawed. As with community care, integration requires a well organized and funded support system. A recent inspectors' report (DES, 1989) on support services stated 'few support services have the accommodation, resources and clerical support necessary for their work' (para. 56). In no LEA was the special needs support service an integral part of an advisory team working towards common goals, as one would anticipate if integration policies were taken to their logical conclusion.

With regard to the integration of children with severe learning difficulties, the national picture is unclear, and reliable and valid statistics difficult to come by. As with policies for all forms of special needs there is considerable local variation. It seems likely that the majority will still be receiving their education in special schools, although some will be in units set up in ordinary schools and others, like Down's children, may be fully integrated at nursery/infant level. The impression from the literature is that in some LEAs partial integration projects have been established involving links between 'normal' and special schools. There are examples of attempts to move from social to functional integration. In the Coleshill Project (Carpenter *et al.*, 1988) joint activities in the non-core open curriculum areas (art, music and PE) were widened to include core/closed areas (see Ainscow and Tweddle, 1979) such as practical number work and early literacy skills. In most of these types of project, pupils remained located in special schools, though links with 'normal' schools were continuous and intended to be sustained throughout pupils' school careers.

The Contemporary Scene: Ambivalent Attitudes

Our own period, therefore, cannot unproblematically be regarded as one where we have reached a 'higher' stage in which progressive policies are under way and humanitarian concerns dominant. Attitude surveys suggest a certain ambivalence of attitude on the part of the general public towards mental handicap. In a survey carried out by MENCAP in 1982 it was reported that public attitudes were by and large positive. Of the sample of approximately 2,000, 62 per cent favoured community care, and that rose to 67 per cent amongst those who knew a mentally handicapped person; 61 per cent would not be concerned if a mentally handicapped child attended the same school as their own children. However, respondents expressed a number of concerns about having mentally handicapped people as neighbours and only 29 per cent felt that mentally handicapped people should marry and have children. The author also commented on the lack of public knowledge of the behaviour needs of people with mental handicaps. Another survey (Weir, 1981) reported that most of the sample were confused about the distinction between physical disability and mental handicap. Only 35 per cent thought that mentally handicapped children should be integrated and 55 per cent felt that they should not.

Perhaps the most disturbing evidence comes from the most recent survey. The findings based on interviews with 450 adults suggested that 25 per cent of the sample were strongly opposed to integrating mentally handicapped people into the community. Another 25 per cent were opposed to integration which would affect their families or neighbourhoods. Of the 50 per cent considered generally sympathetic towards integration, more than half could be swayed against by a local campaign of opposition (Leighton, 1988).

This ambivalence is to be expected given the continuing debate within the humanitarian tradition about the exact nature of the features we all do or do not have in common with people called mentally handicapped. Recent discussion revolves around the question of the definition of 'person' and whether mentally handicapped people can be so regarded. According to Downie (1985) two crucial attributes — the capacity for self-determination and the capacity for morality — are clearly not possessed by many human beings, such as the senile, the severely mentally ill, infants and the mentally handicapped who cannot therefore be regarded as 'persons'. If they are not persons, then they should not be denigrated or treated badly, but they are not the proper objects of respect. Respect means valuing human beings because they have the capacity to become persons.

However, against this is the view that even if human beings do not have these capacities they still have a dignity which demands our respect, in the same way that respect for animals goes beyond mere regard for their sentience. In the modern version of the argument the distinction between humans and animals is not as crucial as it was, say, in the middle of the nineteenth century. It is now considered species-ist to treat even animals as 'brutes' and thus to brutalize them; they too have to be respected for their distinctive 'personality' and deserve sympathy rather than pity.

Downie's point is that people waver between these views, i.e. between the view that dignity is an overriding feature, and the view that to be respected human beings must have a full complement of capacities. There is also another source of ambivalence which relates to the question of determinism. In order to sympathize with people we have to understand their outlook on life and in the case of many people with mental handicaps such empathy is difficult to achieve. In these circumstances we tend to resort to a determinist, 'objectivist' view which assumes that 'what people do is not, despite appearances, freely chosen by them but is governed by forces and factors over which they have no control' (*op. cit.*, p. 38).

The problem is that if a person even vaguely senses that they are not being taken seriously and their choices don't count, then this is not only hurtful but often also self-fulfilling in that they may eventually come to have a negative self-regard and view themselves as 'objects' rather than agents, particularly when this perception is thrust upon them on a daily basis in an institution by people who have power over them. These dangers are well known, but the determinist model is still frequently resorted to by professional practitioners, perhaps because it is the easier option, and thence filters into public consciousness. However, sometimes it clearly is appropriate and necessary from a common sense viewpoint to look at life from the mentally handicapped person's perspective. This is usually always the starting point for the modern humanistic psychologist, and indeed for all those working within the parameters of the humanitarian tradition both in the present and the past. The question 'Just how like us are they?' has been asked both in the hope and the belief that 'they' are much more like 'us' than we in our present state of knowledge can imagine. We never know for certain whether their failure to 'appear' as moral agents is due to alleged intractable features of their nature or our own failures as communicators. Rawls (1971) suggests 'the minimal requirements defining moral personality refer to capacity and not to the realization of it'. How can we be sure we fully understand what these minimal requirements are and know whether the 'being' in front of us possesses them or not?

The School Context: Pupil and Teacher Perceptions

We would expect this ambivalence of attitude to reveal itself in the perceptions of teachers and pupils in schools. A point of reference here would be attitudes towards the inclusion of children with disabilities and difficulties, including severe learning difficulties, in the ordinary classroom. It is likely that such attitudes would not be fixed but vary according to perceptions of the degree of difficulty or disability, the type of teacher or 'normal' group of children involved and the current situation in the school with respect to pedagogical, curricular and material factors. Both pupils and teachers would no doubt have imbibed something of the humanitarian ethic, at least at the level of rhetoric, and would have some understanding of ambiguities and uncertainties in relation to moral issues. Most will possess a moral starting point, but we would also expect their views to be influenced by various social interests (see Barton and Tomlinson, 1984), and cultural expectations derived in part from their experiences of schooling.

(a) Pupils

Variations in attitudes amongst pupils have been demonstrated in quantitative attitude studies. Although peer rejection appears to be a fairly common occurrence, according to Voeltz (1980) much of the evidence from earlier studies is inconclusive. Most earlier studies involved moderately handicapped pupils (see Dunn, 1968; Gottlieb, 1974; Bruininks *et al.*, 1974; Budoff and Siperstein, 1978) and there were very few which focused on the severely mentally handicapped pupil. Voeltz's own study suggested that attitudes were influenced by a number of variables. Thus pupils were more likely to express a desire to interact with severely handicapped children if they (i.e. the 'normal' pupils) were (a) girls; (b) in fifth and sixth grade; or (c) in a school where interaction was possible and occurring regularly. Other studies have reported an increase in peer rejection with severity of handicap (Burton and Hirshoren, 1979), verbal cruelty to pupils whose performance on both academic and social fronts was well below the norm (Jones, 1972) and fear, hostility and aversion to severely handicapped pupils (Kutner, 1971).

However, the cultural meanings involved here are more complex than suggested by attitudes studies. For a further account we need to turn to ethnographic work. Although most ethnographic studies have not examined interaction between children with severe learning difficulties and 'normal' pupils, they have thrown light on the way pupils create their own criteria for assigning status which often differ from those of official school culture. Thus according to Turner (1983) 'swots' (the pupils' term for conformists) are of deviant status from the point of view of the 'dossers' (the pupils term for non-conformists) and 'ear'oles' are deviant from the point of view of the 'lads' (Willis, 1977). But there are some pupils who will be regarded as deviant in the disability or special needs sense of the term. Measor and Woods (1984) found the first year secondary pupils in their study had a notion of the 'normal' pupil. 'The pupils had worked out a concept of "the normal" (to them) pupil and deviations were savagely derided' (p. 127). The authors found that there were two stereotypes with which all pupils wished to avoid being identified, namely the 'too conformist' and 'too deviant' stereotypes. Conformist pupils tended to commit some deviant acts and deviants to commit some conformist acts, in order to avoid being labelled 'too soft' or 'too thick'. Those regarded as 'too thick' could encounter insult, teasing and also aggression. They were frequently labelled by insulting nicknames. Peter, for example, always addressed Mark as 'Hey Goofy Teeth' and those pupils who took remedial reading were known as spastics or 'spassies' (p. 133). Such derogatory remarks about pupils have been noted in other studies and seem to be a reflection of one of the common themes in pupil culture, namely 'competence' (see Woods, 1983, p. 100). It is of prime importance that they themselves feel, and that others feel, that they are growing up as proper persons.

To be a proper, competent person is a sought after identity. One way of displaying this is to avow publicly that certain pupils are the opposite of what one takes oneself to be or, if not the opposite, certainly functioning at a level which clearly is not 'normal' and which is vastly different from one's own level. Woods and other authors (see, for example, Everhart, 1983) in fact paint a dismal picture of peer interactions from the point of view of a pupil with special educational needs. If they are considered 'too deviant', as many in the remedial class would be, then they cannot expect much sympathy or help from peers. Not being considered 'thick' as far as 'normal' peers are concerned is as important as not being considered a 'sissy' if you are a boy or 'butch' if you are a girl. Being classed as 'handicapped' got you the 'sympathy vote', but this also had obvious disadvantages.

In a study by Quicke (1986) it was evident that 'differentiation' along ability lines was experienced by most pupils, not just those with special needs. Moreover views about 'handicap' differed according to the status of pupils. Thus pupils formally designated 'examination' pupils reveal different views from those designated 'non-examination' and 'less able', although they also held views in common. It was felt that pupils' cultural groupings having been set in motion by the organizational features of the school developed forms which were complex, often not fully understood by adults and resistant to what from an adult's viewpoint might seem like radical changes in school practices.

As well as ability, pupils' groupings based on gender would also seem to be relevant in this context. A number of quantitative attitudinal studies have suggested that in relation to all forms of handicap females demonstrate more 'positive' attitudes than males (Horne, 1985) and that this is true for females of all ages (Sandberg, 1982; Voeltz, 1980; Wilkins and Velicer, 1980). It is not surprising, therefore, that in relation to mental handicap similar differences between the sexes have been found (Thomas, 1978), and in studies of the integration of children with severe learning difficulties girls have been reported as more positive in their approach than boys (Evans and Simmons, 1987; Williamson, 1979).

Explanations for these findings have been various, but usually refer either to psycho-biological 'within child' factors or to role socialized traits. Thus, Williamson (1979) explains girls' more successful relationships with 'low functioning ESN(S) pupils' as related to an unproblematized 'maturity' factor and Rose (1981) and Goodman *et al.* (1972) refer to 'prescribed sex roles' with the suggestion that such roles provide girls with various psychological traits, like the 'need to be nurturant', which are functional for the integration of special needs pupils. The limitations of attitudinal studies have been widely acknowledged (Armisted, 1974) and clearly one limitation is the lack of contextualization of attitudes within the social and cultural worlds of the persons under investigation. In an observational study of an integration project in a middle school Evans and Simmons (1987) found that girls made more contact with children with severe learning difficulties than boys did and that in a group situation the latter's attention wandered and they seemed less capable of dealing with the needs of these children. In their discussion of findings, the authors suggest that it may have been the nature of lessons, in this instance PE lessons, rather than 'attitudes' expressed by the boys which should be questioned, because the ethos of the lessons encouraged certain kinds of expectations which were dysfunctional for integration. Thus 'the boys at Lawn Upton expected after a "good" lesson to leave the room exhausted and sweating; if they did not they felt unextended' (p. 117) — which was how they felt after lessons in which cooperation rather than competition was emphasized.

Such findings would suggest that cultural studies might help to illuminate attitudes to mental handicap by examining the relationship between integration policies and the establishment of gender identities. In school the reinforcement of traditional male gender characteristics like 'competitiveness', 'assertiveness' and 'hardness' may have a negative effect on boys' attitudes towards handicap. Such characteristics have always been particularly important in PE and sport. Traditionally boys who have not wanted to participate in sport have been taunted with effeminacy (Roth, 1977) and the myth that male character is built by participation in physically hard team games has a long history (Bell and Grant, 1974). Similarly, it may be argued, girls are viewed as less competitive and acquire stereotyped identities which are more amenable to their playing a positive role in integration. They are thought to be more 'caring', 'mature', 'conscientious', 'passive' and 'sensitive'. As Clarricoates (1980) points out, 'Any girl who is "aggressive" or "independent" and any boy who is "effeminate" or "sensitive" are the exception, the so-called deviants' (p. 39). Conforming to male stereotypes involves boys in dominance behaviour, with girls being on the receiving end of much teasing, abuse and general harrassment, and it is scarcely surprising if girls, therefore, view boys as a potential threat to weaker pupils and handicapped persons generally.

(b) Teachers

Hegarty and Pocklington (1981) report that in a survey of teachers who had had teaching contact with pupils with special needs in ordinary schools, they found that in response to the question 'Do you feel it is appropriate for handicapped pupils to be placed in your school?', 90 per cent of all respondents and 97 per cent of those answering the question indicated that they felt it was appropriate. However, as the authors themselves note, the sample of schools may not have been representative, since some of them had been chosen in the first place because of the positive attitudes of the staff to integration. More crucially, they report that children with moderate or severe learning difficulties (i.e. mental handicap) were less favourably perceived than those who were physically handicapped. This 'hierarchy of preference' towards disability groups has been noted in other studies (Tringo, 1970), and means that mentally handicapped persons are usually perceived as being at the bottom of the heap status-wise. In one recent study quoted in Hegarty and Pocklington, Lair and Sauser (1981) confirmed the existence of such a hierarchy, the order from most to least preferred being as follows:

1. Non-handicapped children.
2. Physically handicapped.
3. Children with hearing impairment.
4. Mentally retarded.

It is also important to note that the high percentages of favourable responses obtained by Hegarty and Pocklington are not a universal feature. In the United States, for example, studies of teachers' and pupils' attitudes to the integration of mentally retarded and other groups of handicapped pupils have stressed the prevalence of negative attitudes (see Horne, 1985; Baker and Gottlieb, 1980). Gottlieb (1975) found that the movement towards mainstreaming has meant more teachers have had experience of handicapped pupils but this has not been accompanied by the development of more positive attitudes by teachers to children labelled mentally retarded. In a study by Moore and Fine (1978) nearly half the ordinary school teachers thought that retarded children should not be placed in ordinary classrooms. Surprisingly they found that those experienced in teaching these pupils held images which were just as stereotyped as those of other teachers, a finding which contradicts that of a decade earlier where more favourable attitudes were found amongst special class teachers than ordinary class teachers (Efron and Efron, 1967).

Further evidence on teachers' perceptions of pupils with special needs comes from ethnographic work. Teachers use 'typifications' of pupils in an attempt to make the world of everyday life cognitively manageable. The content of types will depend on many factors — the life experience of the teacher, the preferred teaching style, wider cultural and social aspects and situational factors such as the need to maintain discipline. Typifications are firmly rooted in processes of interaction in the classroom and in the contextual conditions which structure them. The use of types is thus 'grounded' in the practical circumstances of teachers and relates to their interests.

A number of studies have shown that even if teachers set out to treat children as individuals, they are constrained by circumstances to label them in terms of categories reflecting institutional necessities and external pressures. Sharp and Green (1975) argue that teachers are so constrained that whatever their good intentions they are virtually forced to act in ways which do not match up to their progressive ideals. All children end up being labelled and some will inevitably be placed in low status categories, like 'deviance' (see Hargreaves *et al.*, 1975) with consequent negative, self-fulfilling effects.

The literature on deviant labelling is too extensive to review comprehensively in this brief overview of teacher perceptions. Suffice it to point out that such labelling is yet another example of the hidden curriculum at work. It contributes to the maintenance of a social climate where pupils are not treated with equal respect either by peers or by teachers — a climate, therefore, which is a breeding ground for prejudice.

The Project and Integration Policies for Special Needs Pupils

So far in this chapter we have outlined our interpretation of the humanitarian tradition of debate in the field of mental handicap and examined policies generated by that tradition and the factors that shaped them in practice. We provide historical examples and bring the matter closer to home by considering some of the continuities between past and present. Finally we have looked briefly at cultural features and social processes in schools which influence the way pupils and teachers construct 'deviance', and develop attitudes to traditional concerns like the integration of people with mental handicaps into society and the integration of children with all forms of special needs into mainstream schools.

In this final section we look at the way the Project might relate to integration policies for pupils with special needs, particularly those with severe learning difficulties. The Project itself, of course, is not an integration programme as such. In two of the schools it did not even involve contact with pupils with severe learning difficulties from special schools. In the third school contact was not initially envisaged as leading immediately to either part-time or full-time integration, although this was certainly a perspective that developed amongst some participants. The Project is more accurately viewed as an awareness-raising exercise in preparation for the time when pupils from special schools for pupils with severe learning difficulties are introduced into the mainstream, and as a way of sensitizing pupils to the needs of pupils with various types of special needs who are already in the comprehensive school.

It is important, however, to make clear that we did not view the Project as an optional extra with regard to integration policies. To explain why, we need to examine the kind of integration policy of which we felt the Project should be an essential part, namely the 'whole school' approach to integration. By a 'whole school' approach to provision for special needs in the mainstream we mean an approach which recognizes from the outset that the onus of responsibility for the education of pupils with special needs falls on all teachers, not just those officially designated as support or remedial teachers. The role of the latter is not merely to provide support for the existing pedagogical organization and curricular set up, but involves collaborating with mainstream teachers to develop the curriculum in ways which will abolish the need for a separate category of 'learning difficulties', and which will benefit all children, not just those labelled as having special needs. This is 'whole school' in the sense that the 'whole curriculum' needs to be considered both at the level of the formal and the hidden curriculum.

We would argue that a progressive 'whole school' policy is one where the principle of equality of respect or value is taken seriously. We would urge supporters of integration to think through the meaning of equality for themselves and the implications of the equality principle for practice in the wider context of the mainstream. There has been a tendency for many of us to 'give a reflex-like support for propositions about equality which prevents us following through the logical implications and leaves deep prejudices unexamined'. (Booth, 1988, p. 17). This has happened because the inherent contradiction between the equality principle and the concept of special needs as traditionally defined has not been recognized. Special educators have been welcomed into the mainstream of the comprehensive school but the support they provide has often relied on a psychological paradigm which is outdated and incompatible with the more 'social' view of many progressive mainstream teachers. Underneath the rhetoric of support, the traditional ideas about ability, capacity, deprivation, disturbance, individual differences retain their potency and are in direct opposition to attempts to de-mystify the 'specialness' of pupils with special needs and establish the principle that all children are special.

The embrace of these ideas leads to contradictions and difficulties for the 'whole school' approach. If the intention is to create an educational environment governed by the principle of equality of value, then the overall quality of teacher–pupil and pupil–pupil relationships must not continue to reinforce status hierarchies and competitive individualism, as happened when the traditional curriculum held sway. Moreover, the specific teaching approaches need careful consideration. Bines (1988) argues that certain conceptions of alleged 'good practice' in whole school approaches stress the individualization of work programmes and assessment and thus lead to increased differentiation at the expense of providing common experiences for pupils. Inevitably, because of the practical difficulties involved in tailoring programmes to meet the individual needs of large numbers of pupils, teachers may again resort to grouping by ability and explanations of pupil boredom and 'failure' in terms of deficit models, which is precisely what progressive 'whole school' policies aim to avoid.

One way of breaking down the 'cult of individualism' is to develop collaborative group work as a regular teaching/learning strategy. This may encourage pupils to communicate across boundaries based on class, gender, race and ability differences, to share experiences and develop common understandings. It is these open, exploratory, collaborative relationships between *all* pupils that a 'whole school' policy seeks to institutionalize. Changes need to be wide-ranging enough to alter a prevailing social climate which works against pupils becoming genuinely cooperative. If the ethos remains dominated by competitive individualism, progressive alternatives are likely to be resisted by some teachers and pupils on the grounds that they are merely palliative, and by others who are too frightened or insecure to challenge the status quo. Salmon and Claire (1984) provide some vivid illustrations of pupil conservatism when faced with attempts by teachers to introduce collaborative enquiry into their classrooms.

Thus the aim is to facilitate the creation of an educational milieu supportive of collaborative group work across the curriculum. It is not just a question of introducing a new technique but of building into the whole curriculum a philosophy which values commonality and sociality as much as individual diversity. We have stressed this point because for us if a 'whole school' policy is not based on such concerns then it cannot deliver 'true' integration of children with special needs. However, there is another crucial point which needs to be highlighted. It is quite possible that 'normal' pupils, even if they are not 'conservative' or 'prejudiced', will see no value in working with special needs pupils in collaborative groups. In the particular circumstances in which it takes place the pupil may judge that she or he has other priorities. Given our philosophy of education, we feel we must support the pupil's right to choose, even if this means a complete rejection of collaborative work.

We would like to think, however, that pupils' choices in this matter would be morally informed. Experience alone of contact with pupils with special needs is an insufficient basis for making judgments. Pupils also require knowledge and understanding, derived from discussion of and critical reflection upon their experiences. They need to explore their feelings and think deeply about the issues involved, rather than make choices based on snap judgments about likes and dislikes in the immediate situation. Such matters can be tackled when issues crop up in day to day classroom interactions, but there is also a place for a planned programme within the formal curriculum. The aim of the programme would be to encourage pupils to stand back from the 'here and now' and make judgments based on moral reasoning.

Integration programmes are more likely to succeed if pupils fully understand the moral significance of integration, but also feel they have the right to make decisions about their own participation in such programmes, depending of course on the age and maturity of the pupils concerned. Even with young pupils moral autonomy in this area could be a long-term aim and an important guideline for curriculum development. A framework of trust should be established where pupils feel their decisions are important and where they are encouraged to think for themselves and to act as moral agents. Superficially there often does not seem a great deal of difference between this approach and one where pupils are manipulated into interacting with special needs or any other group of pupils, but it is in our view essential to preserve the difference if we are to challenge prejudice through education rather than indoctrination.

Chapter 3

The Project: An Introduction

In this chapter we describe and discuss the local authority and school contexts in which the Project took place. We then go on to clarify our own involvement and outline and discuss the kind of contribuiton we wanted to make as a Research Team. Finally we briefly discuss and provide examples of teaching and learning strategies developed according to principles elaborated earlier in the book.

The Local Context

To recap: our position was that if prejudice was to be challenged effectively, the traditional curriculum had to be radically changed. To make an impact the Project would clearly have to ally itself with progressive forces in education which had this sort of radical programme. Our intervention would also have to pay some attention to the way the aims of the Project were reinforced and facilitated, or not as the case may be, by the current direction of change in the schools in which we were working. Our hope was that this change would involve a profound improvement in the quality of human relationships in the schools. Whether the Project itself was the initiator of reform or merely part of the general thrust of a reform movement mattered little as long as there was change in the desired direction.

It was fortunate that the local authority in which our schools were located had recently embarked upon a coordinated programme of curriculum reform called the Sheffield Curriculum Initiative (SCI). The main aims of this were outlined in a letter from the Chief Education Officer in December 1985. The authority recognized that despite some attempts to broaden and restructure the curriculum, the old grammar school model still dominated the definition of knowledge and the organization of teaching and learning in the comprehensive school. This resulted in curricula and teaching styles which no longer met the needs of pupils in the late twentieth century. Rather than a knowledge transmission, subject-centred approach the need was for more emphasis on the development of skills, competences and understanding. The revitalization of the curriculum was to be brought about by a number of changes but the main plank of reform was to be the modularization of the curriculum whereby courses were to be broken down into smaller units intended to be more motivating and meaningful for pupils and entailing new forms of assessment, i.e. Records of Achievement, and new teaching approaches.

In order to facilitate the implementation of these reforms, the Authority commissioned five teachers from each secondary school to work with tutorial support from the University or the Polytechnic in a coordinated programme to develop the elements of a modular curriculum. The secondees were expected to work in teams and were briefed to deliver a joint contribution back to their schools. These developments would be supported by additional resources from central government funding in the form of monies from TVEI, TRIST and LAPP.

We felt that the general direction of reforms embraced by the Sheffield Curriculum Initiative were progressive, but this is not to say that we were naive enough to think that all aspects of it were equally radical in conception. The meaning of modularization, for example, was contested within the Initiative. For some it was automatically linked to a 'new vocationalist' perspective (see Pollard *et al.*, 1988) whereas for others the aim was to facilitate the development of liberal education for all. Also as Nixon (1989) points out the Sheffield TVEI strategy of course development through modularization had certain inherent weaknesses due to the nature of the contractual agreement between Sheffield LEA and the Manpower Services Commission (MSC). In the implementation phase there was an overemphasis on course development at the expense of staff development, and on curriculum structures at the expense of classroom practice.

These criticisms raised the question of the extent to which central funding could really be used by the LEA to develop its own Initiative in a way which radically diverged from the original intention at national level. Clearly, what TVEI was in any particular school or LEA would always be the outcome of the interplay between MSC requirements and the existing pattern of practice (Dale, 1983). One suspected that in the final analysis, although all sides engaged in 'subtle manipulation', the national centre's greater financial and political power, plus — in the present circumstances — its more coherent ideology, would make up for the lack of local knowledge and enable it to play a tougher political game.

Be that as it may, from our point of view as a Research Team, we could think of no better strategy than coat-tailing the Sheffield Curriculum Initiative. We agreed with the local commentators about the several advantages of modularization over 'tubular' courses (Krachai, 1987). They enabled 'bite size' curricular units to be constructed, they allowed pupils more flexibility in choice of units and they made pupils' transfer between schools less problematic. Most importantly, they facilitated the development of integrated curricula, helping to break down subject boundaries and enabling the curriculum to be theme-based and thus organized around centres of interest which were appealing and meaningful to pupils. 'Skills and knowledge common to several subjects could be organized into a single module to avoid overlap and the problem of duplication' (*ibid.*, p. 15).

Moreover, the overall direction of change proposed by SCI seemed to be consonant with the values underpinning the Project. Teaching and learning strategies were to be more active, experiential and social. Pupils' experience would be worked with rather than ignored; pupils would have more chance to negotiate curricula and take more responsibility for their own learning. New approaches to assessment would seek to lessen the dominance of the norm-referenced public examination system and broaden the range of pupil achievement that was taken into account. Assessment would be formative and an inextricable part of the teaching and learning process, rather than something that happened at the end of courses when opportunities for feedback were lost. Most significantly from our point of view there was a general concern for the promotion of equality of opportunity, interpreted in the egalitarian sense of providing 'education for all'.

Of course, as suggested in Chapter 1, we expected to find all kinds of inconsistencies and contradictions at the ideological and practical level in this wide-ranging reform. No doubt there would be certain aspects with which we would not want the Project to be associated. But the existence of a movement derived from values similar to our own made the chances of finding allies in the schools that much greater.

Moreover, we were hoping also to take advantage of the anticipated climate of reform generated by the 'returning' secondees. Ideally they should have stimulated change by opening up school-wide discussions about matters like the hidden curriculum, and empowering their colleagues by sharing 'ownership' with them. In the event, in many schools secondees were constrained in playing this role by a variety of factors. Their role was often contested not only by senior management teams but also by colleagues and even by fellow secondees. Despite the rhetoric of 'ownership' and 'partnership' (see Rudduck and Wilcox, 1988) widespread, democratically controlled change leading to reconstructed school cultures was difficult to realize. However, even if we did not find in the schools in which we were working a group of radical 'change agent' secondees or even a readily identifiable progressive faction, we did feel that the overall climate in the authority during this period was such that it would not be difficult to find schools where there would be substantial support for the Project.

It is important to remember that the Research Team working on the Project had no official position in relation to SCI. Our contacts inside the schools were not usually with secondees but with other teachers who had volunteered to participate in the Project because it seemed to fit in with the way they wanted the curriculum to be developed in their schools. In one school the Project was perceived as an ideal vehicle for introducing a modular structure and in another it was perceived as precisely the kind of cross-curricular theme that the recently established second year teaching team wanted to explore and develop with their pupil groups.

In return for agreeing to be involved in the Project, the schools received support from the Research Team mainly in the form of a research worker who visited the school on a regular basis. Her explicit role was to set up a steering group in each school, to support and advise the steering group, to assist the groups in making links with the local and wider community (e.g. MENCAP advisers, parents with mentally handicapped children, social workers), to facilitate the exchange of ideas between the project schools, to provide some resources, to negotiate evaluative criteria and monitor processes and to facilitate liaison between special schools and project schools, where appropriate.

The LEA itself was sympathetic to the aims and objectives of the Project but was able to give only a limited amount of financial and advisory support. This was provided by the special needs sector because of the LEA's interpretation of the content of the Project and the involvement of special schools. On reflection, it was in some ways a pity that the general perception of the LEA was that this was a special needs project, rather than, say, one which also related to broader concerns in personal and social education, pastoral care and equal opportunities. Within the schools the Project was not confined to special needs teachers. In fact in two of the schools there were no officially designated special needs teachers involved and in the third they constituted only a fraction of the total number of teachers who volunteered. However, advisory support tended to come solely from the special needs sector. We felt that this was a reflection of precisely what was wrong with the way special needs provision was handled by LEAs. Integration should be the aim at adminstrative as well as school and classroom level. In the schools the Project attempted with some success to bridge the cultural gap (see Clough, 1988) between mainstream and special provision but failed to do this at local authority level.

A final point about the local context is that although the Project was outside the official framework of SCI, there were many informal links between the two initiatives. The Research Director was in fact involved in SCI as a University tutor, although not in relation to any of the teachers in the Project schools. However, within the University setting links were made with teachers and colleagues working in those schools.

The Schools

In the first year of the Project only one school, School A, was involved. A team of teachers from various disciplines worked on a curriculum innovation which culminated in a module taken by all second year pupils (see Chapter 4). It involved joint activities with pupils from local special schools and study sessions where critical reflection was encouraged. The intention was to establish a 'base' in the school in the first year, before spreading out into five other comprehensive schools in the second year. We were hoping that the teachers from School A would provide a fund of experience on which other teachers could draw.

In the second year five schools were approached and all responded positively to the initial letter from the Director of the Project. In only two of these was there a full-scale implementation of the Project. In School B a team of teachers worked with pupils who had special experience of mental handicap, the aim being to use the expertise of this group to raise the level of awareness in other pupils (see Chapter 5). In School C a module was developed taking up all the time allotted to Humanities for a two week period (see Chapter 6). In both schools the intention was to work with the whole of the first or second year group.

Three further schools were visited (Schools D, E, F) but in each of these the Project was only taken up in a small way. In School D it was housed under Health Education and dealt with under a section on Social and Moral Education. Several lessons with a religious theme were devoted to the topic of handicap and mental handicap in particular. A representative from MENCAP and a parent of a mentally handicapped child were invited to address pupils. The Acting Head of the English Department was contacted to discuss the possibility of coordinated work related to the book *Welcome Home Jelly Bean.* A questionnaire constructed by the Project Director was administered to all second years. However, partly because of lack of time, it was not possible for the Research Team to become further involved with developments in this school.

School E was approached at the end of the first term. At first, a great deal of interest was shown and the Research Team attended several meetings of the second year team where the Project was discussed at length. However, in the end the general feeling was that it was not possible for the school to make a commitment that year. The same was true of School F who agreed to administer the questionnaire, but did not feel able to house the Project that year. There was too much anxiety and uncertainty about the future of the school for staff to feel comfortable about taking on something new.

The Role of the Research Team

It is clear from what has been written so far about our perceptions of the local context that we assumed that most of the teachers who became involved in the Project would welcome it as a potential example of 'good practice'. They would accept the broad aims of the Project because they stemmed directly from values which underpinned their own practice. Thus we did not expect to have to 'sell' the Project to these particular staff at the ideological level. However, this did not mean that within these broad parameters there was not a great deal to negotiate. We were, after all, coming at the issues from a rather different angle than the teachers. We called ourselves a Research Team because we felt we had a responsibility to facilitate a wide-ranging exploration of issues uninhibited by 'political' constraints. Whilst we also hoped teachers would be equally explorative and creative they would inevitably be more enmeshed in the day to day realities of school life and therefore perhaps less willing to take risks. It was nevertheless encumbent upon us to establish a research climate as an integral part of the experience.

Also in the initial stages, although following Biott, Lynch and Robertson (1984) we conceived of our relationship with teachers as a 'partnership', we recognized that certain inequalities would inevitably arise because most of the teachers felt they did not know a great deal about mental handicap and would require considerable support from the Research Team. At the same time, even in this early period, we did not expect teachers to become dependent on us and surrender ownership of the

Project to us. Our view was that teachers would already possess strengths which they could utilize if they had enough confidence to do so. After all, some of them would probably have explored many of the key issues in other contexts — at least, we hoped that this would be the case. Prejudice, discrimination, stereotyping, labelling, empathy, equality, justice — all these concepts are familiar teaching objectives in the pastoral curriculum, personal and social education, multicultural/anti-racist and anti-sexist programmes and in traditional subjects like English and History. They also come to the fore on a daily basis in making judgments about how to handle conflicts in the classroom and human relationships generally in school. We hoped that all this knowledge could provide an invaluable resource for teachers when confronted with the need to teach about another form of prejudice. Our concern was not with inculcating knowledge but with, in a sense, bringing out a commitment that was already there (see Rudduck and Wilcox, 1989). As indicated in Chapter 1, we wanted to nourish an existing moral sensitivity rather than just 'hand over' a few 'facts' about mental handicap.

As far as the evaluative component of the research was concerned, our approach was mainly formative. We were interested in the 'process of curriculum development and the changing perceptions of those teachers responsible for such development' (Nixon, 1989, p. 127) and we recognized that 'the curriculum could [not] be judged solely in terms of the curriculum planners' stated objectives' (*ibid.*, p. 129). There are clearly likely to be many objectives which are not stated but are evident in the implementation either because they are genuinely unintended, secretly intended or unconsciously intended. At the same time, we recognized that this approach did not mean that certain objectives could not be pre-specified and criteria established for assessing whether or not these had been realized. Our position here is explicated further in Chapter 11. Apart from 'conversations with a purpose' (see Burgess, 1984) and what we gleaned from being participants, research activities involved interviewing samples of pupils and teachers using a semi-structured interview technique and developing and administering a pupil questionnnaire (see Chapter 8).

We were not expecting our intervention to be conflict-free. As participants, albeit from the 'outside' rather than the 'inside', we would become a constituent part of the micro-politics of the school. No doubt we would become involved in debates about the best way forward for curriculum development. However, whilst we would negotiate within the framework that had been set up in each school, in the final analysis we saw no alternative to deferring to teachers' judgments since, to put it bluntly, they would be doing most of the teaching.

Being aware of the existence of the micro-political dimension does not mean one necessarily has insights into the politics of any one particular school. It was an important part of our perspective that we should be politically aware, particularly of those conflicts of interest which had a direct bearing on the Project. But we were realistic enough to acknowledge that all the dimensions of 'power play' would not be revealed to us and in any case could only be fully understood after the event, and not even then if people chose to keep quiet. And so our attitude was to pitch in regardless, having taken a few precautionary measures based on our emergent understanding of the 'correlation of forces' in the school concerned. A crucial task was to dispel scepticism about the motivation of the Research Team, a scepticism which for the most part derived from a stereotyped view of university-initiated research.

Teaching and Learning Strategies

Guided by the principles outlined in Chapter 1, we explored with teachers ways in which teaching and learning about mental handicap could be facilitated. There was general agreement that didacticism and 'chalk and talk' should be avoided and that the most appropriate methods would be 'active', 'experiential' and 'social'. There were, however, several important differences of approach between the schools, revealed in the case studies in Chapters 4, 5 and 6 and discussed further in Chapter 11. The most visible of these was that in School A the module and pre-module phase involved prolonged periods of contact with pupils from special schools, whereas in the other schools this did not happen.

Inter-group contact was certainly a strategy which teachers valued highly. Even Schools B and C felt that contact at some stage was indispensable, but decided against it in the initial phase. However, caution is required here because whether such contact is beneficial or not will depend a great deal on the surrounding conditions and circumstances. Some of the factors which should be taken into account are the nature of the activity in which the pupils are engaged, the frequency, duration and variety of contact, the status of the parties, whether the contact is one-off, low status, 'real' or voluntary. Stephan and Brigham (1985) refer to four crucial requisites for productive contact — equal status, cooperative interdependence, support by authority figures and opportunities to interact with 'outgroup' members as individuals. Quicke (1985), on the basis of survey findings, queried whether the aim to demonstrate that persons with disabilities were not an abnormal group outside the mainstream of society was necessarily realized by visits to special establishments. Such visits often involved witnessing behaviour framed within an institutional context which highlighted the 'deviant' status of pupils with mental handicaps and usually provided no opportunities for pupils to interact with individuals outside this context.

Other forms of social and experiential approaches were considered by all three schools and these are elaborated in the case studies. Most of the teaching materials produced were organized around key themes and involved activities intended to help pupils reflect on their experiences and explore issues in greater depth. The following examples of materials, teachers' notes and lesson plans for what was called the 'Working Together Week' in School A give an idea of the kinds of classroom approaches that were planned and in most cases used. These materials were produced by teachers in School A with advice and support from the Research Team and were given to School B and C in the second year to use in their own way, if they wanted to use them at all. Four overlapping themes are highlighted — respect for persons, communication, labelling and the developing tradition in policies towards mental handicap.

Respect for Persons

Respect for persons was a general theme. The main aim of the Project was to draw out the implications of this theme for how we treated people with mental handicaps. The following hand-out for teachers was used in all schools. It was prepared by the Research Team after discussions with teachers in School A.

EXAMPLE ONE
Principles/Aims and Objectives of the 'Working Together' Week
Perhaps the main point to remember is that this is *Working Together* Week and that we are really trying to move on from the ideas of 'doing for', 'doing good', 'doing to feel good' and charity. All of us need, and need to encourage our pupils, to be constantly questioning our thoughts, ideas, feelings and assumptions.

The following are principles, aims and objectives that have developed as this school year has progressed.

Principles
 1. *Children and adults with a mental handicap are individuals*
    We should avoid giving the impression that all of them have similar

personalities and characteristics. It is easy to slip into this, particularly if one begins a sentence with '*The* mentally handicapped . . .'.

2. *Children and adults with a mental handicap are not passive objects of charity*
Anything that reinforces this stereotype should be avoided. They are not those 'less fortunate than ourselves' who need things done for them, but people with rights who need the support of the community — like most of us do from time to time — to help them to lead as full and enjoyable a life as possible.

3. *The families of children with a mental handicap are 'normal'*
Families with a child who has a mental handicap are a diverse group and have no special characteristics which make them different from any other family.

4. *The 'natural' location of all people with a mental handicap is not a special institution*
It is important to bear in mind, for instance, that in other parts of the country some pupils labelled 'mentally handicapped' attend ordinary schools.

5. *People with a mental handicap are not a clearly definable group*
The definition of mental handicap varies from culture to culture and from one historical period to another. In education we do not use the term as an official category, but refer to children as having severe learning difficulties.

6. *No one professional group has a monopoly of knowledge in this area*
Some of us have more experience of working with children with mental handicaps than others, but we are all learning about mental handicap and we are all in an equal state of ignorance about how to teach about this topic in a secondary school.

Aims and Objectives

To develop critical thinking in the areas of handicap/difference/prejudice.
To aid children in recognizing all people's common humanity.
To break down ill-conceived labels and question the whole concept of labelling.
To develop an empathy and understanding of what it is like to have a mental handicap.
To break away from the idea of seeing people with a mental handicap as passive receivers of help; to see them, rather, as needing to develop, have relationships, have choices.

Communication

A second important theme was *communication*. As mentioned in Chapter 2 we never know for certain the extent to which the so-called learning difficulties of people with mental handicaps are due to the failures of 'normal' people as communicators. The following lesson is designed to explore this issue.

EXAMPLE TWO
1. *Introduction: 'we are all individuals'/'warm up'* (10 minutes).
   (a) In pairs the pupils, using the string supplied, interlock their piece with their partners and put loops on wrists. Then they are asked to get free without removing the loops from wrists.
   Some will have found this easy some impossible. Stop game after a short time when a few have cracked it.
   (b) Discussion. We are all different. We all think differently at times. How did those feel who could not see the solution as quickly as others around them? How do those who succeed look on others? Brainstorm of similar situations when you have felt uncomfortable, embarrassed, isolated. We all follow social patterns and certain things are expected of us. If we do not fit into this pattern how are we viewed?
   We continue by trying to put ourselves into the situation of those with a physical or mental handicap.
2. *Trying to share the experience of those people with a physical handicap* (30 minutes?).
   In each of the 8 rooms we will set up before the afternoon session a carousel of activities that pupils will be able to move around and experience. Each piece of equipment will have instructions with it. These can be explained fairly briefly before they begin. If we aim at approximately 8 activities this means fairly small groups working together. The activities will include:

   Safety goggles, heavily taped ($\times$ 2?)
   Industrial gloves ($\times$ 2?)
   (Will depend on availability — maybe more goggles than gloves.)
   Cotton wool to impair hearing ($\times$ 2)
   Mirrors and stands for mirror drawing ($\times$ 2)

   The results of the mirror drawing etc. could go on display.
3. *Look at mental handicap* (10 minutes).
   This is obviously a more difficult experience to share. The idea of the following game is to put someone who can hear, see, etc., quite

clearly into the position where the messages they receive are incomprehensible and this leads to frustration, distress. Also to consider how we react when someone is not understanding us and how we can best help.

(a) Come together after the carousel — in a circle? Send a couple outside (a pair with the confidence not to become distressed!).

Meanwhile we rename certain common objects; e.g. bag becomes pen, desk becomes chair.

On returning the couples are given certain instructions, e.g. put the bag on the desk.

What they do is going to be wrong.

How do we urge them to respond correctly?

Shout? Repeat? Treat them with impatience/disdain?

Help can then be given. What sort of help?

(b) Pull together: discussion — in small groups (15 minutes).

How do we feel when we experience a handicap, physical or mental? How do others respond? How can we help? How should we not respond?

4. *The Practical side: how can we communicate?* (10 minutes).

The idea of this section is to explore methods of communicating without language. With a person who has a communication handicap, often the handicap, physical and mental, is twofold.

(a) The following situation can be presented to the class who will then work in 5 groups approximately.

Child 1 has a communication problem. He/she cannot walk, move his/her hands or arms and has little language but can respond with yes or no gestures. He/she does not understand the names of drinks. Child 1 thinks of a drink they would like (a common drink) but does not say what it is.

The rest of the group know that Child 1 does not understand the names so don't use them.

Instead they explore other methods of communicating the choices to get a yes/no response.

(b) Then the class can put forward ideas for how they managed to find out, and the difficulties and possible solutions discussed. Possible ideas may include:

Good techniques	*Bad techniques*
Miming	Repeating failed methods
Drawing	Getting/looking impatient/cross
Magazine pictures	Shouting

Colour matching	Asking another person what child likes
Encouraging eye pointing	Giving any drink
Being patient, interested	Shifting responsibility of communication on to others

Labelling

Labelling is a key issue because it describes the process by which people are stereotyped and lose their identity as individuals. The 'Labelling Game' described below is designed to give pupils an insight into this process.

EXAMPLE THREE

1. In pairs try to write a short definition of mental handicap.
   In groups of approximately 6 try to see what the definitions have in common — agree a common definition.
   Full class — each group to report its findings.
   Discussion on outcome should show that it is difficult to agree a definition as the term covers a variety of conditions. Therefore it is not helpful to use 'mentally handicapped' as a label.
   We need to think of individuals.
2. Read out the following quote to show what usually happens.
   'A century ago we would have been locked up. Now we can be taught to read and write and we want the right to speak for ourselves. Instead, we are often treated like children, thought to have no ideas of our own, and we are never consulted about anything'.
3. Labelling Game (15 minutes) — to put class members in the same position.
   The class is split into 4 groups.
   Each group has a set of cards, with single words on, e.g. swot, bighead, fatty.
   One person takes a card and without saying anything or showing it to the others gives it to the person it most suits. e.g. one card says 'swot': the person who picks it up gives it to the person that they think it most suits. 'Swot' now picks another card and gives it to someone else in the same way.
   When all the cards have been given out each person introduces her/himself — e.g. 'I'm swot' — using appropriate accent and gestures.

51

After all the introductions —
Discussion
1. How suitable were the labels?
2. How did people feel about being given them?
3. What are some other labels that are commonly used?
4. Why do we use labels?
5. What problems are caused by using labels?

The Developing Tradition in Policies towards Mental Handicap

The following activities aimed to provide pupils with a sense of the developing tradition in policies towards mental handicap. It was extremely difficult to avoid presenting this unproblematically as a 'story of progress'. Some of the continuities with the past were not mentioned in lesson notes, but were explored in discussion.

EXAMPLE FOUR
The History of mental handicap
AIMS
1. To examine the way in which mentally handicapped people throughout history have been denied their needs.
2. To consider what are some of the important needs that should be met *today*, so that mentally handicapped people can live as full a life as is possible.
3. To develop the idea that mentally handicapped people are *people* first and handicapped second, and that mentally handicapped people have the same needs as the class members themselves — love, acceptance by others, opportunities to develop and grow, relationships with others, etc.

1. Pupils list some of the things they think are their most important needs in life, working in a small group, or as a class. (Record their ideas on the board for use at the end of the lesson.)
   e.g. Food, clothing, medical care, something to do, love, belonging, friendship, acceptance by other people, learning things.
2. Remind students that throughout history these needs have been denied to certain people, or groups of people, in our world. Can they think of any?
   e.g. Jews in Germany, Christians in Russia, Blacks in South Africa. Throughout history these needs have also been denied to mentally

handicapped people. In this lesson we shall be looking at four different periods in history and finding out how mentally handicapped people were treated, and what needs were denied them.

3. Divide the class into 4 groups and present each group with information about a particular period of history.

The Ancient World

The Middle Ages

16th Century to 18th Century

19th Century and early 20th Century

In their groups they have to read through the information and:

(a) decide on how they are going to present the information back to the full group, and prepare the presentation: e.g. drama, newspaper article depicting typical situation;

(b) state which needs were being denied.

4. Each small group presents their work to the full group. Discussion.

EXAMPLE FIVE

The idea *today* is that mentally handicapped people who do not need special medical facilities and nursing should be moved from the hospitals where they are now into the community. They could live with families, in group homes, hostels, flatlets and foster homes. What kinds of things do you, as a group, think will be important to mentally handicapped people moving from a hospital? Read through the ideas below, and add any ideas of your own. Then write down the 10 most important things, in order of their importance. If you have time, say why you have chosen them.

1. To live in a community with other people.
2. To live in my own personal accommodation.
3. To decide how to spend my free time.
4. To have my own bedroom.
5. To be able to move away from my parent's home if I wish.
6. To have holidays away from home.
7. To spend time with people my own age.
8. To live with not more than 10 other people.
9. To be paid for the work I do at a fair rate.
10. To have friends who are not handicapped.
11. To go to school in a place away from where I live.
12. To live with people of the opposite sex.
13.
14.
15.

Concluding Comment

This chapter began with a description of the context in which the Project was located and the suggestion that this context was a favourable one as far as the Research Team were concerned. At an early stage, prior to actually working in the schools, we anticipated that 'reality' would not match up to rhetoric and the penetration of the Sheffield Initiative at classroom level would probably be limited, although the picture would vary from school to school. However, in a sense, the rhetoric was enough for us! At least, it meant that some of our focal concerns would be high on the agenda in several schools.

In the next three chapters we describe what took place in the three schools in which we were the most heavily involved. The intention is to provide a blow by blow account of how the Project was implemented in each of the schools rather than an in-depth analysis. As case studies, therefore, they are rather restricted in scope, but give a general impression of the particularities of the take up in each school.

Chapter 4

School A: Inter-group Contact in a Changing Curriculum

The School

The school is a comprehensive with about 1,100 pupils aged from 12 to 18 years. It is set in a green, pleasant environment on the outskirts of the city. There are five main feeder schools, three of which draw their intake from a mixture of private and council housing, and two from mainly council estates. The majority of pupils are from white, 'working-class' homes, there being very few from ethnic minority families. The area is stable — many families are related and many parents themselves attended local schools.

In 1986/7 the Second Year Curriculum consisted of the following subject areas: English, Mathematics, Science, Languages, History, Geography, Home Economics, Art, Design Studies, Social and Personal Education (SPE), PE, Music and Activities. SPE and Activities were introduced in 1983. Activities offer a choice of experiences (e.g. making music, working in the community) to enhance pupils' development outside the traditional academic curriculum. In 1987/8 the curriculum consisted of English, Mathematics, Science, Languages, Humanities, Creative Studies, PE, Music and Activities.

Although some staff were happy with this structure, others felt that changes needed to be much more radical, with a move away from subject-based learning and whole-class teaching to 'modules' and cooperative group work. This meant that there was a good deal of enthusiasm and support for the 'Teaching About Mental Handicap' Project from the management team initially, which gave the school an opportunity to develop a cross-curricular module and gave the staff the chance to work in inter-disciplinary teams.

There was also a great deal of interest from teaching staff, although time had to be spent in encouraging staff to commit themselves to the Project. The main reason for this was dismay at an ever increasing workload. As well as the tremendous amount of extra time spent by staff at School A on curriculum development, meetings, pastoral care, and out of school activities, staff were also involved in the implementation of GCSE and in-service activities attendant upon School Focused Secondment (SFS) Programmes. One said: 'The project sounds wonderful and we'll do all we can to be involved, but we won't have much time because of GCSE, SFS, etc., and all other new developments. I don't know how we'll get through the workload.'

As well as workload pressures, there were other reasons for holding back: a suspicion that the University was just using the school for research, with no follow-up support, and that this was just another 'innovation' for the sake of gratuitous experimentation; lack of resources for the Project to be carried out properly; personal qualms, such as feeling inexperienced, unsure, and embarrassed; having conflicting feelings about handicap; and being put in a position with School A pupils of not having sufficient knowledge to encourage meaningful interactions or learning.

The twenty staff who did become involved gave several reasons for doing so which are discussed at length in Chapter 10. Despite staff commitment, the Research Worker felt that she had to spend time encouraging involvement in the Project and this meant that she tended to be seen as the 'organizer', and that the amount of work that staff would eventually be involved in was underestimated, which led to tensions later in the Project. Another factor here was that the Project outgrew its original modest intentions and so demanded more and more of those involved. In effect, everyone had to contribute more, but the organizational issues became disproportionately onerous and time-consuming to discuss and effect. It also raised the question of how and whether totally new learning areas can be introduced into schools without outside agencies being involved.

The way in which we react to handicap and the chances we offer people with handicaps depend upon the value systems operating within institutions and society at large. Comprehensives with examination systems and the need for a degree of conformity could be anathema to a project which was partly about acceptance of people who weren't going to achieve academically. School A, however, did seem to have created a value system in which academic achievement was not upheld as being more important than any other sort of achievement. All pupils interviewed felt that personal qualities and 'trying hard' were the main things valued by staff. Many staff also believed in child-centred learning and making 'fun' and appealing to pupils. There were exceptions, however, plus occasional references to some pupils as being 'thick' or 'stupid' by a couple of teachers involved in the Project, although the Research Team recognized that it was simplistic to read off from such habitual vulgarities a prejudicial attitude to non-academic pupils.

Aims and Objectives of the Research Team

School A was chosen to host the Project initially because of the enthusiasm and support of the senior management team; its reputation for being at the forefront of change; its desire to adopt cross-curricular teaching methods; and the good relationships which had already been established between the Project Director and the School.

An outline of the sort of issues in the area of mental handicap that staff might want to consider was initially established by:

a. The research findings of the Project Director presented in his initial article, which explored how schools dealt with and taught implicitly and explicitly about handicap (Quicke, 1985).
b. Issues raised by the Research Worker during her employment as Head of the Special Needs Department in a comprehensive school, and as a youth worker in charge of a MENCAP Gateway Club.
c. The outcome of discussions with two Education/Training and Employment Advisers from the Royal Society for Mentally Handicapped Children and Adults.
d. Observations by the Research Worker of lessons already taking place in the school.

Some of these findings laid the basis for the way in which what turned out to be a 'Module Week' was structured. It was felt that doing community service, or merely making visits to institutions, could increase prejudices and only present people with handicaps as 'those less fortunate than ourselves to whom we must be kind'. Experiential work was thought to be important, but perhaps only if linked to critical thinking.

It was also thought that links needed to be made between different areas of the pupils' experiences. Staff attitudes were important here. Fortunately, there was a group of staff who were interested in finding out what could be achieved by changing from subject contributions to an integrated week format and who were critical of the strait-jacket hold the period structure had on schools.

Other issues were used as a basis on which to build the module activity and study sessions, and in-service staff 'training'. These included looking at the whole process of labelling; linking the historical attitudes and treatment of those with a mental handicap to present day attitudes; self-advocacy; age appropriateness; definitions of normality; charity and handicap. Two initial meetings with one of the management team involved in the Project established two important factors:

1. That the Project would take the form of a two week module (later reduced to one week as it was felt it might be difficult to sustain interest for two weeks, and the planning for that amount of time would be enormous).

2. The module would take place in the summer term as that was when fifth year pupils would have left, leaving more room in the school, teachers with a lighter workload, and the chance to increase staff/pupil ratios.

At an initial meeting with interested School A staff the above plans and ideas were put forward. Reactions were:

1. They wanted to be given some issues to think around as they felt themselves to be totally inexperienced in the field of mental handicap. However, they strongly felt that they wanted the Project to be 'theirs', i.e. belonging to staff at the grass roots, and not management or University controlled, with information merely passed down to them.

2. They wanted to involve School A pupils in the planning. This idea was reiterated several times during the year, but never came to fruition, partly because not all second year form teachers were involved, and feedback meetings would need to take place during form periods; and partly because nobody felt able to spare the time for the organization involved.

3. They also wanted the Project to be a massive in-service course for staff.

4. They felt excited that the Project would be about staff and pupils cooperating and using their initiative.

Module Week aims were eventually defined by the Research Team and were:

1. To develop critical thinking in the area of handicap, difference and prejudice.

2. To break down ill-conceived labels and analyze the whole concept of labelling.

3. To aid children in recognizing all people's common humanity.
4. To develop empathy and an understanding of what it is like to have a mental handicap.
5. To break away from the idea of seeing people with a mental handicap as passive receivers of aid, but rather to see them as people who have the same needs for love and personal development as the rest of us.

School A staff felt that they could not really define the Project aims as they were too inexperienced and unaware of all the issues. The aims were discussed as a group, and the intention was that they would be altered accordingly as the Project progressed. However, this was never done, mainly because there were so many issues for staff to discuss that some very important ones were neglected. The problem was that although aims were agreed upon at the level of rhetoric, in practice a consensus was difficult to achieve. This, of course, characterizes every curriculum initiative, even the most successful ones! On the positive side there was no doubt that a working agreement was achieved amongst staff and a remarkable degree of solidarity and coherence did emerge.

The aims of the Research Team in carrying out the Project were initially to see if pupil attitudes could be affected by a teaching programme. However, as the Project progressed it became clear that we were looking at many more issues, including teacher experience and attitudes; how and whether curriculum change can take place; divisions and collaboration within schools; relationships between schools; teachers' fears, resentments and self-evaluation; integration; community involvement; and differences in teacher and pupil attitudes to children with special needs within the comprehensive and to those in segregated settings.

The School Staff

After a few initial meetings, School A staff, despite their enthusiasm, felt as if the Project was not progressing fast enough, and that they'd never be able to organize the module in time for the summer. Consequently they asked for assistance from the Research Worker and made further demands of the Project Coordinators (two School A teachers had been cast as coordinators). This is what tended to happen, although the drawbacks were that there was a danger that staff confidence would be undermined and they would feel it would stop being their project, something they had specifically said they wanted to avoid. This was unfortunate, but not surprising in view of the inevitability of some division of labour. There was a tension, characteristic of every enterprise like this, between staff wishing to act independently and at the same time wanting someone in authority to take on the organizational responsibilities they 'hadn't got time' to fulfil. The main determinant here seemed to be the structure and organization of the curriculum, although personalities undoubtedly played a part. From a psychological viewpoint the tensions were experienced in different ways by different teachers — an aspect which is explored more fully in Chapter 10.

There was much positive interaction between staff from different subject areas, and this was an aspect of the Project that many staff said they enjoyed. There were some problems — staff not really having time to get together or never being available at the same time; occasional feelings of resentment that another member of the 'team' had more time, or was paid more and ought, therefore, to be doing more; a lack of agreement on the angles that ought to be taken; a reliance on one of the team who might be more senior or more able to meet deadlines; and forgetting to involve a member of a team from a very different department.

Problems for staff, perhaps, were also to do with the fact that teachers are often essentially alone and divided by salary, and that promotion still depends on individual performance; this makes genuine team work difficult. Despite these problems, School A staff did work together well. Many of the staff met socially and were friends, and were therefore able to work as equals. The current Headteacher encouraged a non-hierarchical school structure and open-door policy, which without doubt encouraged team work.

The attitudes of staff not involved in the module were important. There was generally a great deal of support for the Project, perhaps because of the 'sentimental' appeal of 'handicapped' children and because it dealt with 'real' issues. Some criticisms were that people would be using involvement as a spring-board for promotion; that it was 'just another' development; that it could be a back door approach to integration; that during the week, their own subject areas were being neglected. Staff involved occasionally said, 'The project has got to succeed to silence the critics', and one member of staff was put under quite a strain by her department who wanted her to make sure that her part of the module was purely about her subject area. Apart from the personal problem here of not receiving support, it also meant that she couldn't really develop a cross-curricular area. However, many other staff were extremely keen to be supportive, offering help and support to staff involved, or becoming involved on the sidelines, as the English Department did by using a novel about a child with a mental handicap.

Staff were very keen to participate in as much 'training' as possible in the limited time they had. When asked what form of preparation they would really like to have for teaching such a module if time were no problem, they mentioned working within special schools; living with a family who had a member with a mental handicap; working in training centres; attending meetings, awareness courses, video evenings; and gaining background information.

The Research Team provided a variety of books and teaching packs for the school. The Research Worker went through each book to give a summary of the content and to point individual staff to appropriate chapters or page numbers. Each member of the team was given a folder containing any relevant articles, worksheets, or ideas, and these were added to as the year progressed. An introductory evening meeting was held at which videos were shown and discussed. The Central Library mounted a book display at this meeting, and a parent, social worker, special school teacher, and a MENCAP representative came along to talk to the group as a whole, and then to smaller groups. Regular meetings were held at which issues were discussed, but as the year progressed, these became mainly organizational meetings. Staff talked to each other, although time restrictions meant that very valuable exchanges of experiences and ideas were lost, and they also talked formally and informally to the Research Team, who were a regular presence in the school. Most important, however, was the setting up of links with two special schools, and with the 'community', i.e. parents, social workers, school advisers, and MENCAP representatives.

The Research Team felt that staff were sometimes looking to experts too much, and underestimating their existing range of knowledge and experience which could be applied to the Project, e.g. what it feels like to be different, where we get our ideas of normality from, the influence of advertising and the media, and family life. However, it did seem that a degree of experience and knowledge of all the issues about mental handicap was vital if any really in-depth education was to take place. On reflection, it would have been better perhaps for the first year simply to have concentrated on staff training and awareness, although this would have been difficult because of the design of the Project, and because some staff felt that they would learn better alongside the children. Perhaps many of the problems of the Project could have been solved with more time for thinking about issues, establishing links and experimenting with different teaching strategies; although it could also be argued that the

Project would not have moved so far, so fast, if it had been a two year programme.

The Module

There were eight second year classes at School A, with an average of twenty-six 12- to 13-year-olds per class. The final structure of the Module Week was as follows:

DAY ONE — Introductory Day
Registration
Lessons 1 and 2: Introduction to the week
                 Discussion: 'What is Mental Handicap?'
                 'Causes of Mental Handicap' (Part 1)
Break
Lessons 3 and 4 'Causes of Mental Handicap' (Part 2)
Lunch
Registration
Lessons 5 and 6 'Language and Communication'

DAYS TWO TO FIVE (inclusive)
The mornings (lessons 1–4) were spent on 'Activities'. Four classes were on a carousel of the following four activities: Art, Music, Cooperative Games and Plans (simulation exercises to see the problems School A threw up for people with handicaps and how these might be overcome). Three classes remained doing the same activity each morning: Video, Computers and Toys (designing toys for people with specific handicaps). One class remained to take part in the Drama activity. The Theatre in Education Group who were running this Activity only wanted seven or eight School A children each morning. This wasn't known until the Module Week was almost upon us, so two other activities were devised for the remaining nineteen or twenty children:

(a) Magazine Activity — putting together a magazine of the week;
(b) Trips Out Activity — visits to places such as an integrated nursery, the Advocacy Project and a hostel.

Each class of School A children was joined by a group of children from one of the two special schools, the same class and group working together each morning. This was with the exception of the Plans Activity and Toys Activity.

The afternoons (lessons 5 and 6) were taken up with Study Sessions involving just School A children working in their class groups. Areas covered were: The History of Mental Handicap; Mental Handicap and Family Life; Labelling; Ante-Natal Care (originally part of 'Causes of Mental Handicap' but tending to be used separately). The final afternoon was a sports afternoon.

Activities were selected as ones in which all children could participate and which were feasible in terms of space, equipment and planning time available and also, in some cases, to satisfy departmental demands.

Initial plans were to hold the Activities on 'neutral' sites or to divide them between the three schools. This was eventually abandoned as the organizational effort needed to effect this would have been enormous. The two special schools could have catered for no more than one class of children from the comprehensive school; and the logistics of transporting children to alternative sites, especially when it involved large numbers of School A children, proved too problematic. However, in future years the school would still like to pursue the ideal of using 'neutral' sites.

Originally each class was going to follow the same activity each morning, but as four staff felt they'd prefer to work with a different class each day, the carousel arrangement was adopted for four of the eight classes. Although this meant children had a wider variety of experiences and staff could prepare only one morning's work to alter accordingly, it also meant arrangements were more complicated and that School A staff were working with lots of children and adults they hadn't had time to get to know or coordinate with beforehand.

The overall feeling of the school in the morning was of fun, joy, and energy — one teacher described it as 'buzzing'. There was a great deal of excellent interaction among pupils, staff and community links, and some positive and, it is to be hoped, lasting pupil relationships between School A pupils and those from special schools. Many adults and pupils felt it was the 'best thing' to happen all year, and all, with the exception of a few teachers from one of the special schools, were eager and keen to develop the Project over a few years.

One of the problems was that some of the special school staff felt excluded and that they hadn't been consulted sufficiently. Consequently they felt some activities were inappropriate or underestimated the needs of their pupils. There were also a number of 'technical hitches' due to last minute room changes, transport problems, the effects of teachers' industrial action and classes from special schools being changed or substituted, for a variety of reasons, at the last minute. School A staff were themselves so involved, that no one was available to welcome and organize visitors and sort out any problems. The size of the comprehensive school classes was occasionally overwhelming for the small groups of children from special schools, and this is likely to remain a problem for any such integrated project due to staffing levels and room availability.

There were a number of areas which could have been covered in the study sessions. The ones eventually developed were chosen because clarification of certain issues was needed by some pupils. It was felt that some skills necessary for the week could be taught, such as alternative forms of communication in 'Language and Communication'. The choice of study sessions also depended upon staff preference and the availability of material from which to draw ideas.

The staff producing the study materials had a difficult job as there were few existing resources which could be used as a base or guideline. They also felt vulnerable as the work they produced would be seen and used by all other staff and community links. The other staff saw some of the material as it was being produced and offered encouragement. Had there been more time available, and had it been possible to create a feeling of group responsibility for everything that was organized or produced, it would have been easier for staff to have worked on material together, offering suggestions from their specialisms.

Staff found it difficult to complete the material until two weeks before the module began. This was frustrating but May/June was the peak of the examination period and staff were hard pressed. The material then had to be correlated, photocopied and distributed. This meant there was very little time for staff to be fully acquainted with what was a vast amount of material. The Local Education Authority gave them ten days supply cover so teachers had some time to look at the materials, but they could not always look at them alongside the teachers with whom they would be working. There was not time for School A staff to arrange for the Community Links to come in and look at the materials with them, although Community Links were sent copies.

Some of the study sessions were described as being far too 'heavy' and containing too much information. In fact, in the end, there was a problem of over- rather than under-preparedness, which given the situation (non-specialist staff, new content, etc.) was scarcely surprising. Some staff didn't feel confident enough to select from the material available or to abandon it and follow an alternative discussion should it arise, and consequently some good opportunities for extending understanding of issues raised by pupils were lost. In some cases excellent material was underused as the significance of it was not fully explored, and chances to relate back to pupils' own experiences and feelings were not always pursued. Some staff felt that the study periods should have come in the morning when people were less tired, although the original intention of having them in the afternoon was that experiences from the morning could be discussed, and because the school worked a timetable of two-thirds in the morning and one-third in the afternoon. Perhaps, as well, some staff did not feel the study periods were relevant or the right way of discussing issues, preferring full day contact with the special schools. Some pupils would also have preferred this, one saying 'Can't we have some more games?' when asked to read and discuss a worksheet. This raises some interesting questions about the best way to foster reading, questioning, discussion and reflective activity generally in a module with a heavy experiential component.

There were, however, many positive aspects to the study sessions. Staff said they felt rewarded and that they and the pupils had learnt a great deal. Pupils were often very involved, asking perceptive questions and making in-depth observations. There were many opportunities to be involved in a variety of learning situations, e.g. whole class, group work, role play. Both staff and pupils enjoyed working alongside each other and particularly liked the presence and contributions of the Community Links. Sessions where parents of children with mental handicap talked and were questioned about their experiences were highly successful. All the Community Links were extremely enthusiastic about the sessions, and they and the staff frequently said how they'd been amazed by the maturity and involvement of School A pupils.

It was recognized that there needed to be a lot of preparation in the school before the actual module week. Again, time available was limited, and the actual workload it was possible for teachers to take on board was prohibitive, but much did seem to have been achieved. There was continual discussion of the module week between staff and children, sparked off mainly by the initial pupil interviews conducted by the Research Team. The Research Team provided two sets of the book *Welcome Home, Jellybean* by Marlene Fanta Shyer which the English Department read, discussed, and used as basis for creative work with each second year class.

A group of children from each class made visits to both special schools. These proved extremely successful. Care was taken to make sure the children from School A were fully involved in the host school's activities. Ideally all children would have been involved, but it was too much to arrange for 210 pupils to make visits, so the groups who did go 'reported back' to their class colleagues. Comments were often perceptive and sensitive, but some children were playing to their audience and exaggerating the behaviour they'd witnessed. This often had the effect of emphasizing the differences rather than any similarities between themselves and the children in special schools. This was just one instance where, through lack of experience, staff were on the verge of inadvertantly encouraging prejudice and stereotypes rather than leading pupils on to question their ideas.

Other plans which were not used this year, although the school was hoping to develop them in future, were looking at related issues such as prejudice, difference, physical repulsion, bullying, value systems; 'pen-palling' children in School A with children in the other two schools; and using videos and visiting speakers to raise issues with pupils.

Collaboration with Special Schools and the Community

School A had already developed and was continuing to develop links with their immediate community. Upper school pupils worked in the community one afternoon a week. There was a recently formed school–community committee: and one of the management team was attending a course on 'Schools and the Community'. It was therefore natural that staff should request links with parents and families of children with a mental handicap. It also seemed unfair to think that meaningful courses could be developed without the involvement of people who were involved on a day to day basis.

The Research Worker knew the city and already had extensive links with parents of children with mental handicap, and professional workers with such children, and took on board the job of involving them in the Project and keeping them informed. The links included parents, social workers, advisory teachers for children with special needs, speech therapists and a games therapist who became involved as the Project progressed. Their involvement seemed to have been successful. All of them were extremely positive about the Project, and said it had given them a great amount of joy and thought it was invaluable. They were linked to specific School A teachers to act almost as 'trainers'.

It was felt that for the Project to have any real meaning, contact with children with a mental handicap was imperative. There were three schools within the city which children with 'Severe Learning Difficulties' attended. Two catered for the pre-school to 13-year-old age range, and one for the 13- to 19-year-old age range. All were approached. Two responded positively immediately and these two became involved.

Involvement with one was hugely successful whereas there were several problems surrounding the involvement of the other. These were due to a variety of factors, including complex issues within that school, as well as problems about the dissemination of information which led to some misunderstandings. There was a natural affinity between School A and one of the schools, which led to a neglect of the second school and a misunderstanding of the aims of the Project. On reflection the Research Team could have done more to prepare the ground here.

However, there was overwhelming support from the first school and from some teachers in the second school to continue and develop the links, and a feeling that despite some of the problems raised, the outcome had been exciting, positive, and of great benefit to both children and staff.

Concluding Comment

There are many constraints on the development of a project of this nature — practical, financial and political. Psychologically, these aspects of the context are experienced as pressures which vary in intensity depending on the time of year, the number of competing demands being made and the salience of organizational conflicts. However, the general impression was that School A staff had derived benefit from the Project. The nature and origin of their commitment is discussed at greater length in Chapter 10. We were hoping that the experience of the Project would deepen this commitment and this appears to have happened, although we were unable to carry out post-module interviews to explore this further.

The original idea was to run the Module again in the second year but we decided against this partly because many staff felt that it was unnecessary to repeat it in this form and partly because we were uncertain what demands would be made on the Research Team. If there was too much further involvement with School A it would drastically restrict the time we could give to the new schools. However, in School A the skills, knowledge and experience gained in year one were put to good use in year two. Contact with one of the special schools was maintained and pupils continued to visit the school in Activities periods. The suspended timetable in year two consisted of a variety of activities, one of which involved children from the special school and School A participating in joint activities. The English Department continued to use *Welcome Home, Jellybean* and the topic of mental handicap was dealt with in Humanities. Some of the teachers involved in the Project left at the end of the year. This was unfortunate from School A's viewpoint, but we felt that it might mean that further seeds would be sown in other schools.

As for the pupils in school A, their development is discussed at length in Chapters 8 and 9. Suffice it at this point to note that there was a general feeling amongst staff and pupils that most pupils had enjoyed participating in pre-module activities and the Module Week. Some children clearly felt they had learned a great deal. Several wrote that they felt 'nervous' or 'scared' at first and didn't know what to expect but soon felt at ease. One girl concluded that she had 'grown closer' to the special school pupils by the end of the week. All referred to the special school children by name and most clearly regarded them as individuals with wills of their own. As one girl put it:

> The handicapped girl I was with, Fiona, didn't enjoy painting. She was more interested in when she was having her lunch. She told me she would be having fish and chips. During the lesson we went for a walk. She was talking and laughing all the way.

The most difficult feature of all to evaluate was the impact of the Project on special school pupils. Clearly, at the time many seemed to enjoy the module activities, although not all participated to the same degree. Hopefully, some lasting contacts between School A children and special school children were established. Some School A children explicitly requested that they be allowed to continue the relationship in some way.

On the negative side there was a suggestion that children from the special schools were being used as 'teaching aids', as some teachers from one special school put it. Their curriculum had been disrupted in order to develop the curriculum of School A children. The Research Team also noted that very few participants suggested this might be the beginning of a full scale integration programme. Indeed, there was a certain confusion over this which though anticipated was never fully resolved. In future the question of whether such inter-institutional contact consolidates or dismantles segregated provision must be confronted.

Chapter 5

School B: A Child-centred Approach — The 'Ripple Effect'

The School

School B is an 11–18 comprehensive on the northern outskirts of the city. The pupils are from white 'working-class' backgrounds, with few ethnic minority families. Many of the families are long established, with second and third generation families living in the locality. Unemployment in the area is high.

Close to the school an Adult Training Centre offers recreation, work and education opportunities for adults with a mental handicap, drawing adults mainly from the north side of the city. The centre has maintained contact with one of the feeder schools and to some extent with the comprehensive school. A Health Authority hostel also within the area provides supported living accommodation for adults with a mental handicap. Adult Education uses part of the school building and provides a number of daytime and evening courses plus basic skill courses for those with severe learning difficulties.

The school supports an open access policy. The building is designed to offer access to people in wheelchairs. A number of children with physical disability are fully integrated at school. The school also encourages adults to attend although as yet few adults have actually done so. During the previous year three adults with mental and physical disabilities residing at a local hospital were supported in first year classes but this has since stopped. One of the city's special schools is located in the immediate area of the comprehensive.

The first year are organized into four classes and ten smaller tutorial groups. An inter-disciplinary team of teachers known as the first year team and consisting of four tutors and one liaison staff take the pupils for most of the week but each member of the team has other responsibilities around the school. The pupils and teachers are based in four connecting rooms in school. The curriculum is based on an integrated, thematic approach rather than organized into subject areas. Pupils go 'out of team' for design, PE and swimming and some Music. Part of the music curriculum is integrated into the Performance Arts Unit. Most staff are happy with this structure, supporting the move away from subject-based learning.

Curriculum Development

Curriculum planning always involves the full team. Members contribute ideas and discuss initiatives. Individuals may then offer to be responsible for a particular project. Regular feedback is encouraged through team meetings held once a week and since staff have considerable contact with each other throughout the week, ideas are frequently exchanged at other times. Small tutor groups allow for the pupils to discuss curriculum issues and contribute to planning as well. Staff, at least at the level of rhetoric, appeared committed to a pupil–staff team approach to curriculum planning and development.

The move toward an integrated curriculum with a mixture of skill-based and theme-based learning was still relatively new in the school. Staff however were positive about its benefits. They felt, for instance, that the flexibility arising from such an approach allowed for certain areas of learning such as the 'mental handicap awareness' project to be taken up and developed more easily. Timetabling and organizational issues, for example, did not become disproportionately time-consuming. Many staff also felt that overall pupils clearly benefited more from this way of working. One teacher commented: 'The kids seem to have a more mature attitude to learning: they seem more mature in their surroundings; they ask if they're not sure and enjoy finding out; they know they are listened to.'

There are, however, some problems with the approach: occasional conflicting interests over curriculum content; taking on equal responsibilities when some staff are paid more, have more time, etc.; staff feeling that they lack expertise or that they are inadequately experienced in certain topics; difficulties in communicating all relevant information to all team members; and other pressures arising out of tutors' other responsibilities within school.

Development of the Project — Aims

At the outset there appeared to be considerable enthusiasm for the Project. The school had been contacted by the Director of the Project and a member of the first year team had been assigned coordinator.

The initial meeting took place between the school coordinator and the Research Worker. The coordinator acted as liaison teacher between the University and team. There were a number of issues raised at these meetings which it was anticipated would, when discussed with the team, provide the basis for developing aims and structuring teaching. Some of the issues raised were:

1. Community involvement through parents, youth workers, adult education workers. The coordinator felt that by setting up community links it would not only benefit the Project within school but would have a 'spin off' effect to youth clubs, adult education groups and community activities.
2. Recognition of the pupils' experience of mental handicap. If a child-centred approach was to be adopted pupils' experiences should be used as a basis on which to build activities.
3. The decision to implement curriculum changes entailed by the Project rested with the first year team. For the Project to 'take root' staff at the school should feel that they 'owned' it.
4. At the time of the Project there were no pupils with severe learning difficulties attending the school. A long-term aim might be the integration of those children, the Project preparing pupils and staff for that process. One suggestion was that pupils and staff at the comprehensive 'twin' with pupils and staff at the special school. It was recognized that an integration programme as such was not within the boundaries of the Project since the decision to integrate individuals rested with the education authority.

Other issues which were discussed were the ten year strategic plan for mental handicap services and its effect on the local community, particularly the imminent closure of nearby hospital units; labelling and the use of language within the pupil culture; age appropriateness; and perceptions of normality.

Despite the initial enthusiasm and commitment, the Project at the school seemed to progress slowly until Easter. It became increasingly difficult for the Research Worker to meet with staff. There were a number of possible reasons for this. The coordinator left the school at Christmas on maternity leave. The new coordinator was for a long time unsure of her role. The first year team were feeling pressured by other departments in the school and by the increasing workload as initiatives were developed. There was a reluctance to 'take on any more'. Another reason for holding back was that some staff felt inexperienced and inadequately trained in the area of mental handicap. As one member of staff said: 'I took a back seat for a long time not through lack of interest but lack of time etcetera. Also an in-built fear of not knowing myself how to relate to mentally handicapped people.'

The team, however, finally did meet with the Research Worker and the Director of the Project. It was decided that a complete teaching programme could not be planned in advance but would gradually develop during the course of the summer term according to the response from the pupils. The starting point would be the questionnaire which had been completed by all first year pupils in the first term. Staff were to discuss the questionnaire in small tutorial groups and decide the next development through consultation with the pupils. Staff and pupils would be learning together. They were keen that the Project should not be seen as something separate but should develop as an integral curriculum concern. The issues surrounding special needs and mental handicap in particular should, staff felt, be viewed in the same way as multi-racial and gender issues.

Any feelings of never having 'owned' the Project, or loss of ownership, were dispelled in these meetings. This was an important turning point. Throughout the Project the Research Team had attempted to act as facilitators and to be as non-impositional as possible. The roles of the University and Project coordinators were clearly defined. The Research Team were seen as initiators, a source of information, observers, commentators and providers of feedback and liaison with other establishments. At all stages a sharing of responsibilities for planning and teaching by the team was encouraged.

After these meetings staff met regularly, feeding back information, evaluating work and planning the next stage. Some staff had developed the Project further than others, either because of personal interest or because the response from pupils in their small tutorial groups had required it. Information about mental handicap provided by the Research Team had been read by some staff. One teacher had begun reading *Welcome Home, Jellybean* by Marlene Fanta Shyer with his group and another was using pupils' experiences of mental handicap as a basis for creative writing.

The Teaching

The teaching programme eventually consisted of four interconnected stages — each stage developing from the previous one.

Stage One

The first stage was exploratory. Some of the first year pupils were given back their questionnaires and asked to discuss their replies in small tutorial groups. Some discussions were taped. The structure of the groups lent itself readily to discussion of this kind. The groups numbered approximately 8–12 and met in small rooms such as the headmaster's office twice each week with their staff tutor.

The activity varied according to the curriculum emphasis at the time, but mainly it was seen as a discussion session or a forum for pupils' opinions. Children were encouraged to evaluate teaching activities and their own progress. It had been found that such activities were difficult in large groups. To enable small group tutorial sessions to operate, other first years were involved in large group activities such as swimming.

Most pupils seemed happy to share their knowledge and experiences of mental handicap with others although obviously there were some who lacked confidence or found it difficult to articulate their feelings.

Experience and images

The findings of the questionnaire has shown that experience of mental handicap amongst first years was extensive. The discussion also indicated that those experiences were extremely varied. For instance, in one tutorial group alone, one pupil had an aunt with a mental handicap and made weekly visits to the hospital where she was living; another lived opposite a hostel for adults with mental handicap and frequently spoke to some of the residents; another had simply seen a group of adults from a unit using the canteen and still another travelled on the same bus as an adult attending a training centre. An interesting observation was that, in the main, accounts of experience of mental handicap referred to adults. Behavioural descriptions from responses to the question 'Write down three things about them' were punctuated during the discussions with accounts of pupils' reactions and feelings towards adults with a mental handicap. For instance, one girl *wrote* 'She lives in a hospital, she needs help to feed herself', and *said* during discussion 'I help to feed her, she seems happy.' A boy *wrote* 'They make a mess when they're eating', and *said* 'It puts me off my dinner.'

Integration and 'being picked on'

The questionnaire responses indicated a mixture of views on integration. Little was added during tutorial sessions except that many agreed that problems arising initially in an integration programme would probably be overcome in time. Being picked on emerged as a major concern both in interviews conducted with pupils by the Research Worker and during discussions in small tutorial groups.

Calling a person names intended as an insult, blocking somebody's path, ordering them to do things they didn't want to, and threatening physical abuse all constituted 'picking on'. The pupils felt that they themselves had all been picked on at one time or another although they agreed that only a minority consistently picked on others. Most pupils seemed confused about or could not articulate the reasons why this sort of behaviour should occur at all, although jealousy, fear, thinking it was funny or clever were all mentioned. The general response was 'I don't know why, it just happens'.

Pupils were far more able to articulate what they felt were the reasons why a person with a mental handicap would get picked on. They felt that such a person was more vulnerable, might not understand the verbal abuse, might not be able to fight back, might look different and might behave differently. It was suggested by the staff tutor that these could equally apply to a young child. Clearly pupil expectations and age appropriateness needed further examination, and could be used as a basis for broadening understanding of mental handicap. As for sex differences, it was agreed that girls picked on someone mainly by ignoring them or excluding them from their activity whereas boys appeared more aggressive, using physical and verbal attack. Where help was needed both boys and girls agreed it was more likely to be the girls that offered it.

Debating the issues: language

An encouraging aspect of the small group tutorial sessions was that pupils challenged each other's language. In some instances discussions became heated. Although nobody objected to the term 'mental handicap', other terms were questioned. For instance, in one session a pupil referred to someone he knew as 'being mental' and another referred to the 'funny farm where they live'. Others in the group objected and challenged the users to provide an explanation of why they had used the term. Another pupil spoke of someone he knew as 'daft' and 'thick in the head'. Another objected, 'That's not fair. He's not daft, he just hasn't learnt some things.'

It was noted that the 'challengers' tended to have had greater contact with people with mental handicap than the challenged. Challengers were also seemingly well aware of the significance of language in what they considered faulty perceptions of mental handicap. They were not merely being compliant with the teachers' views and values. They objected to the terms used on the basis that they devalued the people they knew and were 'unfair'.

Stage Two

Twelve pupils were identified during Stage One whose experience and knowledge of mental handicap was considerable. At a planning meeting of the first year team following small group tutorial sessions it was decided that the twelve individuals would meet as a group to work intensively on the Project. The aim was that a core of expertise would develop. The core would be used as a focal point for work with other pupils. The group was allocated a staff tutor (the coordinator of the Project) to work with them. It was hoped that this would be the beginning of what was described as the 'ripple effect'.

The structure of the work was designed by the staff tutor, after negotiations with the pupil group. One of the curriculum emphases at the time was a 'creative writing project' and it was intended that the Project would link in with this. The group would meet to discuss ideas and talk about their experiences of mental handicap. They would produce illustrated stories, written interviews, written accounts of their experiences and fact sheets which could be typed and collated to form a booklet. The booklet would be duplicated and distributed to other first year groups and a copy provided for the library. The aim was that pupils would work together, in pairs or as a group, drawing on their particular creative strengths. Thus one person might illustrate another's story. The idea was that pupils would work collaboratively.

Observing these activities, the Research Worker found that some pupils showed a reluctance to participate. Some were very quiet during discussion sessions and needed considerable encouragement to articulate their feelings. The boys seemed particularly reserved and did not interact with the girls much. It was also felt that there was an undercurrent of conflict in the group and some pupils seemed isolated. Although there was some degree of cooperation the sessions were not a good example of collaborative group work. The staff tutor spent time encouraging her pupils, convincing them of the value of their experiences and raising confidence. When interviewed the pupils were not prepared to discuss their reasons for holding back. These were articulated much later in the second set of interviews held after Stage Three.

There were positive aspects to these sessions. Some pupils were 'open' with the group; pupils worked together and produced the booklet and when given the choice at the end of the first week all pupils wanted to continue their involvement with the Project.

Stage Three

A company of actors based at the city's main theatre who had been involved in the Project the previous year were invited to place an actor in residence at the school for two weeks. The company were embarking on a series of 'Actors in Residence' (A in R) projects aimed at creating closer links with educationalists, community workers and young people in the city in a variety of formal and informal settings. The company participants consisted of three actor/teachers, an education liaison officer, a young theatre leader and a stage manager. The actor/teacher placed at the school had had mainstream experience and had also worked in special schools in the city with the company.

Staff at the school were struggling at this point to find a way forward with the Project to meet the aims of extending it to all first years. They felt they needed an input from another source and they therefore welcomed the opportunity of A in R involvement with great enthusiasm. It was then suggested that he might extend work with 'the twelve' and begin work about mental handicap with other pupils.

At a planning meeting it was then decided that the Mental Handicap Awareness Project would be linked with a first year Environment Project developing concurrently within school. The aims as defined by the actor in residence and the first year team were:

1. To look at the fears and prejudices that surround disability in a supportive environment in order to raise the level of awareness within the school.
2. To raise the level of awareness within the community.
3. To see people with disability as being part of our community.
4. To use the expertise of 'the twelve' and develop this beyond their immediate environment.

5. To make the knowledge of the twelve important (the role of the expert) and encourage the responsibility of sharing this across the first year.
6. To explore people's relationship with the environment, focusing on the senses and the creation of facilities to meet particular needs.

The final component of the residency would be to work in small tutorial groups on the 'hidden language' surrounding disability. The final structure of the week was as follows:

Day One
Morning   : Sensory Workshop with 'The Twelve'.
Afternoon : Small group tutorial sessions.

Day Two
Morning   : Workshop to tie in with the Performance Arts Unit.
Afternoon : Small group tutorial sessions.

Day Three
Morning   : Workshop on environments with 'The Twelve'.
Afternoon : Small group tutorial sessions.

Day Four
Morning   : Planning meeting with the first year team.
Afternoon : Small group tutorial sessions.

Day Five
Full day   : The twelve would build environments and masked 'performers' would explore those environments.

The structure was repeated the second week although some workshops and small group tutorial sessions were not included.

The culmination of the week's intensive work with the twelve pupils was the Friday 'performance'. Whilst one half of the group prepared for a masked 'performance' the other half built an environment in the drama studio. Neither half had any contact with the other whilst the preparations were going on. When the stage had been created the studio was put in darkness apart from lighting for the stage itself. The masked 'performers' entered the studio one by one and explored the hitherto unknown environment set for them. The only directions they had been given were that they were not to speak and their actions should be slow and exaggerated so that the people watching them could see their reactions clearly. The actor in residence then asked questions of the performers —

who they were, how they felt, whether they knew each other, what they thought of their environment, etc. Once on stage each pupil had clearly become the character of the mask.

Stage Four

The intention had been that the Project would be extended across the first year. The expertise of the twelve would be used to raise the level of awareness in other pupils. Staff encouraged a sharing of ideas and knowledge but unfortunately a structural plan for the fourth stage was never completed.

Preparing pupils for the fourth stage had been done through small group tutorial sessions. The questionnaire had been discussed with a number of groups in Stage One. The actor in residence had looked at perceptions of normality and the 'hidden language' surrounding disability with pupils at Stage Three. Some groups had been looking at provision in the community for those with a disability, others had been looking at the accessibility of the school building and another group had been reading books about disability.

Work continued in small group tutorial sessions in the fourth stage. The twelve returned to their respective tutorial groups to take part in follow-up discussions on disability. Extracts from pupil diaries were used as a basis for these discussions. Pupils were encouraged to impart knowledge and recount experiences and occasionally teach skills to the rest of the group.

It was unfortunate that work with pupils was started so late in the school year that it left little time for the fourth stage to develop beyond those few discussions. Staff and pupils became involved in end of term activities and not surprisingly had little time or inclination for interviews and questionnaires. The researcher felt that valuable information had been lost because of the timing.

Concluding Comment

The intention behind the teaching strategies deployed at School B was to harness the 'ripple effect'. It was hoped that a group of pupils who had special experience of mental handicap and who had worked on that experience in small groups would create 'ripples' in the rest of the year group. Unfortunately, for practical reasons, this process could not be completed and the momentum built up over a number of weeks was lost. However, the general feeling was that up until Stage Four the project had been successful and that a useful working model for curriculum innovation in a sensitive area had been constructed.

The Research Worker observed that the group of twelve eventually began to share their experiences and work collaboratively. Any reluctance to become involved had been replaced by an obvious enthusiasm and excited anticipation of further sessions with the actor in residence. Their perceptions of the value of their work had altered and they began to feel the Project was important.

Staff also noted changes. One wrote:

> The pupils became highly motivated. They were very enthusiastic, eager to get down to the sessions each day. They felt privileged to have spent so much time with the actor in residence — proud of their part in it. They became more comfortable with their position, more open about knowing someone with a mental handicap.

The pupils who had worked with the actor in residence were interviewed one week after the work was completed. Small groups of two to five were asked to describe their experiences, evaluate the sessions and reflect on what they had learnt.

All the pupils had clearly enjoyed the sessions and were eager to comment, needing little encouragement to do so. There was a relaxed atmosphere in these interviews. Pupils seemed comfortable with each other and with the Research Worker. They interacted well and the separateness of boys and girls, noticeable in the pre-project interviews, was not apparent. Some individuals' confidence to contribute to the discussion had increased. The sense of hidden conflicts of interest was not felt and the pupils referred to each other with a certain affection and understanding.

Some agreed they had initially been reluctant to participate in any of the early sessions. The reasons they gave for holding back were that they thought it might be boring; that they didn't really see any value in the Project or in their knowledge of mental handicap and they didn't want to miss other activities in school. Some were worried about 'getting on' with the rest of the group; some felt they might be ridiculed by friends not involved and some were concerned about discussing the source of their experiences because they were unsure if 'it was right'. Many of the comments hinted at views expressed within the pupil culture — views which, as noted elsewhere in the report, are difficult to extract and are therefore inadequately researched.

No one felt their reasons for holding back were justified in the end. The overall feeling about the sessions was that they were 'really good' and 'great fun'. Pupils' comments on individual sessions varied. They recognized a developmental process, seeing their own actions and feelings as the consequence of the previous day's experiences. For instance one pupil commented: 'At first it was really hard to trust someone to take me round the room when I was blindfolded but after I had to do it I learnt it was all right.' Another said: 'We had to build environments together — we talked about it first. I don't think we could have done that at the beginning of the week but we'd done some games and things by the end.'

The way in which events were recalled by the pupils demonstrated that pupils were not only thinking about isolated activities and their reactions to them but also connecting their thoughts and reflecting critically on issues surrounding handicap, and mental handicap in particular.

They were asked to list the things they had learnt. One boy just said 'Lots!' In the area of handicap most felt they 'experienced' disability during the sessions — what it felt like to trust someone to do things for you that you want to do for yourself; frustration; fear; loneliness; feeling isolated; inability to coordinate your movements; not being able to speak; having your reactions misinterpreted; hiding your feelings; and experiencing joy and relief when problems were overcome. Pupils also spoke of skills they had learnt or developed to help each other such as taking responsibility and finding a means of communication.

It was encouraging that pupils were critically reflecting on their experiences. They had examined their existing knowledge and experiences of handicap in the light of the new experiences offered to them through the activities. One boy, referring to people with a mental handicap, concluded: 'I hadn't thought about it like that before. They're just the same as us really.'

When asked about the future, pupils said they were prepared to use their expertise to extend the Project to other first years but they were uncertain as to how to carry out this role. All, however, welcomed an opportunity to be further involved, particularly if involvement included more sessions with the actor in residence. They felt others would also benefit from similar sessions.

Chapter 6

School C: A Module within Humanities

The School

School C was a large 11–18 comprehensive on the south-eastern side of the city and was due to be amalgamated with a neighbouring school next year. In the not too distant past the catchment area of the school had been altered to include some of the better off parts of the city. The social class distribution was skewed towards the middle and low middle class end of the spectrum. Originally a secondary modern school, it worked hard to create a more academic image and was pushed further in this direction by parental pressure. Now with an active PTA and a reputation for academic success it was considered to be the 'best' school in the neighbourhood. The curriculum was subject-based and teaching methods tended to be traditional, but under the impact of LEA initiatives changes were taking place. Amalgamation and redeployment were major concerns for the teachers at the time of the Research Team's involvement with the school and this has to be borne in mind when evaluating the intervention.

Staff Involvement: Some Problems for the Project

During the first year of the Project a member of the school staff became involved in the module at School A whilst seconded as Education Liaison Officer for a company of actors from the city's theatre. She was keen to develop the Project in her own school when she returned to her position as Drama/Humanities teacher in September. Subsequently the Head of the school decided that the Project would be 'a good thing' and passed the information he had received from the University to the Head of Humanities. It was discussed with the teacher on her return to the school and she assumed responsibility for the Project and acted as coordinator between school and University.

The Humanities Department was formed in 1985 combining Geography, History and Religious Education. The English Department was also linked after the first year as it was decided that an English teacher was to be allocated to each class for at least one lesson in Humanities a week. Consequently most classes had three teachers for Humanities. Many staff expressed dissatisfaction with the structure. Some felt that they did not have sufficient opportunity to build relationships with their pupils which they considered important for good teaching. Others felt that some areas of work were repeated while other areas were left out completely because there was little time to discuss with colleagues which aspect of the curriculum they had taught. Some staff were not committed to the integration of subjects and saw more benefit in continuing to work within traditional subject boundaries.

The Project was introduced into the Humanities curriculum because, as the coordinator said, 'it is the only area of the school curriculum flexible enough to take it'. This tended to happen in this school to initiatives which crossed subject boundaries. The Head of Humanities felt that the Department was expected to take on too much. Whilst staff were committed, there was a certain amount of resentment about the fact that they were the ones who were always expected to take on new projects. A senior teacher said: 'Everything's a bit rushed. For some teachers who are good but used to a bit more traditional teaching, every time there's a new project it unsettles them. Teachers like to feel in control of knowledge. It is also complicated by the number of teachers involved.'

Most staff when interviewed stated that they would have liked to become involved at the developmental stage, but that lack of time had prevented this from happening. Many were involved in the implement-ation of GCSE, as well as other curriculum developments and out of school activities. The timing of 'free periods' seemed to influence involvement as well. Some staff were concerned that many of their free periods were spent covering for absent staff. What free time was left did not coincide with the free periods of other staff involved in the Project. Consequently, since they were often attending lunch time and after school meetings, there was little time for the exchange of ideas and information between staff. It seemed impossible to organize a time when all members of staff involved in the Project could meet.

Throughout the year there was an increasing tension amongst staff over the amalgamation with the neighbouring school in September 1988. The amalgamation was the result of post-16 developments in the city. Staff felt under pressure to justify their roles and by the second term were being interviewed for posts in the 'new' school. Some staff were to be redeployed and concern about their futures created considerable tension and competition between staff. Because of the way teachers' careers are structured, there is always an emphasis on individual performance, but the additional pressures this year made team work even more difficult. Commitment to the Project was also affected by other uncertainties created by the amalgamation programme. As one member of staff stated: 'There's a difficulty anyway now with people moving buildings and the amalgamation. This year has been *the* most hectic and disorientating for years.'

Though there was general support for the Project some staff felt unqualified to assist in its development. The coordinator and the Research Worker tended to be seen as the experts. In order to deepen staff's understanding of mental handicap, they were invited to a seminar at the University where School A staff described what happened at their school the previous year, and the development of the Project was explained and resources displayed. A parent, special school teacher, MENCAP representative and Educational Advisor for Special Needs talked to the group. Although all staff from School C were invited, few were able to attend.

At the initial meeting of the Research Team and school staff it was decided that in-service training sessions would be set up at the school and staff would in addition make arrangements to visit a special school. Unfortunately, although five such sessions were planned for the term, only one took place because of the difficulty in finding time for staff to meet.

It was at this point that the Research Team queried whether or not the Project should be continued in this school. Clearly, the staff did not feel that they 'owned' the Project and there were many indications that the result of continuing might be counter productive. However in the end we felt justified in supporting the Project in this school. In the first place, although staff may not have assumed team ownership, within the Humanities Department they had at least agreed that the Project should be included in the curriculum. They all wanted it to 'happen'. Their acceptance indicated the importance they attached to the topic. Second, the Research Worker felt that to have withdrawn from a school because staff did not immediately wish to take up ownership was to ignore the possibility that ownership might eventually be established. The system at the school seemed to operate in such a way that it was usually an individual member of staff or an outsider who initiated curriculum changes and took responsibility for ownership and development of materials and staff training. Only after a project had been taught for a while did the Humanities team assume more responsibility for it. This had happened in the past in relation to other 'sensitive' areas of the curriculum. Third, the Research Team was impressed with some of the findings of the questionnaire and interview study, particularly the latter which suggested that pupils' and teachers' value systems were more compatible with the aims of the Project than had at first been thought. Initially, we had doubts about the value system operating in the school. Academic success as measured by examination results seemed to be the most important definition of achievement, and traditional subject-centred methods of teaching were favoured. Staff in general felt that this orientation was still dominant. Some felt that it was partly due to parental influence which was interpreted as 'support' or 'pressure' depending on which staff perceptions were being considered. There were clearly a number of staff who were not happy with the present system and expressed a desire to move towards child-centred learning and integrated curricula. Moreover, interviews with pupils suggested at least the possibility of an alternative value system becoming established. Almost all pupils interviewed felt that 'trying hard' was perceived by teachers as more important than academic achievement and the rewards for 'effort' were greater than those for 'getting a high score in a test'. Friendship groups did not seem to be based on achievement levels as might have been expected in a traditional school. As one child put it: 'She's better than me at lots of work at school but it doesn't matter. She helps me sometimes. We're in a different set for maths. But we're still friends and I help her sometimes with other things.' Moreover, personal qualities were considered by pupils to be one of the main things valued by staff. In fact, being friendly, trustworthy and able to share were valued by pupils and staff.

Setting up the Module

Some of the findings of the questionnaire and interviews were fed back to staff at the school at a meeting held at the beginning of the second term. These findings were used as a basis for structuring activities. Staff felt that there was a need to increase understanding and fill gaps in their own and the pupils' knowledge of mental handicap; to involve 'outsiders' as much as possible; to set up contacts with special school pupils; to introduce activities which were 'experiential'; to look at speech and alternative methods of communication; and to involve all first year pupils. It soon became clear that contacts with special school pupils could not be set up properly in the time available, and so this aim was abandoned.

As the Project progressed the organization of timetabling became the main concern and overcoming the difficulties was time-consuming. Staff wanted all the children to participate in each activity and this wish had to be matched with the varying amount of input that outside links were able to offer and the availability of resources. In addition the need for limiting the size of the group, rooms available and the constraints of the existing timetable had to be taken into account. Unlike School A, School C did not consider it necessary to have a suspended timetable. Nevertheless, there were a number of similarities between the schools in the way the Project developed. For example, as the coordinator's workload increased the Research Worker took on more responsibility for organizing the structure of the module and contacting outside links. We felt that this had implications for curriculum initiatives of this type. Can new 'sensitive' topics be introduced within the existing structure of most secondary schools without the involvement of outside agencies? Can organizational difficulties be overcome by joint responsibility? Can teachers effectively organize a project of this nature with a full timetable commitment?

It was finally agreed that the module would extend over two weeks. All Humanities lessons during these weeks would be concerned with disability awareness with particular reference to mental handicap. Each of the ten first year classes of approximately twenty-five children had six lessons per week in Humanities. These were mainly in the form of three double lessons lasting 1 hour 10 minutes. At some time during the two weeks most children were to be involved in the following:

1. Drama: 'Experiencing disability', taken by a member of the school staff.
2. Dance: 'A lesson for children with severe learning difficulties', taken by a teacher for children with special needs and organizer of a centre for arts for the disabled.
3. Family Life: taken by a parent of a child with special needs.
4. Communication: 'Using Makaton', taken by a speech therapist.
5. Simulation Exercises using equipment designed to simulate disability: taken by the class teacher.
6. Looking at Moral and Philosophical Issues: taken by the class teacher.
7. History of the treatment of people with a mental handicap: taken by the class teacher.
8. 'How We Learn', implications for those with learning difficulties: taken by the class teacher.

9. Looking at case histories: taken by the class teacher.
10. Prejudice and Language: the use of labels and how they affect perception: taken by the class teacher.
11. Building Design: access to the school for those with a disability: taken by the class teacher.
12. Reading a story about a person with a mental handicap: taken by the class teacher.

Staff and Pupils' Views on the Module

Staff

In general staff felt that the Project had been successful. They themselves had learnt a lot and the pupils had responded well. The staff agreed that the most effective contributions depended on the involvement of outside links. The pupils were interested and obviously enjoyed themselves. They talked about their experiences amongst themselves and with their class teachers. Some staff, who had previously been worried about the pupils' reactions, were pleased that their pupils were sensible and cooperative with 'outsiders'. Others were amazed at the ability of the outside links to 'hold the class together' and maintain interest throughout the sessions. One teacher commented after a dance session: 'It was really beautiful to watch — even the most difficult pupils were totally involved and relaxed.' In these sessions, the class teacher had the choice of becoming an observer or an active participant. Either way staff felt that they had benefited greatly from the experience as they rarely had an opportunity to observe others teaching.

Some staff felt that they had employed new skills or new approaches with the pupils during the Project. For instance one teacher commented that one of the lessons required the children to be involved in a number of separate activities at the same time, which was a new experience for her. Some felt they had used existing skills in a different way.

Not all comments were positive. Staff were critical of a number of aspects of the Project. The main concerns were:

1. The Project was weakened by being spread out over a fortnight. Many staff felt it would have been better to suspend the timetable for a week and intensify the input for that week.
2. The Project was 'anaesthetized' by not including such issues as the right to live, and the quality of life for those with a mental

handicap and their families. It was felt by some that the 'real issues' surrounding disability were not represented.

3. Some of the materials were too difficult for first years.

4. Although they recognized the organizational difficulties, some felt that a few pupils working together with children with a mental handicap, feeding back and sharing those experiences with others would have been more effective than a course on mental handicap awareness for the whole first year.

5. The material for the lessons involving the class teacher was given to staff too late for them to feel confident about using it. Consequently some material was underused and some misused.

6. Some staff felt that both they and the pupils had been 'bombarded' with information. Some sessions might have been better spent discussing issues, sharing experiences and reflecting critically on the activities.

Pupils

Many of the pupils said they had enjoyed the module. Some agreed that it was very different from other Humanities lessons. Their main enjoyment seemed to have been derived from the activities involving 'outsiders'. They referred to them by name and gave detail accounts of those sessions.

Pupils were able to reflect critically about the sessions. Several pupils talked about their feelings of embarrassment or fear at the beginning of some of the sessions. One girl commented: 'In the dance I felt really silly and embarrassed to start with and then I realized that that was what I was supposed to feel. It was all part of it — feeling handicapped.' Another boy said: 'In one game I had to go out of the room and when I came back they'd changed the names of things like tables and chairs and meanings of words like 'on' and 'under'. I felt really frustrated, not being able to understand. That's what it must feel like if you're handicapped.'

When asked what they thought they had learnt many said that their image of a person with a mental handicap was that 'they were just like us'. Of the skills they had developed their comments were mainly about using sign language. Many said they had been practising signing at break time. Some felt it was like having a secret language.

Concluding Comment

Many of the problems mentioned by staff might have been overcome had there been more opportunity for staff to meet beforehand. For instance, the coordinator had seen the materials she had provided for staff as merely suggestive, to be used as a basis for exploring teaching strategies. Some staff on the other hand had thought they were for immediate use with pupils. Had they been able to discuss materials with colleagues or even to have worked on producing materials together this might not have happened. Similarly, staff might have been able to offer more suggestions based on their specialist knowledge. One teacher did in fact make good use of his specialist historical knowledge to produce a stimulating lesson on the history of mental handicap, and it was felt that more of this kind of thing should have been done. Clearly, more sharing of ideas would have been beneficial.

With hindsight it might have been better to have concentrated on pre-module in-service training this year, although it could be argued with equal force that staff needed the experience of teaching about mental handicap for training to be effective. Staff certainly seemed more enthusiastic and committed after the Project and clearer about what they would like from in-service training. In fact, there was generally more enthusiasm for the Project after the module had taken place. Staff seemed to have 'warmed' to the topic. To some extent, the initial hope was realized that teachers would gradually wish to take on more responsibility.

Chapter 7

Three Views of the Research Process

This chapter consists of three personal accounts of the research process written by members of the Research Team. The aim is to give an impression of what it felt like to be working on a project of this nature. Up until now in this book, it is the 'we', i.e. the consensus view, which has been speaking. This 'we' is now unpacked into three separate 'I's. We felt it was important to do this because although we agreed on many things, and had many experiences in common, certain experiences were unique to the individual and deserve to be included in the 'story'.

These accounts give an extra dimension to the case studies in that they provide a clearer picture of certain aspects of the micro-politics of the schools concerned. To some extent what also comes through are differences of interest between members of the Research Team. We often think that research teams should present findings as if they all spoke with one voice but this is derived from a basically positivist view of research and is a reflection of the hierarchical nature of most teams. Clearly there is a risk involved in separating out the views of researchers in this way. It is possible that the coherence hopefully achieved in the text so far will now be revealed as essentially a compromise rather than a genuine consensus amongst the Research Team. Our view is that this is a risk worth taking, even if it does raise more questions than it answers. We are confident that despite a few loose ends our narrative does hang together, but the readers must judge for themselves.

Karen: Research Worker, Year One

I was delighted to be appointed to the post of Research Worker on the Project. I'd spent five years teaching children with special needs within three different comprehensives (the last post being as Head of a Special

Needs Department), and a year as Youth Worker in charge of a large club for children and adults with mental handicaps run by a charity.

Throughout this time I had a rapidly increasing sense of frustration and anger about the system in which I had been working. As a practitioner, working directly with children and adults with special needs, I had lots of questions to ask about what I saw as the faults inherent within institutions and their management structures. But as a practitioner, and a female one at that, the workload, the lack of access to people making major decisions and the low status nature of my work were totally prohibitive to allowing opportunities to research these questions and have my views taken seriously. The job came just at the right time. I desperately wanted a chance to reflect on my experiences and use this as a spring-board to create change. I felt that my worth and potential had been recognized by the appointment. I agreed with the Director that experience and awareness of relevant issues were more important than research skills, which could be acquired on the job.

Like many of the teachers with whom I was going to work, I'd always regarded the University as something of an 'ivory tower'. This was partly to do with a sense of injustice that university lecturers were so privileged. Such people were far removed from the stresses of 'grass roots contact' and had nothing to offer practitioners. On the other hand I wanted to be in a position which afforded chances to learn, reflect and affect change — and that is what some people working in universities also do.

I thus came into post fired with enthusiasm but also with some pre-conceived ideas about schools; about what issues I felt needed to be looked at and how I'd present myself as a Researcher, with 'hands-on' experience. On reflection, I feel that the way I came across as an accessible 'expert', with a seemingly vast 'knowledge' about the issues to do with mental handicap, must have added to the organizer role into which I later felt pushed.

The Director of the Project had already approached a school which seemed willing to take the Project on board. I had a few qualms and feelings of unease as it was the school in which I'd spent my probationary year and which I felt I knew too intimately. According to accounts I'd been given over the years by people who still taught there, the school had been fraught with inter-personal problems. There was a bitter split between some staff who were seen as 'ambitious and pushy' and those seen as 'the old guard'. The previous management had seemed unaware of some of the bitter feelings amongst staff, adding to them by seeming to have a favoured group. The school had always seemed to adopt any 'new' idea. This also caused bitterness amongst staff who felt the adoption of new schemes was more to do with personal promotion than improving teaching. In addition there was a tradition of resistance amongst the staff to initiatives they saw as 'management inspired'. I was also worried as to how I'd be viewed and how seriously I'd be taken by people who had only known me as a young and inexperienced teacher, as well as how a couple of remaining staff, with whom I'd had some problems, would view me.

I think, however, that the solution lay within myself. As a Research Worker you are certainly 'up front' but not a part of the institution. It doesn't own you any longer. You can walk away from it and see any difficulties as interesting data. Being a Research Worker seemed to call upon lots of human skills such as being able to keep relationships open and not responding personally to anything that happens or is said. And you need personal confidence. Anybody who's worked for any length of time in situations where they've been on the outside of rooms listening to the clink of coffee cups from within knows how easy it is to lose confidence, to feel intimidated and undermined by people in authority. As a Research Worker you'd be working with all sorts of people. It was imperative to achieve a state of quiet self-confidence which couldn't be shaken when dealing with people who had suits and offices and power on their side. I'd discussed my qualms with the Director and he was willing to find another school should my unhappiness continue. This made me feel that I wasn't being forced into a situation in which I felt unhappy, and that I had some control. The decision to stay with the school was a positive choice.

And of course there were advantages to having intimate knowledge. I knew where a lot of the potential problems, bitterness and mis-understandings lay. I was aware of not presenting the project as 'management inspired' or letting it fall into the ownership of one or two individuals, hence isolating other staff.

Being seen as 'one of them', however, is not without problems. In a sense as a Research Worker you aren't really 'one of them', as you're there to observe, record and comment. I felt I needed to keep reminding staff of that so that they never felt they'd given me information under false pretences — either in intimate moments or because they forgot I was there. I often found myself sitting in union and departmental meetings, as I was just seen to be one of the staff. But I needed to avoid becoming attached to one group too closely and I also needed some of the status that being part of the University afforded. Without this and without the involvement of the Director of the Project, I wouldn't have been taken so seriously. I needed access to staff rooms, to private offices, to people in authority. This meant maintaining independent status.

Talking with a variety of people not only in different positions of authority but with also very diverse outlooks means a lot of adaptation. People won't respond to others whose attitudes seem very different from their own, or who don't seem to have empathy with them. The permanent need for sensitivity, awareness and self-abnegation could be a terrible strain sometimes. The need to be sponge-like, to be continually absorbing and observing whilst not responding is very difficult. I was lucky in that I had a room at the University to which to retreat, a research colleague with whom to discuss the day to day process and a sympathetic Director with whom I could speak. Doing research is often lonely. It's sometimes tempting and easy to talk in an over-personal way or complain to those whom you're researching. Once that starts to happen you stop being independent and objective. People will perhaps stop trusting you so much or seeing you as someone who can be objective. I came close to 'losing my grip' on a couple of occasions as the year wore on. Demands of staff were growing, I'd been pulled into a heavy organizational role and felt used and exhausted. One of the management team who was involved was particularly open, approachable and sympathetic. It would have been very easy to complain to him, like a worn-out member of staff. I just managed to hold back.

There was another issue which it became obvious I needed to confront from my first entry into the school as a Research Worker, accompanied by the Director. That was the issue of how I would be perceived and how I would handle gender issues. On the first meeting the Director's hand was shaken, mine wasn't. This could be interpreted in several ways. I think the way I took it was that I wasn't being taken as seriously as the Director — a man — although this could have been because he was known, or that men sometimes don't feel it is appropriate to shake hands with women. On other occasions during the course of the Project I was referred to by male staff as 'this young lady' and had my hair playfully tweaked. I wasn't, in this situation, interested in making statements about the situation of women in society and in institutions, but I did need, for research purposes, to work out how to handle over-personal approaches or situations which might restrict my role as a Research Worker. I didn't want to antagonize or put down men or make any political statements. I also wanted to make sure I avoided entering into any flirtations, however mildly. This was sometimes a temptation as a way to coerce people into doing things I wanted or to deflect antagonism, but it certainly wouldn't be good research practice and inhibits people from being open or relaxed.

I did feel that, because of the uniqueness of the Project, some mistakes were made at the outset. These were: not clearly defining my role; not forming a clear consensus about the 'point' of the research; not having really worked out if this was Action Research or 'Participant Observer' Research; and all the issues to do with ownership and control which surrounded those decisions. I also felt that some wrong assumptions had been made by the Director about how much support teachers would need. The great majority of the staff had not had any close contact with people with mental handicap. This instantly put me in a position of having to set things up for people. There were other things that also defined my role for me. We had funding for a year and it had to take place in that time. I knew schools and I knew that school. I had to instigate something or not only would nothing happen but, worse, it would let down the people who had enthusiastically taken the Project on board partly in the face of cynicism. More importantly, schools have children in them sitting in rooms waiting for things to happen. Things have got to happen. You can't just go in and say, 'Sorry kids, mental handicap's off, you'd better go home.' I had been given responsibility for twenty or so teachers and well over 200 children. As well as this, I knew they weren't aware of the issues, needed experience and information and that the only way they would get this would be through me.

The idea of 'ownership' was often bandied around but I never felt this was clearly defined. The staff said they wanted 'to own' the Project and didn't want it to be 'management inspired'. We said the same things, but we did want to own it to some extent. I felt very strongly that there were some issues that staff must address. Some of them could be said to be commonly agreed issues by people involved in the world of mental handicap, others were ones that I felt very strongly needed addressing because of my own work and experiences. I was therefore trying to direct attention to those issues and was constantly worried that staff, most of whom felt very vulnerable, might reinforce prejudices rather than challenge them. This linked to our worry that the Project might be 'hijacked' by groups or individuals, who would try and push it in a certain direction.

One thing we perhaps should have 'controlled' at the beginning were the schools' plans which were far too ambitious and meant that as well as taking on a new issue they wanted to use the opportunity to see how 'modular based' learning, cross-curricular planning and base group teaching would work out. There was a vague expectation that extra material resources were available from the University, which was partly true. There was a sense in which this was seen by some as the school's reward for taking part. I had sympathy with this, because in the early stages I was not sure how much the Project was about the school's needs. Certainly by the end of the year I felt that our contribution had been more than just material and we had given a lot to the school. Nevertheless, it was evident that many people had put in a tremendous amount of unrecognized work. There were some positive, 'vibrating', exciting parts of the Module Week — but what did the teachers gain from it? Some gained professionally and personally, but I'm sure, as always, some people felt 'used' and felt that the University 'didn't really care' about people with mental handicaps.

Finally, perhaps the role of the researcher as ambassador needs mentioning. For all the exciting and creative aspects of research one always feels a little out of control. As a research worker you become the 'front person' of an institution and of a Director. Sometimes you find you have to do or not do things against your better judgment. Sometimes people are let down because meetings are cancelled because of the wishes of other people. I found that aspect very difficult to cope with. It was compounded in this project because of the involvement of other schools and groups and individuals from the community. I found myself as the link person, having to handle people's frustration, anger and annoyance when they had been let down or not contacted. This is another aspect of needing to be a 'sponge' — one that absorbs everything but releases nothing even when squeezed.

Caroline: Research Worker, Year Two

Negotiation and Access

The initial negotiations with the LEA and access to the schools had been sought by the Director prior to my appointment. I had been working as a peripatetic teacher with special responsibilities in the area of mental handicap and had experienced a frustrating three weeks while my leave of absence was decided. I therefore arrived at my new post feeling very fortunate to have been released from the constraints of a full teaching commitment, and enthusiastic and excited at the prospect of the research, but confused about the nature of the relationship between University, school and LEA and my role within that.

At the time the involvement of the LEA was not seen as a priority issue. My understanding was that their involvement in the Project would be marginal and that any further support would be negotiated when necessary throughout the year. It was considered more important to establish my role as a researcher within each school, particularly as the opportunity for reassessment would be limited because of the increase in the number of schools involved in the Project. The differences between the schools required a flexible approach. Some aspects of the role would be easier to fulfil in one school than another. I was to encounter difficulties at some stage in all schools in establishing and fulfilling my role and it was only later that I realized that some of those problems stemmed from the early crucial negotiating months of the second year.

At the time, and certainly with hindsight, I felt the 'marginal support' from the LEA needed definition. Even with financial support from the University, which in any case was limited to covering minor expenses, it became increasingly difficult to get staff to give time to the Project. I sympathized with some staff over their resentment of both the University and the LEA that they were expected to take on new initiatives without additional resources being made available. Sometimes I felt that resentment directed towards me. 'At least you've got time off to do it', was occasionally said. In some ways I regarded such comments as positive statements because it indicated that staff were identifying with me as a practitioner, a position I frequently found useful during the research. In other ways that view was another contributory factor in the difficulty I had establishing myself in the role of 'researcher' (a point I return to later).

Apart from the lack of financial support available for teachers to cover their classes in order to attend meetings, work on resources and maintain 'links', the advisory role of the University, LEA and myself caused me continuing worry. It was apparent from the previous year that staff were likely to need training for the Project to 'happen'; and indeed in the schools involved in the second year, few staff felt confident about their abilities to deal with issues in the area of mental handicap. The Research Team had hoped that staff from School A would be able to 'induct' others and that all schools would be able to meet regularly to exchange ideas, and advise each other. The Research Team would input this with additional advice and resources. On the occasion when it was possible to set up such a meeting it proved very successful but it became impossible to repeat the exercise. I was frustrated at my attempts to set up further meetings and concerned at the amount and depth of training requested by staff. I had hoped that 'support' from advisers of the LEA might have included some assistance with training but this was not forthcoming. In one conversation the adviser to whom I was speaking was surprised that there was a problem in this area since her view was that sufficient training had already been given to staff.

The 'Take Up'

The way that the Project was 'taken up' was markedly different between the schools, as were the staff perceptions of my role as researcher. I will therefore need to examine separately each of the two schools with which I was most involved. But before doing this I should point out that in each school the result of the initial negotiations was that the Headteacher took information about the Project to a senior member of staff who then chose a member of staff to act as liaison teacher. My first contact with the school was with that teacher. There was some advantage in this. Access to the school was made easier for me in that I had a named person who would be directly involved with the Project at grass roots level and who was anticipating meeting me to discuss the immediate task of administering the questionnaires. I also had the satisfaction of knowing that at least the Project had been agreed in principle. Even as a member of staff within a large institution such as a secondary school it can sometimes be difficult trying to contact other teachers, and as an outsider it can be very time-consuming getting hold of the appropriate person.

I felt, nevertheless, that there was a 'missing stage' in the process of the uptake of the Project. Staff had usually only been given 'half the story' and accepted the Project without understanding the full consequences, as I saw them, of being involved in an action research project. Unlike the first year, which was a pilot year in any case, there was not so much urgency for schools to take the Project on board. Furthermore schools themselves had registered an interest in the Project by the second year and I felt that it was less a University-instigated initiative and more a project that was actively wanted by schools. There was, therefore, more space for the 'research' aspect of my role. I wanted staff to be involved in a collaborative partnership, including a clear commitment to the necessity for critical dialogue with the University. Perhaps this was too ambitious an aim for some staff who had to learn about mental handicap, plan and take part in the teaching of the Project and deal with a number of other new initiatives at the same time. Also, the staff's expectations of my role were not compatible with my own and I sometimes found myself in a state of tension and uncertainty about what I knew had been negotiated or not negotiated, what I had hoped staff would do and their expectations of what I would do.

Here I must distinguish between the two schools. In School C teachers were expecting to be involved in the teaching during the Module Weeks, and possibly some of the planning, but only in an organizational sense. Research and evaluation of the process and the content was my domain and the majority of the content planning was the responsibility of the liaison teacher. This was clearly linked with ownership. The Humanities team never did 'own' the Project. True collaborative activity between staff and the University was never really achieved.

As the Module Weeks approached I became more involved with planning the curriculum, editing content and organizing outside links. I felt a responsibility towards the liaison teacher, knowing that if things did not 'go well' the finger would be pointed at her first. She had put a tremendous amount of work already into the Project and I felt I had to offer maximum support if the module was to run as she had hoped it would. I also felt a responsibility towards the children, particularly one class whom I had got to know well through interviews and involvement in their classroom activities. There were certain promises that had to be kept — an expectation that something different was going to happen in those weeks. I did not want them to be disappointed. On one occasion this sense of responsibility went too far when I 'covered' for an absent speech therapist to take a lesson on alternative communication and the use of Makaton.

I found it was difficult not to fall into the role of organizer. My time was more flexible. It was easier for me to contact outside links many of whom I already knew and had contact with in any case. Also, I had considerable experience and knowledge of mental handicap and felt confident with the subject. I could focus more immediately on the relevant issues. I knew the pressures that the liaison teacher and others were under. At one point I discussed the problem of ownership and control with the Director, and considered the possibility of withdrawing, but decided against it. We both understood that this meant I would continue to have to offer support as an organizer and curriculum adviser.

The result of all this was that it was sometimes hard to be independent and objective. I never quite lost sight of my role as researcher but at times I felt that the staff had, and I was in the position of having to renegotiate my ground.

Negotiation was difficult as it was nearly always on an individual basis or through the liaison teacher. I had wanted a formal mechanism for feedback. I think perhaps this should have been made clear in the early stages. Once staff had accepted the Project on the understanding that they would be involved in the teaching only, with an occasional interview with me, it was unfair to expect them to negotiate ways of recording data. There was a possibility of my feeding back information from interviews and questionnaires on written sheets, but this seemed not only wasted effort (written information was never well received or read) but also too directive and impersonal. Consequently, exchanges between myself and staff tended to be informal, individual and *ad hoc*, e.g. chance meetings with staff over lunch. Because of lack of time I found I was having to be too selective, making rash decisions about which was the most important data to feed back. There were several crucial omissions. At times I felt uncertain about the best way forward.

As far as evaluation of the Module Weeks was concerned, I wished that negotiations had been a little more productive, but I did feel that staff were learning so much themselves and focusing so intensely on new content areas and new ways of teaching that it would not have been possible for them to be more actively involved in any additional data gathering exercises. I had attempted to involve staff in observing their own and others' lessons, using a formal framework for observations. There were a lot of concurrent activities during the Module Weeks, and even with the support of the Director, we were not able to observe as many as I had hoped. However, staff had been critically reflecting on their experiences and there was certainly an eagerness to communicate their thoughts to me in the interviews that followed.

School B

I still felt that, as with School C, there was somehow a missing stage in the negotiations which may have contributed to the long gestation period in this school. The first year team seemed less eager, however, to take up the Project without a full discussion and agreement about their role in the partnership. I was generally much happier with my position/role at School B. There were a number of possible reasons for this:

1. Though never discussed formally, I gained the impression from talking to individuals that there was an understanding of the concept of a 'research project' and the role that outside bodies like the LEA, University, community agencies, etc., might play in it.
2. The second year team had already been involved in similar projects and had experience and knowledge of action inquiry.
3. Inquiry into classroom/curriculum practice and process was ongoing with a formal structure for discussion, feedback and dialogue.
4. There was flexibility in the structure of the curriculum which allowed staff and pupils considerable freedom to test out new strategies.

5. Staff perceptions of my role seemed compatible with my own so that constant individual negotiations about what I *should* be doing and what they *should* be doing were unnecessary.

6. There was an openness to learning and knowledge. There was a sense that ideas, experience and knowledge could be shared in a productive learning process. I did not fall into the unwanted role of 'the expert from the ivory tower'. Neither did I pick up any feelings of resentment or ridicule directed towards me, which I had experienced elsewhere. I felt that this positive, open approach was also reflected in the staff's attitudes towards children.

7. It was easy to move around the school and gain access to classrooms, partly perhaps because of the architecture of the building itself but also because the school was used to adults other than the school staff being around. Entering a teacher's classroom whilst he or she was teaching was not viewed as an intrusion.

Objectivity — The Researchers' Role

In establishing myself within the schools I felt that I had to become known, because to gain a real understanding of processes, I had to have easy access to a number of areas. If I was going to interview staff and children I wanted them to feel comfortable with my presence and not threatened, as I thought they might be by the intrusive nature of my role. These were people on whom the Project depended for success. Without their cooperation, information, thoughts and ideas the Project could not be implemented. I spent time building relationships, engaging staff in conversations, explaining my role and something of my history, establishing common ground and getting to know how the system worked. With the children, I wanted to empower them, to give them a real sense of the importance of their views, and yet to make them feel relaxed about being interviewed. Also I wanted them to keep diaries and be cooperative in other ways. I needed their trust and I had to earn it. They were curious about my role but I was able to demystify my position when I got to know them better. It was a satisfying experience for me not to be bound by the rules of the teacher–pupil, or for that matter mother–child, relationship. That is not to say that I didn't employ the skills of a teacher and of a mother on occasion but to be able to step outside those roles was invigorating.

I tried to view everything with a researcher's eye but I was aware that there was a danger of becoming too familiar — of collusion mainly with staff but also to some extent with children. I was concerned some degree of separateness should be maintained in order to be objective. I did not want to become so involved that I 'went native'. A lot of time was spent becoming a familiar enough figure not to be regarded as a stranger or intruder, and yet at the same time I felt being a stranger was important for the research process. There were times when I felt the balance was 'not quite right' but I was able to discuss my worries with the Director and withdraw to the University! The fact that I was researching more than one school meant that I was forced to limit my involvement in any case.

Then there was the moral question. For ten years I had worked in schools and other institutions, with children and adults with special needs. I was committed to confronting prejudice, to increasing awareness of the issues surrounding mental handicap and to bringing about situations where these issues could be properly debated. To me the Project was not just a very interesting and exciting piece of research but something I really cared about, yet I had to explore the nature of my own commitment and bias from the outset. In doing so I heightened my self-awareness by constantly questioning my motives.

The Final Verdict

I suppose I left the Project feeling a little frustrated. We may really have only touched the surface. I wanted to return to my job in the full knowledge that we had helped to get the topic of mental handicap on the curriculum for good. It was by no means certain that we had achieved this aim, though a start had been made.

John: Project Director

I was very pleased to receive a grant from the Mental Health Foundation (MHF) and MENCAP City Foundation to research and develop a project which was to be called 'Teaching About Mental Handicap in Secondary Schools'. I felt that the previous work I had carried out in the area of teaching about disability could now be put to use in a more practical way in schools. In my careers as a teacher, an educational psychologist and a university lecturer, I had always been involved with special needs pupils, but in recent years my interest had a more specific focus on teachers' and pupils' attitudes towards disability — which I regarded as the key to successful integration programmes.

Some of the conventional approaches to teaching about disability irritated me. They were often based on dubious assumptions about the nature of the disability concerned. I was suspicious of the motivation of 'experts' from charities who were invited into schools to talk to pupils (though I did not feel this about the two MENCAP representatives who became involved in the Project). Much of the material I examined and the practice I observed did not tackle the real issues or relate to the rest of the curriculum. Arguments were unsophisticated and critical reflection not encouraged amongst pupils. In comparison with practice in other equal opportunities areas — e.g. multicultural/anti-racist education — the standard of debate was low. Pupils were really being emotionally black-mailed into adopting certain kinds of attitudes.

And so my ambition was to set up a curriculum project which avoided some of the pitfalls of previous attempts, which was derived from a coherent rationale, which had critical bite and was based on knowledge about how schools worked. Having been an in-service education lecturer for many years, I had many contacts in schools and it wasn't difficult to find a volunteer school which would house the Project in year one. I expected to know personally several teachers in the chosen school, and indeed I did.

My first task, however, was to appoint a Research Worker. I had some qualms about this because I actually feel uncomfortable about employing someone as a 'research assistant', given the usual interpretation of the role. In the current period, the old career route from research assistant to lecturer has really been blocked off. In reality we are employing persons on low salaries and short-term contracts with no job security, who, it could be said, do the 'dirty work' for the grant holder. Moreover, because they are dependent on other people — people like me! — to obtain funding, their academic freedom is jeopardized. And so I wanted to make sure that (a) the person selected had no illusions about research as a career, and (b) had a job to go back to at the end of the Project. In fact two Research Workers were employed — one in each year. One attained leave of absence from a teaching post, the other did not want to return to teaching anyway. Both understood the short-term nature of the job.

In both years I had in mind a person who (a) had teaching experience in secondary schools, and (b) had a great deal of knowledge and experience of mental handicap. Fortunately, two applicants fitted the bill perfectly. I wasn't too concerned about research experience. The job had so many odd features that it was difficult to say what would have counted as relevant research experience.

From the beginning I found my own role problematical. I didn't want to hand over completely work with the schools to the Research Worker because, after all, I was interested in the 'nitty gritty' of how the schools took up the Project, and I didn't want to lose touch with the process. I paid visits to the schools, I interviewed pupils for several days on end, provided some support for teachers in conjunction with the Research Worker, attended meetings, wrote handouts and constructed a questionnaire for pupils and an observation check list for teachers. Inevitably, however, I drifted 'off the pace' and at times must have a seemed remote figure to the Research Worker, particularly in the second year. I was an extremely busy lecturer in a thriving Division of Education. I had irons in a number of fires, and was always short of time — and often, too, of breath! No doubt most research directors claim the same thing — and no doubt most research assistants are sick of hearing it! However, by the end of the first year, I honestly felt I had managed to keep a grip on the Project — in the sense of understanding 'what had been going on'. In the second year it was harder to do this because more schools were involved, but I kept abreast of events.

Another aspect of the role which I thought about a good deal was my relationship with the Research Workers. I didn't want to be a 'director', but to work in a team situation (although for certain public relations purposes the title of director was useful). Fortunately each member of the Research Team had a similar perspective on most of the key issues, and so shared understandings were not difficult to achieve at an ideological level. My strategy was to play the role by ear. Research Workers clearly require space if they are to be creative, yet should be supported when necessary. I felt I gave regular informal support but was prepared to provide a more structured form of support if this was required. Thus, there was clearly a need for a deeper understanding of approaches to research and evaluation. I provided photocopies of articles and chapters on curriculum evaluation and discussed notions like 'action research' and 'participant observation'. But I was not happy with this aspect of the role. Certain differences between us on the nature of research, on the role of teachers in research and the definition of action research required further clarification and discussion. But there was never enough time to do this.

Another difference between myself and the Research Workers stemmed from our different histories prior to involvement in the Project. My memory went back to the early 1980s to a run-down Teachers' Centre somewhere in South Yorkshire where a group of Special Needs advisers turned down my proposal for a DES Regional Course on 'Teaching About Disability' on the grounds that it was a Personal and Social Education rather than a Special Needs topic. Since then I have roamed around secondary schools asking if I could observe any examples of practice which were to do with teaching about disability. My aim was to find out what existed in the locality. I eventually got round to carrying out a survey of practice, which gave me a more comprehensive overview. I felt the topic was important. Other people agreed but I still felt I was banging my head against a brick wall. The grants from MHF and MENCAP came like bolts from the blue. I didn't expect to get them. Things could now really start to happen. Despite obvious flaws in the design of the Project in each school it was in every case infinitely better than what I had seen before in other schools. Merely to have got a module — of all things! — off the ground was an achievement. I wanted to accentuate the positive and perhaps had a vested interest in doing so. After all a large part of my research identity was bound up with all this.

Both the research workers had had more 'hands on' experience than I had prior to their involvement with the Project. They were hot foot from the scene of the battle and were keen to get things done properly! In a way, coming at it fresh, so to speak, they tended to be much more critical of how the schools operated in relation to the Project. What I saw as achievements, they tended to play down, although not always. In a way, they helped me as much as I helped them. They kept my feet on the ground, and I provided them with support when they required it.

It dawned on me quite early on that the job I was expecting them to do was daunting. They were to be change agents, curriculum developers, advisers, participant observers and evaluators all rolled into one! It was difficult enough to work in one school; when more than one school was involved — as in the second year — the job was almost impossible. That they achieved what they did was a minor miracle. The main problem was that I had overestimated the amount of support the Project would receive in schools and from the LEA. As far as the schools were concerned certain assumptions I had made were correct. There certainly were, in the schools, some progressive activists who were sympathetic to the Project's ideals. Such teachers became involved in the Project and were a source of inspiration to everyone. In my more euphoric moments I imagined that we could return to the 'good old days' of the late 1960s and early 1970s, when groups of radical teachers democratized their schools and created a genuinely educational environment (or, at least, almost did). However, although the commitment was there and up to a point people were willing to work in teams, nobody had enough time to think beyond immediate issues. I was hoping that in each school a steering committee of 'hard core' activists could be set up who would have acted as a support for the Research Worker as well as being supported by her. This committee would then have linked up with similar committees in other schools. A bit of romanticism, this, I think! There was some 'good' organization and coordination happening in each school, but a certain dynamism was lacking and cross-school communication was minimal.

One of my jobs was to keep the LEA informed of what we were doing and try to get as much support as possible from that quarter. I should make clear that the LEA was fully committed to its own programme of change and there was no reason to expect that any resources at all could be redirected towards our Project. We were 'extra' to what was going on already. But we did expect some help and got it up to a point. I was secretly hoping that the LEA would recognize the value of our work and, in a sense, take over the Project in the second year and incorporate us into a 'disability awareness' policy framework. This was discussed but never materialized, and for me was the one big disappointment of the whole exercise.

Finally, I ought to mention some doubts I had about the Project as a whole. It was called 'Teaching About Mental Handicap'. I chose this title because it was readily understood by teachers. But it could be construed as patronizing towards people with mental handicaps. Perhaps we should have been talking about 'sharing experience' rather than 'teaching about'. School A's title for the Project — 'Working Together' — was better. A related point is that I don't think we discussed the idea of self-advocacy often enough or in sufficient depth. It was there in the programme — see Example Three in Chapter 3 — but not given priority.

In the end, who really benefited from the Project? — a question asked by my research colleagues and others who were personally involved with people with mental handicaps. The teachers and the Research Team no doubt improved themselves morally, and also, perhaps, career-wise. My own view is that it was better for the Project to have taken place in the way that it did than not to have taken place at all.

Chapter 8

Judging Pupils' Progress

The purpose of this chapter is to present a comprehensive picture of pupils' knowledge and understanding of mental handicap and explore some of the changes which did or did not take place in 'attitudes' between the pre-module phase (Time One) and the post-module phase (Time Two) in School A. In the next chapter we explore the pupil perspective using an interview method, but here we use the findings from a questionnaire which was administered on two occasions to all second year pupils.

Attitude studies often assume that since an attitude is 'an acquired orientation towards or away from some object, person, group, event or idea' (Thomas, 1982), it is a relatively easy and uncontroversial task to judge whether a particular response is positive or negative. Such an assumption is usually unwarranted. The findings of these studies are often inconclusive because they fail to make their assumptions explicit or to explore the taken-for-granted consensus about what constitutes worthy attitudes to mental handicap.

It is not consensus itself to which we object, but the lack of discussion about reasons for holding certain views and making certain assumptions. For example, when studies like that of Williamson (1979), Goodman *et al.* (1972) and Rose (1981) describe girls' attitudes to handicap as more positive than boys' and claim that girls are more 'caring' we suspect that the criteria for establishing this difference are derived from false assumptions about the needs of persons with mental handicaps although we have no way of knowing because the matter is not discussed.

Researchers therefore should clarify why they consider a response to be positive or negative, and we would argue that they will not be able to do this unless they discover *why* the person responded in a particular way. In short, our evaluation of attitudes must involve ascertaining whether or not the reasons for holding a particular attitude are 'good' reasons. It would be difficult to describe a particular attitude as 'positive' that was not underpinned by such reasons. On the other hand an allegedly negative attitude might be derived from 'good' reasons and therefore be, in a sense, positive. Of course, there is, if we adopt this view, every danger that negative expressions could be judged acceptable. However, it is unlikely that the rejection of people with mental handicaps will thereby be validated. What we assume, usually correctly, is that a negative attitude towards a person with a mental handicap is *not* based on 'good' reasons. It is often the case that such an attitude springs from ignorance of the nature of mental handicap or assumptions about people so labelled which are false. The attitude can be described as prejudiced in that it involves judgment with scant regard for the evidence.

When considering attitudes it is always important to tease out the cognitive aspects and to clarify the reasoning *within* those attitudes. We need to ascertain not whether it is 'positive' or 'negative' in a superficial sense but whether it is rationally based. Pupils should be asked to provide reasons for their responses, and it is this reasoning which has to be evaluated. An examination of reasons may lead to a categorization in terms of 'stages of development'. Miles (1983) in his study of attitudes in Pakistan revealed that views on the nature of public opinion and required policies could be divided into three stages of development that bore some relation to developmental psychologists' work on moral judgment. Whilst this approach is open to the objection that it relies on an unproven notion of a fixed sequence of development, it does at least suggest that some views are based on sounder **arguments than** other views and that it is possible to develop criteria **against which** to judge progress.

The Questionnaire

It was intended that the questionnaire data should have two purposes. First, it would provide information of which the teachers and others could make use when planning and implementing the module. Second, a base line could be established at Time One (T1), the pre-module phase, against which progress could be assessed at Time Two (T2), the post-module phase. Both purposes were realized to some extent but in each case the procedure was more complex and muddled than these neat descriptions suggest. It should be emphasized that the questionnaire was seen as a contribution to ongoing processes, as part of an action research strategy (see McCormick and James, 1983, p. 315) rather than as an external measuring instrument in a before and after experimental design. The intention was that the data would feed into these processes and influence teaching approaches rather than remain unknown to teachers. Since teachers work in different ways it was not surprising that they each made different use of the questionnaire. For some it merely supplemented other sources of information used in introductory discussions with pupil whilst for others 'filling in the questionnaire' was seen as the main way of introducing the topic to pupils.

As for the base line, since the questionnaire was administered some time after the start of the Project, some pupils had already had preliminary discussions about mental handicap and visited special schools, and all pupils therefore were not in the same position when completing the questionnaire at T1. This was not unexpected. Having obtained the teaching staff's cooperation by emphasizing their 'ownership' of the Project, the Research Team felt that they should not then start directing staff as to how and when to introduce the topic. If the Project was to 'take off' at all, teachers had to be allowed scope to make their own judgments about timing and content, particularly in the initial phase.

However, the questionnaire did provide at least a superficial overview of pupils knowledge in the whole of the year group. It was envisaged that this knowledge could be used for comparison purposes at a later date. Since one of the aims was to assess changes between T1 and T2, what happened before T1 could not be taken into account in this aspect of the evaluation. A further point here is that if the concern was to measure the effectiveness of the module, ideally, a control group of pupils who did not participate would have been required. But for various reasons to do with the school's expectations about the Project it was not possible to arrange this.

In its final form the questionnaire (see Appendix at the end of this chapter) consisted of eleven questions which were designed to reveal pupils' images of people with mental handicaps; their experiences of such people; their knowledge about mental handicap; their views about integration and the reactions of boys and girls; and their feelings about mental handicap. These were all aspects which had been referred to by pupils in exploratory interviews and seemed to relate to their existing way of thinking about handicap in general, but they were also readily relateable to the overall aims of the Project.

The piloting of the questionnaire was carried out with half a dozen or so older pupils not involved in the main study and it was then administered by the Project Director to eight second year classes on a class by class basis at T1. At T2 the questionnaire was administered by a number of teachers approximately one year after the module had taken place. There were 179 pupils involved at T1 and 190 at T2.

The findings are presented in two parts. In the first we chart the knowledge, experience and understanding of the pupils at Times One and

Two. We try to convey a sense of the range of views amongst pupils. We expected pupils to have imbibed something of the humanitarian tradition (see Chapter 2), but we also expected that many would hold stereotyped views and be ambivalent in their attitudes, particularly towards 'integration' because this policy affected them personally. The picture as a whole has 'negative' and 'positive' features. This is scarcely surprising because although prejudice is rife in our society and deep rooted at a cultural level, there are countervailing tendencies. We strongly agree with Taylor and Bogdan's (1989) criticism of the notion that because prejudice is a dominant cultural feature it follows that 'communities' will always reject people with disabilities. In their study they found that 'a significant number of ordinary community members are willing to accept people with severe disabilities if given the opportunity' (p. 33).

Changes that occurred between T1 and T2 are also referred to in Part One, but the criteria used for evaluating the direction of change are left until Part Two which consists of an analysis and discussion of responses to the open ended parts of two questions.

Part One

Experience

In the pre-module phase (Time One), of the 179 second years who completed the questionnaire, 119 (66.5 per cent) circled 'Yes' in response to the question 'Have you ever met anyone who has a mental handicap?' We were disinclined to take this response at face value. Even if pupils were 'telling the truth' they may not have understood exactly what 'mental handicap' meant. Nevertheless we were heartened by this response because it suggested that as far as these pupils were concerned mental handicap was not perceived as an esoteric phenomenon outside their experience, as conventional wisdom might have led us to believe. They saw it as part of their 'reality'.

In the post-module phase (Time Two), 93 per cent gave a 'Yes' response. There are significant differences here between T1 and T2, which is hardly surprising in view of what took place in the Module Week, but it is probable that such gains would not have been recorded had the Project not taken place at all. Both boys and girls benefited but the gains for boys tended to be greater. The percentage of boys circling 'Yes' rose from 60 per cent to 90 per cent; girls from 75 per cent to 97 per cent. Of course, those absent at the time of the module were more likely to be boys than girls.

Images

Respondents were asked to write down three things about a person with a mental handicap. Images of mental handicap were diverse but most descriptions were behavioural, referring to problems with talking, e.g. 'They have trouble speaking', followed by problems with movement, e.g. 'They walk slow'. About two-thirds of the responses referred to 'problems' and about a third referred to positive attributes, e.g. friendly, kind. There were a few negative or derogatory comments, e.g. stupid, impatient.

The intention of this question was to elicit images of mental handicap. In general, a deficit image was dominant. The pupils saw mental handicap in terms of what people so described could not do. Interestingly, they did not, in the main, refer to intelligence or cognitive aspects (although see below). The descriptions were functional and were perhaps a reflection of pupils' own priorities in relationships at this stage. Thus second years are more likely to refer to behavioural features like 'talking' and 'movement' because in terms of their perceptions of peer relationships competence in these areas was important. Maybe this also reflected the 'social' orientation of the pupils who were said by some of the teachers to be highly sociable if not high fliers academically.

At T1 and T2 the differences between the sexes were maintained with girls on both occasions providing proportionately more references to positive attributes. However, there were some differences between responses at T1 and at T2. Although 'problems with talking' accounted for over 20 per cent of the deficit responses on both occasions, the second largest category which referred to intelligence or cognitive aspects (e.g. 'Their brain is slow') was 5 per cent at T1 compared to 17 per cent at T2. This suggested that pupils at T2 were more aware of aspects specific to mental handicap, i.e. that it was 'mental' as opposed to 'physical'.

An analysis of girls' responses revealed a dramatic increase in references to mentally handicapped persons being 'affectionate' and 'loving' (21 per cent of positive responses at T2 as opposed to less than one half per cent at T1). Although, as experienced workers know, not all physical contact which seems 'affectionate' is necessarily a demonstration of genuine affection, it would be wrong to regard this development in girls' perceptions as derived entirely from a sentimental view of persons with mental handicaps. For many people so labelled as well as for 'normals' affection is sometimes expressed physically and it is quite possible that the girls' responses were an accurate reflection of the kinds of relationships that were established.

Another change noted at T2 was in the number of responses which might be described as expressing the common humanity idea, e.g. 'They're the same as us', 'They look as normal as us', 'They're no different'. This was interpreted as 'progress' because it was felt that pupils were attempting to emphasize similarities rather than differences between themselves and persons with mental handicaps. Also, in most cases it was clear from their other responses that they were not intending to convey the notion that there were no differences at all.

Knowledge

Responses to the 'knowledge' questions produced no evidence that pupils at T1 or T2 were harbouring bizarre or grossly incorrect views on the nature of mental handicap. At both times the overwhelming majority (80 per cent) thought that a person with a physical handicap was more likely to use a wheelchair than a person with a mental handicap or mental illness (Question 9). There was therefore no evidence here to support the commonly held view that many 'normals' confused physical with mental or emotional handicap. Similarly there was no evidence that these pupils thought that all people with mental handicaps lived in hospitals. The majority (T1 70 per cent, T2 79 per cent) also did not think that such people all had the same 'personality', but there was clearly a substantial minority who did think so — fewer at T2 than T1, suggesting at least some progressive development on this point. No sex differences were evident.

In response to Questions 4 and 5 about whether someone with a mental handicap could learn to talk, read, play games and sports, feed themselves, look after a pet, earn a living, have children, live by themselves if they wanted to, travel on buses on their own, get married, the overwhelming majority at T1 and T2 circled 'some can' rather than 'they all can' or 'none can'. There was some variation between questions. Thus at T1, 24 per cent felt that none could live by themselves, whereas less than 1 per cent felt that none could learn to talk, read, play games and sports and feed themselves. These differences largely disappeared at T2 where 'some can' was circled even more frequently. The only significant increase (1 per cent level of confidence) was on Question 5 (ii) where 59 per cent at T1, and 75 per cent at T2 thought that 'all of them' could get married.

Their views on the causes of mental handicap (Question 11) likewise suggested no bizarre beliefs. These views could be placed in two main categories; first the view that people with mental handicaps were 'born with it' (2/3) and second that it was due to an 'accident' (1/3). In the former, various features were mentioned — problems to do with mother (e.g. 'Mother has a disease', 'Mother has german measles', 'Rubella'), problems with the birth itself (e.g. 'Brain not getting enough oxygen') and problems to do with heredity/genetics (e.g. 'Mum and dad had too many or too less chromosomes'). In the latter, car crashes, being dropped on the head, and falling and injuring the head were mentioned.

However, causes were limited to 'physical', with no acknowledgment of 'social' explanations. Since one of the aims of the Project was to encourage pupils to be critically aware of labelling processes, it was hoped that such processes would be included as 'causes'. The fact that this did not happen suggests pupils may have retained a conventional notion of cause.

Feelings

In response to the question 'How do you feel when you see or hear about someone with a mental handicap?' 78 per cent at T1 and 63 per cent at T2 said they felt 'sorry for them' or words to that effect. Some felt curious, a few felt scared, a few pondered on how lucky they were not to be handicapped. Some admired the courage of the parents. Some felt upset. A few qualified their statement of sorrow with 'but I would try to treat them as normal'.

The most interesting responses came from three pupils who each said they knew a person with a mental handicap very well. A boy whose brother is at a special school for pupils with severe learning difficulties wrote in response to Question 10 'Nothing really'. A girl also wrote 'Nothing', but went on to explain — 'Because I work with handicaps I really like them, my cousin's handicapped'. Another girl wrote 'I don't really feel anything. I don't look at them because I'm used to them'.

The difference between T1 and T2 was significant at the 1 per cent level. At T2 more pupils qualified their statement about feeling sorry with a phrase like 'but I would treat them as normal', indicating an awareness of the need for a less patronizing attitude.

Integration

Overall the responses suggested that the integration/segregation debate was nicely balanced amongst pupils at T1 and T2, although sex differences were noted (see below). The reasons given for their responses were interesting. Taken together they represent a wide range of views on integration. In fact nearly every argument in the current debate was deployed here. The responses could be grouped into approximately five categories with an equal number of responses in each category. The percentages in each category were remarkably consistent between T1 and T2. What might be described as the pro-integration categories (1 and 2) accounted for exactly 36 per cent of the reasons on each occasion.

1. Productive learning experience for mentally handicapped pupils

Many felt that being in an ordinary school would give pupils with mental handicaps a chance to meet 'normal' people, to make more friends and to 'mix'. They could also learn from other children. As one put it, 'It would give them a chance to see how we got on with our work'; and another wrote, 'If they are watching children whose brains do work, they will pick up what's right and wrong (within reason).' They would learn to speak more, to pick things up quicker and learn to do things for themselves. They would get used to 'normal' children and see what they are like. It would give them confidence and they would learn not to feel different. According to one girl, 'It would teach them how to handle the world and they would not feel like an outcast.' They would learn some of the things that 'normal' children learn.

2. Benefits to 'normal' pupils

For some 'normal' pupils it would be a 'good experience' and 'interesting'. Others felt it would help them to understand these pupils, e.g. 'We would all be able to learn from the person and would be able to understand a mentally handicapped person better.' One girl thought that if ever they, i.e. 'normal' pupils, became parents of handicapped children, this experience would 'help them to cope'. Another also saw the practical benefits — 'It would enable us to deal with situations like this and learn from it.' The joy of helping was also mentioned — 'We would learn how to help them'; and 'I would like to look after one.' Another saw the importance for integration policies — 'It would be good for other children to learn and to show that handicapped children can grow up with normal children.'

3. The need for a special environment

A number of respondents used the term 'special', e.g. 'Pupils with mental handicap would learn more at a special school.' Indeed, some thought they would prefer to be 'with people like themselves'. Also, at the normal school there were not 'proper staff'. They required 'special teachers' and 'special teaching', plus special facilities and equipment, special attention and special work. One boy stated his opinion that 'Normal schools are not for mentally handicapped people and they'd be better off in a mentally handicapped school.' However, even though he wasn't sure if he liked them, he, along with a number of other respondents, thought they ought to be given a 'test trial'. References were also made to stairs and corridors and mentally handicapped pupils' vulnerability in crowded areas, e.g. 'They might fall down in a corridor when it was crowded and hurt themselves.' This was rendered more possible by the fact that 'in this school we move from class to class up and down stairs in mad rushes'. Some felt that they wouldn't be able to join in the fun — 'In our class we have a laugh by running about and other things, and they couldn't.'

4. Being 'picked on'

Many felt that pupils with mental handicaps would be picked on or called names, tormented, teased, made fun of. Most were not specific about who would do the teasing. One or two thought it would be the 'older boys', and generally the impression given was it would be others and not they themselves who would indulge in this sort of aggressive behaviour. In this connection, it is important to note that a substantial minority thought it was by no means certain that such pupils would get picked on, and that in any case, as one girl pointed out, 'they might get picked on sometimes but sooner or later mix'. Many were doubtful, e.g. 'Yes [they should come to our school] because we would help them'; 'No, because they might get picked on.' A few felt that the majority would help them and only the minority or a 'handful' would pick on them. For others, however, it was a definite 'No' to such pupils attending ordinary schools because they would be 'teased too much'. At least one boy emphasized the importance for his or her future life of such a pupil learning to 'take the rough with the smooth'. Experience of ordinary school was necessary 'so when he grows up he would know how nice and how horrible people could be to him or her'. For another, it was a puzzle — 'Some people are spiteful to handicap, I don't know why.' Only a few mentioned the possibility of a gender differences, but see below.

5. Not a productive learning experience for either party

According to one girl it would be a 'big responsibility helping them walk, eat and answer the teacher'. Several felt it would involve a 'lot of work'.

One boy stated that though they'd be 'fun' it would still be 'hard work'. More important for many was the feeling that they would 'slow the pace down'. It would prevent 'normal' pupils getting on with their work, and they would hold the rest of the class back. Also, they would demand too much attention from the teacher. Some felt the teacher would lose patience and get annoyed with them. Doubt was expressed about the capacities of pupils with mental handicaps for learning in an ordinary school — 'They wouldn't understand lessons', the work would be 'too advanced' for them and there were 'many things they would not understand in class'. One of the main problems, according to some, would be communication difficulties — 'They wouldn't understand us, we wouldn't understand them.' Other pupils made similar points, but were not as adamant. They pointed out that it applied to some but not all such pupils and depended on personality factors, e.g. 'depends on whether he or she is nice to talk to or nasty'.

As far as progress between T1 and T2 is concerned, overall there were no significant changes in the percentages responding 'yes', 'no', 'don't know' to Question 7 — 'Would a child with a mental handicap benefit from going to your school?' On Question 6 — 'Would you like to have a child with a mental handicap in your class?' — there was a significant increase in the 'no' percentage.

When these responses were broken down by sex it was evident that

(a) at T1 boys were just as likely as girls to circle 'no' in response to Questions 6 and 7;
(b) boys were mainly responsible for a significant increase in the 'no' percentage on Question 6 between T1 and T2;
(c) girls' 'no' responses on Question 7 dropped between T1 and T2 whereas boys' remained the same.
(For further details see Quicke, Beasley and Allen, 1989.)

Thus, boys seemed to become more pessimistic about the potential benefits of integration whilst girls became more optimistic. At T2 approximately *one* fifth of girls expressed a negative view, whereas approximately *two* fifths of the boys did.

However, girls did not become more optimistic about boys' behaviour. Question 8 asked about the attitudes of other pupils in the class towards pupils with mental handicaps. The focus was on 'picking on' behaviour which all agreed would occur, but from the girls' viewpoint the boys would be mainly responsible for it. Although overall 58 per cent felt the boys would pick on such pupils more than the girls, when this result was broken down by sex it was found that 80 per cent of the girls but only 42 per cent of the boys agreed with this statement at T2.

Part Two

At a later stage of the analysis of questionnaire responses, we felt that percentage differences between T1 and T2 may have underestimated the amount and nature of the changes, either progressive or regressive, that had taken place. For instance, did those who responded 'yes' to Question 7 at T2 contain the same individuals as those who responded 'yes' to the same question at T1, or could it be that the T2 percentage contain some who had responded 'yes' previously plus others who had responded 'no' or 'don't know'? An analysis of movement towards the 'yes' category on Question 7 at T2 revealed that of the 'yes' responders just under half had responded 'yes', a fifth had responded 'no' and roughly a third 'don't know' at T1. Further analysis revealed that over half the pupils changed their responses between T1 and T2 on the multiple choice parts of Questons 6 and 7.

However, a potential problem with this analysis is that it assumes that if a person changed his or her response, say, from 'yes' to 'no', this would be a valid indicator of psychological change. Likewise, if the same response was given at T1 and T2 it would be assumed that no change had taken place. Of course, this applies to all responses on the questionnaire requiring a choice between 'yes', 'no' and 'don't know', but the problem is particularly acute in relation to Questions 6 and 7 because the nature of the questions is such that responses are likely to be more complex. Thus when designing the questionnaire space was provided for an open ended question which asked respondents to give reasons for their choice of 'yes', 'no' or 'don't know'.

Even a cursory glance at the reasons was enough to suggest that to examine 'change' purely in relation to the multiple choice responses at T1 and T2 would not have given a true picture either of the amount or the direction of change. Further analysis of the multiple choice responses on Questions 6 and 7 was therefore abandoned in favour of a closer examination of the responses on the open ended parts of these questions.

These responses were particularly important because they provided data on pupils' *moral reasoning* which, as pointed out in Chapter 2, was a key focus for the whole project. Moreover, these two questions were closer to home, so to speak, than most of the other questions, perhaps evoking a similar sort of reaction to asking someone if they would like a person with a mental handicap living next door. Pupils were being asked to look at 'integration' from both their own and a mentally handicapped person's perspective and it was felt that they would reveal more in the process of doing this than when responding to purely factual questions. In fact Questions 6 and 7 were potentially so productive in this respect that responses to them were considered to be the most valid indicator of 'progress' or the lack of it. They could with some justification be considered separately from responses to other questions.

Judging Pupils' Progress

We were aware that making judgments as to 'progress' was clearly a controversial matter. To demonstrate how we proceeded let us examine the responses of girls in class X and boys in class Y. In the female group in Example One (Table 8.1), although mostly 'yes' and 'don't know' were circled, a striking feature was the apparent lack of movement or change in the group between T1 and T2. Only four out of eleven changed their responses on the multiple choice parts of Question 7 and only five on Question 6. However, it was found that when a judgment was made on the quality of reasoning at T1 and T2 and the data from both questions combined, at least nine and possibly all eleven could be said to have changed their perspective. Moreover, they were judged to have changed in a 'positive' direction. By way of contrast, Example Two (Table 8.2) provides an illustration of a group of boys whose change or movement between T1 and T2 was judged to be in a 'negative' direction.

The notion of 'positive' here means the same as progress or improvement and is derived from criteria which are consonant with the overall aims of the Project. But clearly, application of these criteria to particular instances is no simple matter. In order to clarify how judgments were made details are provided in Tables 8.1 and 8.2 of the responses of six of the girls (Example One) and five of the boys (Example Two). The responses to Questions 6 and 7 are combined because it did not seem appropriate that differences between questions should be allowed to cancel each other out. Change in one component, either the pupils' perceptions of the desirability of integration from their own viewpoint or their perception of its desirability from the viewpoint of a child with a mental handicap, was sufficient to establish that the overall view on 'integration' had changed. The responses on Questions 6 and 7 were interrelated and had to be judged together.

Evaluation of Responses to the Multiple Choice and Open Ended Parts of Questions 6 and 7

Question 6 Would you like to have a child with a mental handicap in your class?

Question 7 Would a child with a mental handicap benefit from going to your school?

In the tables the multiple choice response — 'yes', 'no', 'don't know' — plus reasons at T1 and T2 are given in full in the first two columns. In the third column a judgment is made of the direction of change — positive, negative or ambiguous — plus a brief explanation as to why that particular judgment was made. Our intention has become more evaluative — a move from a concern with 'change' *per se* to the quality and direction of change. A fuller explanation is provided in the discussion below.

Discussion

The impression given by the figures in Part One of this chapter that very little change had taken place between T1 and T2 was dispelled in Part Two by further analysis of findings on two key questions. Pursuing the analysis further has involved taking into account the quality of reasoning behind the responses and this has inevitably meant moving to a more controversial phase of interpretation. Given that change has taken place how do we judge that this was in the 'right' direction? How do pupils' reasons relate to the overall aims as discussed in Chapter 1? In Tables 8.1 and 8.2, in the third column, an attempt is made to evaluate pupils' reasoning. Clearly, the judgments are arguable and require further explication.

Recognition of the value of 'mixing' is regarded as a progressive development (see, for instance, KF, AG) and we consider this to be a relatively uncontroversial judgment. Even if it was felt that integration was not possible for practical reasons, few people would argue that 'mixing' in itself was not desirable. Awareness of the idea of a continuum of handicap (see KF and LL) is, however, more difficult to evaluate. One could argue that the notion of a continuum of handicap reinforces rather than punctures stereotypes because the barrier between 'normal' and 'handicapped' is retained in this idea. Persons may be categorized as mildly, severely or profoundly handicapped but they still have a

Table 8.1: Example One — Girls

Class X		Time One	Time Two	Evaluation of Development
KF	6	Yes, because we could see what it is like and what they are like.	Don't know. It would depend on how badly handicapped they are. If they are very bad they would be hard to control.	Positive. At T2 she is aware of practical difficulties but clearly committed to the value of 'mixing'.
	7	Don't know. Some of them would but others might not know what we are talking about.	Yes, the children would be able to mix with children without a handicap.	
LL	6	Don't know. I don't know. I haven't thought about it before. I would feel sorry for them.	Don't know. They would be picked on. And we have got loads of stairs. We haven't had enough experience with them.	Positive. At T1 a more patronizing attitude is evident. At T2 shows more awareness of the social and physical environmental problems of integration, but clearly does not rule integration out. Also at T2 shows more awareness of a continuum of handicap.
	7	Yes. It would make them feel accepted. But some may not like it because they'd be picked on.	Don't know. Some would, some wouldn't. If they weren't too handicapped, yes.	
AB	6	Don't know. I have not thought about it before.	Yes. It would be a good experience and we would make good friends.	Positive. At T2 she shows that she has now thought about some of the issues. Recognizes benefits for 'normal' children. Optimistic. Aware of idea of a continuum of handicap.
	7	Don't know.	Don't know. It depends on how mentally handicapped they were.	

AG	6	Don't know. The class has never really thought about it.	Yes. It would give us chance to mix with one every day. It would probably benefit the child and us too.	Positive. Has now thought about it. Sees possibilities for mutual benefit. Recognizes at T2 the value of mixing. This an advance on the idea of mere acceptance at T1.
	7	Yes. It would help them to think they had been accepted by normal people.	Yes. The child would be treated along with normal children instead of all handicapped children.	
JW	6	Don't know. It depends on their personality.	Don't know. It would be good if they were because they would be treated normally but people might pick on them and there would be no special teachers or anything.	Ambiguous (possibly no change). Emphasizes 'normal' treatment but emphatic about special teachers.
	7	No. People might tease them and they might find it hard to learn.	No. No special teachers or facilities to look after them.	
RW	6	Don't know. I don't know because it depends on their personality.	Don't know. It would depend on other people. Other people may reject them.	Ambiguous (possibly no change). At T1 the problem is 'within the child', at T2 the problem is 'within society'. On the other hand, she shows more awareness of the practical problems of integration, she is not optimistic.
	7	No. Because it would need special trained people to help them with subjects.	No. They would need to work a lot faster. They may need special help in difficult cases. May get picked on.	

Table 8.2: Example Two — Boys

Class Y		Time One	Time Two	Evaluation of Development
MH	6	Don't know. People might not help them.	No. Might interfere with my education.	Negative. More aware of practical difficulties but has moved from uncertainty to a more emphatic 'no'.
	7	No. Most people would laugh and ignore them.	No. He'll get beaten up every day.	
RF	6	Don't know. I don't know because some people might take the mickey and some people might not like them.	No. Some people might pick on them and it will slow my reading.	Negative. Less concern for 'understanding'. More aware of practical difficulties but has moved from uncertainty on Q.6 at T1 to a more emphatic double 'no' at T2.
	7	No. Because people would not understand him. Boys would pick on them. There is no mental handicap classroom.	No. You might get picked on.	
DH	6	Don't know. I don't know how to get on with them.	No. Slow your class down. Have to wait for them. Need special teachers. Get away with things.	Negative. More aware of practical difficulties but lack of optimism at T1, even more marked at T2.
	7	No. They wouldn't learn properly.	No. We would be doing work which they wouldn't be able to cope with.	
DHa	6	Don't know. They could mix with more people and get friends.	No. Because they change your life and sometimes they have to go to special places.	Negative. Recognition of practical difficulties but seems to have abandoned 'mixing' principle.
	7	Yes. They would mix with more people.	No. Because the school would not have the equipment that a handicapped school would.	
LT	6	No. Because it will slow us down in lessons.	No. Because they would get more attention and they would get away with things we don't and they would disrupt our lessons and they would slow us down.	Negative. Mh pupils even more of a 'threat' than previously. More pessimistic.

handicapped identity. On the other hand, a clearer idea of degrees of handicap may represent the first step towards understanding individual needs and towards regarding 'the mentally handicapped' as persons, and this was how we interpreted it.

Another controversial judgment was of the degree to which an attitude might be considered patronizing. A number of pupils were credited with moving away from such an attitude if they did not repeat a 'feeling sorry for' response (e.g. LL). But is there anything wrong with 'feeling sorry for'? Might it not be a first step towards genuine empathy and understanding? After all, pupils could have reported that they just did not care at all or had no sympathy whatsoever for handicapped people. However, whilst it can be sincerely felt, 'feeling sorry for' is often an insincere, unthinking, stylized reaction to handicap, placing people with mental handicaps immediately in a dependency role. Some respondents were aware of this difficulty. As one girl put it, 'I think I would feel sorry for them in my mind but most of them would not want to be felt sorry for.'

This last idea is connected to another which recognizes that the benefits of integration are not just one way. 'Normal' children may also benefit from the experience in various ways. Recognition of this was regarded as a positive development even if there were doubts about the benefits to people with mental handicaps (see AB). Conventional, stereotyped thinking usually precludes recognition of the learning experience for 'normals' and the notion of mutual benefit (see AG).

As for integration, many of these pupils became more aware of some of the problems that such a policy would encounter — stairs, not enough facilities, 'picking on' behaviours, teachers' lack of experience, lack of appropriate lessons, etc. Our view was that the development of such awareness was not necessarily negative. At least it meant that pupils were thinking critically about the school environment as a place where certain needs could or could not be met. However, it would only be clearly positive if the commitment to integration, despite some uncertainty, remained. If integration was ruled out altogether, statements about practical difficulties might merely be a rationalization of prejudice rather than a sign of progressive development. In general, we felt that some underlying sense of optimism was desirable. Whilst naive and uninformed optimism is ultimately counter-productive because it masks the intractable nature of certain problems and creates illusions about what is immediately achievable, a belief in the potentialities of mentally handicapped and 'normal' persons to create positive and productive interchanges in the school environment must be at the heart of the matter.

A further point here is that not all statements about difficulties were equally segregationist in their implications for policy. To say teachers required more experience was one thing, to say that pupils with mental handicaps required special teachers and special attention was quite another (see JW). One of the main purposes of the exercise was to get away from the notion that some children were 'special' and others 'normal'. Many pupils seemed to recognize this in their enumeration of facilities that would be needed, but still stressed the need for 'special' labelling.

Another controversial area was the pupil view of where problems were located. For RW they were 'within the child' at T1, and at T2 'within society'. 'Within child' descriptions are usually associated with policies which employ official labelling. RW refers to 'personality' at T1 and 'rejection' by others at T2. It was assumed that a shift in emphasis to factors within the environment of pupils with mental handicaps, despite the limited conception of environment, was a positive move because it would then be possible to understand the significance of labelling processes.

In Example Two it is evident that the majority of the boys were clearly worried that their own education would suffer in the event of pupils with mental handicaps attending ordinary schools. This is probably based on a realistic appraisal of present circumstances, but when not coupled with a concern for the education of pupils with mental handicaps or any awareness of possible benefits for 'normals' it seems to be rather egocentric. We felt that to include consideration of one's own and one's friends' interests in the moral equation is not necessarily self-centred, but merely to assert these interests with no attempt to understand the point of view of pupils with mental handicaps *is* self-centred. Some awareness of dilemmas and unresolved conflicts of interests is surely desirable? Even if pupils felt that on balance they would lose more than pupils with mental handicaps would gain, and rejected integration on those grounds, this would at least have suggested that some critical thinking had occurred.

An alternative view would be that 'interfere with my education' is not purely egocentric, since it may imply a concern for the right to be educated. But even here we would expect pupils to refer to the rights of pupils with mental handicaps as well. Clearly, however, there is no principle of mutuality or reversibility involved; that is, involving the ability 'to actively or imaginatively take the part of the victimized person or the judge who has to resolve the dilemma' (Lynch, 1987, p. 123). Likewise the principle of provisionality which 'assumes the imperfection of human knowledge and a willingness to review judgment' (*ibid.*, p. 124) does not seem to be applied by many of the boys who tended to move to fixed positions at T2, frequently from 'don't know' to 'no'. Judgments had been revised from T1, but the new judgments seemed couched in terms which were less open to change.

Findings for the Whole Sample

The above analysis gives an indication of how judgments of responses to Questions 6 and 7 were made. Clearly, some controversial decisions were taken, but it was felt that having gone through this exercise the process of categorization of responses as positive, negative or ambiguous could now be pursued with greater confidence in the sample as a whole. The responses of all 162 (73 girls, 89 boys) pupils who completed questionnaires at T1 and T2 were then examined and percentages calculated for three categories:

(a) those whose development was 'positive' and where progress seems to have been made;
(b) those whose development was 'negative' and for whom the outcome does not appear to have been successful;
(c) those whose development was ambiguous.

The results (see Table 8.3) present a rather different picture from the one described in Part One. First, whereas the latter suggested little psychological movement between T1 and T2, the figures in Table 8.3 reveal that at least 70 per cent of girls and 66 per cent of boys clearly and unambiguously changed in some way during the year. Second, although only 38 per cent moved in a clearly positive direction, this was a better result than that indicated by the slight but noticeable decline in the 'yes' percentages on Questions 6 and 7 in the earlier analysis. Third, the increase in the 'no' percentage for boys is not reflected in Table 8.3, where 'negatives' are cancelled out by 'positives'.

Table 8.3

	Total	(N = 162)	Boys	(N = 89)	Girls	(N = 73)
Positive change	a	38 %	b	33 %	c	45 %
Negative change	d	30 %	e	33 %	f	25 %
Ambiguous (i.e. possibly no change)	g	32 %	h	34 %	i	30 %

* (a, 30.7–45.3)   ** (c, 30.04–59.96)
* = significant at 5 % level   ** = significant at the 1 % level

Summary and Conclusion

What do these findings tell us about developments between T1 and T2? Unsurprisingly a much larger number of pupils at T2 than at T1 acknowledged having met a person with a mental handicap. By and large, however, the image of mental handicap in the sample as a whole remained roughly the same, with a deficit image remaining dominant. Certain changes were noted in relation to knowledge of the nature of mental handicap and views about affectionate behaviour and 'normality', but it could not be said that involvement in the Project had produced any dramatic alteration in pupils' perceptions. A similar point could be made about views on the performance of certain activities like playing games or looking after a pet. There were no striking differences between responses at T1 and T2 but the continuity noted was at least positive.

As for integration, pupils as a whole remained ambivalent, but if anything they were less in favour at T2 than T1. A breakdown of the figures by sex suggested that boys tended to be more pessimistic on this point than girls. Reasons given for responses to the 'integration' questions could be grouped into five roughly equal categories at T1 and T2: productive learning experience for mentally handicapped pupils; productive learning experience for 'normal' pupils; the need for a special environment and different facilities; being 'picked on'; and not a productive learning experience for either party. Sex differences were noted on questions asking about 'picking on' behaviour. Thus, more girls than boys at T1 and T2 agreed with the statement 'The boys would pick on them more than the girls'.

Some progress was evident in responses to the question about personality and mental handicap. At T2 fewer thought that people with mental handicaps had the same personality. As for 'feelings', fewer pupils at T2 gave an unthinking response, like 'I feel sorry for them', although on both occasions the majority did. Knowledge of causes did not change noticeably between T1 and T2.

In Part Two of the analysis the focus was on the two questions relating to the integration issue. The percentage of pupils changing their responses from T1 and T2 was calculated and from this the amount of psychological change in the sample as a whole was inferred. It appeared that there had been much more volatility than suggested by the initial analysis. On balance this was considered to be a positive occurrence in itself whatever the direction of change. Some prejudices may have been confirmed by the experience of the Project, but we felt most pupils were at least beginning to think about the issues. However, it was evident that more pupils did in fact move in a 'positive' than a 'negative' direction between T1 and T2, and of those proportionately more were girls.

APPENDIX: QUESTIONNAIRE

NAME: _____   CLASS: _____

The purpose of this questionnaire is to find out what you know about mental handicap. If you don't know the answers, it doesn't matter. Have a go! Try to guess the answer.

In question 1 put a circle round your answer.

1. Have you ever met anyone who has a mental handicap?
   (a) Yes
   (b) No
   (c) Don't know

2. If your answer to question 1 was 'Yes', write down three things about them.
   1. _____
   2. _____
   3. _____

3. If your answer to question 1 was 'No', what do you *think* a person with a mental handicap might be like. Write down three things.
   1. _____
   2. _____
   3. _____

In questions 4, 5, 6, 7, 8 and 9 put a circle round your answer.

4. What do you think children with a mental handicap can learn to do? Can they learn
   (i)   to talk?   Some can/They all can/None can
   (ii) to read?   Some can/They all can/None can
   (iii) to play games and sports?   Some can/They all can/None can
   (iv) to feed themselves?   Some can/They all can/None can
   (v)   to look after a pet?   Some can/They all can/None can

5. What do you think an adult with a mental handicap can do? Can they
   (i)   earn a living by doing a job of work?   Some can/They all can/None can
   (ii) get married?   Some can/They all can/None can
   (iii) have children?   Some can/They all can/None can
   (iv) live by themselves if they want to?   Some can/They all can/None can
   (v)   travel on buses on their own?   Some can/They all can/None can

6. Would you like to have a child with a mental handicap in your class?
   (a) Yes
   (b) No
   (c) Don't know
   Give reasons for your answer in this space

   _____
   _____
   _____

7. Would a child with a mental handicap benefit from going to your school?
   (a) Yes
   (b) No
   (c) Don't know
   Give reasons for your answer in this space _____

   _____
   _____
   _____

8. What would be the attitude of other children in your class to a child with a mental handicap?
   (i)   Some would pick on them   Agree/Disagree
   (ii) The boys would pick on them more than the girls   Agree/Disagree
   (iii) Some would help them   Agree/Disagree
   (iv) The boys would help them more than the girls   Agree/Disagree

9. (i)   Which of the following are more likely to use a wheelchair?
         (a) A person with a mental handicap
         (b) A person with a physical handicap
         (c) A person with a mental illness
   (ii) Most people who are mentally handicapped have the same type of personality
         (a) True   (b) False
   (iii) Most people with a mental handicap live in hospital
         (a) True   (b) False

10. How do you feel when you see or hear about someone with a mental handicap?

   _____
   _____

11. What do you think are the causes of mental handicap?

   _____
   _____
   _____

Chapter 9

Pupils' Cultural Meanings

An important part of the social context in which attitudes to mental handicap are located is pupil culture. In working with teachers and pupils in schools we were constantly aware of the possibility that both we and the teachers knew only a fraction of 'what was really going on' amongst pupils. We knew that out of earshot of teachers, researchers and other adults, some pupils would be discussing the Project amongst themselves and interpreting it in their own way. The cultural meanings generated by this interpretive activity were important because they gave an indication of the kind of impact the Project was making on the social world of the pupil.

Pupils' interpretations would be influenced by their experience of social organization of teaching and learning. If the Project was interpreted as 'just another lesson' with all that this implied (i.e. teachers setting the agenda and doing most of the talking and pupils' existing knowledge being ignored or even downgraded), then pupils would be less likely to view the material or the process as having anything to do with their real concerns. At best they would be bored, at worst they might see the 'lesson' as another occasion on which to resist teacher authority, perhaps even deliberately expressing and cultivating prejudiced attitudes. Such resistance has been noted in studies of working-class youth's attitudes to anti-racist policies (see Bardsley, 1987; Cohen, 1980).

School-structured identities will also be influential. Any form of streaming or banding will create hierarchically ordered identities of which most pupils are only too aware. Thus along with the officially proclaimed diet pupils imbibe other things (see Quicke, 1987). They learn about their status in the institution from the way teachers react to them and from their experiences of school life generally. All become aware of what teachers expect of them and how this is similar to or different from what they expect of other pupils. Whilst some will enjoy school, others may come to understand that school is essentially a place where they are relatively powerless and where they often feel demeaned or alienated. Some may feel sponsored by the official culture of the school, so that they see themselves as superior to other pupils. Others experience school as a place where they are made to feel inferior. Boys and girls may experience school differently because of the way gender identities are reinforced by school practices.

To many pupils, therefore, lessons about attitudes towards disability may seem paradoxical. On the one hand the teacher is encouraging critical engagement with ideas and practices which discriminate against persons with disabilities, whilst on the other the very same teacher may be identified with an authority which generates discriminatory attitudes of another kind. A classic example would be a situation where teachers discussed 'labelling' on a social education course in a streamed school with no attempt to encourage criticism of the streaming system or be seen themselves to be opposed to this system. Another example would be a school where a 'disability curriculum' was introduced with scant regard for the way the hidden and overt curriculum fostered gender divisions based on stereotypes.

Interview Study

It was in an attempt to acquire knowledge of these underlying meanings that one of the researchers carried out interviews with a class of pupils, 2RG, at School A. Detailed observation of pupil behaviour in a variety of contexts was not possible to do systematically on a large enough scale, mainly because the researcher's time was limited. It was felt that the next best thing would be unstructured interviews or, more precisely, freewheeling conversations with groups of pupils in a non-threatening atmosphere. If good rapport could be established, then there was some hope that pupils would express views which were 'genuine'.

Only two themes were introduced by the researcher, namely 'school' and 'disability'. Pupils were encouraged to talk around these topics and introduce other topics if they wished. The first set of interviews was less structured than the second set which took place a year after the Module Week. On the second occasion the interviewer asked specific questions about what they remembered of the module. Even here, however, the interviewing style was mainly non-directive.

2RG was chosen originally because the form teacher felt it would be an interesting class in view of the fact that one of the boys had a brother who was at a school for children with severe learning difficulties. It was also interesting because at T1 it contained more boys than any other class who denied that they would be any more aggressive than girls to pupils with mental handicaps. A further feature was that, paradoxically in view of the boys' responses, the girls seemed even more certain than most other girls in the second year that pupils with mental handicaps would *not* benefit from integration and at T1 were more adamant about the extensiveness of negative behaviours amongst the boys. The following description consists of (a) 2RG's interview responses before the module; (b) their behaviour before and during the module; and (c) their post-module (i.e. a year later) interview responses.

Pre-module Group Interviews

The pupils were asked about disability and handicap in the context of an exploration of their attitudes to school. Most expressed a positive attitude to their new school, which they preferred to the middle school because of the varied curriculum and the fact that they had different teachers for different subjects. For instance, Jane felt:

> In this school, you do different subjects — not do the same things. At the other school we had one teacher for everything. Here we've got lots. If you get fed up with one, you can always look forward to the other one.

Although they were 'bossed about' at this school, they felt that the teachers treated them as more grown up. For instance, the dinner arrangements allowed for more choice of meals and they would go 'through the cafeteria' rather than sit at a designated table and be 'served by servers'. Also, they appreciated being allowed to stay inside at break rather than being 'forced' into the playground as they had been at the other school. They liked their form teacher and had good things to say about many of the other teachers. Maths was a popular lesson, particularly amongst the girls. Karen described what she liked about it.

> It's different here from other schools. Here you can mark your own books. We have these booklets and answer booklets and that, and then marks are put into a big folder. It's not all about one thing. You can change, if you tell the teacher it's too hard, he'll take you off that booklet.

English was also popular because as Jenny said:

> You don't always do writing. Sometimes you do writing,

sometimes you go to the drama room, sometimes you read, sometimes you work in groups.

Activities was another 'subject' which was mentioned by most groups. One of the activities involved helping to look after pupils at a local nursery and infant school. This was extremely popular with girls, but two or three boys also did it. Other activities included pet care, swimming, exploring Sheffield and community service. Donald summed up what he liked about this school:

> You get away from your desk quite a bit in this school. The subjects are interesting. There's more freedom in this school. You have to carry your things around with you but I prefer that to leaving them in a desk.

Negative comments about school were few and far between. Some subjects were less popular than others, but 'dislikes' tended to refer to method and content rather than teachers.

The topic of 'gender' surfaced without prompting from the interviewer. It was clearly a focal concern which, since it arose in discussion about the integration of 'disabled pupils', seemed to be relevant to attitudes towards mental handicap. In view of the significance of gender, the girls' and boys' responses will be described separately.

View from the girls

Nearly all the girls seem to have had some direct experience of handicap of some kind, and a substantial minority, of mental handicap. This experience was limited but significant and suggested that most did not have to rely entirely on 'second hand' knowledge when talking about handicap. Some had attended an integrated youth club, others knew neighbours who were 'handicapped' and others had 'handicapped' relatives. The quotations selected are intended to give an impression of the variety of their experiences:

> JANE   I've got an uncle. He's not all that handicapped, but he's a bit backwards. He's 19 and he can't write properly and read. He used to be in a home but because he used to break windows and everything, he's living with a social worker. He usually comes to our house every Sunday. I get on with him all right. When he's in a bad mood, he sits down and cries. When he goes out people will torment him but it doesn't bother him.

JENNY I have a cousin who is 21. She had her birthday in January. She didn't know what were happening at party. She goes to this special school and they invited some of her friends from there, but she didn't know what were happening. I don't see her much. At weddings and parties, I see her.

JULIE I've worked with [mentally handicapped] already at Wesley youth club. On Wednesday, the handicap bus brings them. They play table tennis with ordinary children. I used to go but there was a boy who grabbed hold of my head and tried to hit it against wall, so I stopped going. I don't know why he were handicapped. He looked the same as anybody but he were cheeky. There were all different ones at Wesley. There were ones who didn't grow, who were right small but he were all right. His mum were small. She had Down's Syndrome; her face were just same all the way round.

ANNE I know a deaf person, Louise. She's at Guides. She doesn't like anybody saying, 'Louise, do you understand this?' when we're playing a game. She doesn't like people bossing her. My grandad's got a lady friend who's handicapped. Her knee is disjointed and she has to walk on crutches. She has to go upstairs forward and downstairs backwards. She hasn't got no bones in her knees and kneecap.

KAREN I know somebody who is deaf. She's about nine or ten. She lives near us. Every time she sees me she says hello. You have to speak up for her a bit but she just seems normal. When you saw her you wouldn't think she was deaf. I think she goes to a special school but I don't know. Mental handicap is a bit more serious. I don't know anybody... There's a boy across our road. He wears special shoes. I see him every day. He talks a bit funny, but he's all right and gets on with a lot of people. You don't have to be brainy to knock about with friends.

In all the interviews the questions of 'mixing' or joining in arose spontaneously and the interviewer took his cue from this to introduce the idea of 'handicapped' pupils attending an ordinary school. From the girls' viewpoint, the boys would sabotage attempts at integration because they would be the ones who would be mainly responsible for teasing and bullying a pupil with a handicap. As one girl, Jean, said:

> Most of the girls would be all right. I don't know about the lads though. They're always messing about. They're always making fun of people.

She described how one boy, David, who was rather 'weak and slow', had been picked on recently because he had a skinhead haircut. Another girl, Pat, described how David tried

> to act hard but when he had a fight he still ended up with a broken nose. None of the lads wanted much to do with him, so he comes to the girls. I feel sorry for him sometimes...

The girls' views here were clearly derived from their experience of boys' dominant behaviour towards girls and towards 'weaker' boys. One group accused boys of 'walking past you and bashing you on the head' and thinking 'it's right good to come over and hit you on the back'. For another group a boy called Ian was clearly one of the main villains of the piece.

JANE   Boys like to show off in front of fourth and fifth years... especially Ian.

JENNY   Ian, yes, he's always showing off. Tries to be top dog. Everybody does things to please Ian.

JULIE   Ian only has to say 'Do that' to some boys, like dead weak boys...

JENNY   ...and they'll do it. He'll just say 'Go and get me this and go and get me that' and they'll do it.

INTERVIEWER   Is this Ian the footballer?

GROUP   Yes.

Other groups had similar things to say about boys' attitudes and behaviours, although most insisted that not all the boys were equally 'irritating'. Some boys were popular with the girls. Paul, for instance, the only black boy in the class, was liked because 'he talks a lot, he's always making you laugh and he's a nice person'. Others were 'right idiots', but could be all right depending on what mood they were in.

Such comments were usually a prelude to a discussion about strategies for dealing with boys' aggression. These were various, but there was a general feeling that girls should 'stick up for themselves'. This was typified by Anne, who seemed a dominant force in the peer group partly because of her militant approach to boys but also because she wore fashionable clothes and was considered to be attractive. She believed in giving as good as she got and hitting boys back. In contrast, Karen's attitude was more supine than the others. She clearly objected to the behaviour of a certain boy — 'He squeezes you and everything... and he punches' — but she felt it was not easy to know how to react to this. She recognized that some girls like Anne would stick up for themselves and punch the boys back, but queried whether this was ultimately a useful strategy...

> After all, it just starts a fight so you might as well pretend that he
> is not there because if they punch you and you punch them back
> — it just goes on forever.

She seemed to have accepted that there was not much a girl could do about all this other than just take it. Later, she also admitted to worrying about losing friends amongst the boys if she retaliated to their teasing. If she responded aggressively, they would tease her even more and she would feel 'embarrassed'.

After much talk about boys' behaviour, the characteristics of different boys and what made a good boyfriend, the conversation typically began to revolve around the question of 'looks', in particular what they thought about their own 'looks' and what they wanted to look like. This topic usually arose spontaneously and was pursued vigorously without much prompting from the interviewer. For example, in one group there was an extended conversation about dieting, size, make-up and hair.

In summary, it was apparent that in an unstructured interview situation where topics were allowed to surface with minimal prompts from the interviewer, conversations amongst the girls drifted towards concerns other than 'handicap' reflecting links between cognate areas of experience, particularly those relating to gender. Conversational highlights included handicap, mixing, joining in, integration, boys' behaviour, boys' personalities, strategies for dealing with male aggression, themselves, 'looks' and body image, usually but not invariably in that order.

View from the boys

What soon became apparent in interviews with 2RG boys was that many of them had had as much first hand experience of handicap in general and mental handicap in particular as the girls.

DONALD   My brother has to go in for a test on Monday. We think he might have *petit mal*, that gives you fits. Our David has

temper fits; he goes blank and stares into space. He's 7. He's got
to have an EEG or something like that. They've got to keep him
up all night so that his brain's under stress and then if he goes to
sleep during the test it doesn't matter. If he's relaxed before the
test it will be harder to find out what's wrong with him . . . *Petit
mal* is a mild form of epilepsy.

NICK My friend is a bit deaf. His eardrums haven't broken.
He's thirteen . . . He's got two hearing aids. If he jerks his body,
they make a bleep. He doesn't like it when this happens.

PAUL Yes, I know someone who is handicapped. He's got to
have all these soft toys to throw about because he sometimes hits
his head with these rattles and so he had padding around them.
He goes around in a wheelchair and he's got to be brought home
in a green van. He's my friend's brother. I think he's 6.

One of the boys, Stuart, had a brother Allen who was a pupil at a
school for pupils with severe learning difficulties.

STUART If you're handicapped you've got something wrong
with you and you can't do certain things . . . [My brother] doesn't
like dinners at his school . . . they have to write it in a book. They
wrote that he didn't eat his dinner yesterday. If he came to this
school people would make fun of him but he'd be all right . . . I
think it would be a good idea if he came to a big school like this,
because he'd be able to mix with other people. He couldn't do our
work. He'd try and draw things. He draws at home — he could
do that. He likes doing jigsaws.

Several of Stuart's friends in this class had had contact with him. Ian,
the boy described by the girls as 'top dog', a tease and a bully, had this to
say about Allen:

IAN Stuart's brother Allen is all right. We have fights with him
and that. We mess about with him. He's right strong. He's a good
laugh. You can get on with him right well. Whatever me and
Stuart do he just joins in with us. Just because he's mentally
handicapped it doesn't really bother him, he just carries on like
us. I haven't seen him play football. Stuart doesn't, so he doesn't.
He goes swimming.

Thus, while some of these boys were, from the girls' viewpoint, likely to be insensitive to the needs of pupils with mental handicaps, the boys did not in the main perceive themselves in this way. In fact, some of them felt it would be the girls rather than they who would have more difficulty in relating to such pupils because, as one of them put it, 'they might be frightened of them'. Two boys, John and Peter, explained how girls had started crying at a disco when some 'handicapped had grabbed one of them'.

JOHN   [Handicapped] aren't like us in their selves. They don't know what they're saying half the time. 'Cos I go to this integrated youth club, I used to go to it. They [handicapped] used to come upstairs and they don't like it and used to start crying. Girls who are not handicapped started crying. They're frightened of it. Handicapped people are at the disco downstairs, we play badminton upstairs.

PETER   They [i.e. girls] seemed to be frightened of them but they don't do nowt, do they? One lives off my road. He's fun, he chases you. He's 17. He sort of speaks to you. He slavers a lot. He's friendly. He doesn't frighten us. Girls (mostly) seem to think that he's going to hurt them but he doesn't, but they don't know him as well as us. He has a brother at this school — fifth year. He looks like him. He's all right with him. He just ignores people if they call him names. At youth club, there's about twenty handicapped. They come from all over. They have special minibuses for them. Our old teacher at last school used to run it. She used to get people to go to it. We used to go to play badminton, and if there wasn't a game we'd sometimes come down. We saw quite a lot of them.

As far as 'picking on' was concerned the boys in general did not think pupils with mental handicaps would be teased a great deal by anyone in the class, either boys or girls. Although they admitted boys messed about more than girls because 'they liked to show off and liked to look big', there was a general feeling that there would only be the odd one who would 'call them names'. When the interviewer pushed them on this, there was an admission that if any one picked on them it would be boys rather than girls, but that in any case 'picking on' was not as bad as it seemed. As Ian pointed out, 'tormenting' others was often just a joke, particularly so in relation to girls. However, they felt that most boys would be careful about teasing pupils with severe learning difficulties because 'it might upset them', and though they might call them names behind their backs, they would never do it to their face because they probably 'couldn't take it'.

When the question of 'looks' was raised by the interviewer, most of these boys clearly had their own ideas as to why girls went on diets. Peter felt that they did so because they wanted to look slim. He felt that boys did not need to go on diets because they were slim already. John pointed out that boys were slim because they did a lot of sport, but girls only did 'one or two sports and didn't get enough exercise and that's why they get fat'. But there was no suggestion here that girls should therefore be encouraged to play the same sports as boys. It was just a fact of life that girls wanted to play 'softer' sports.

Observations of Behaviour Before and During the Module Week

Like other clases, 2RG read *Welcome Home, Jellybean* and had various other curriculum inputs on disability throughout the year. According to the English teacher, they enjoyed reading the novel, but the work they produced on it was not particularly imaginative. Four of the pupils, two girls and two boys, visited one of the special schools involved in the Project once a week for two terms. The researcher observed them there on at least two occasions. They joined in activities, struck up relations with the special school pupils and seemed to enjoy themselves.

During the Module Week, this class was involved in the Computer Activity. Pupils were divided into groups with one or two special school pupils attached to each group. Adults observed that interaction between School A and special school pupils was two way, although sometimes it was necessary for the former to help the latter, e.g. loading a disc. Such helping behaviour was more typical of some groups than others. On the whole groups were not adult-dependent, although sometimes adults needed to supply computer programs and explanations. Observers felt the emotional atmosphere was enjoyable, exciting and purposeful for most of the time, although one teacher felt that the atmosphere 'became a little flat at the end of a tiring week'. Verbal communication between pupils was mainly task-focused. Other forms of communication noted were gestural, tactile and facially expressive. Some of the adults felt that the most important learning taking place was 'awareness'.

Interestingly, it was noted that the boys of 2RG settled more easily to working with the visiting pupils than the girls, perhaps due to their greater confidence in using the computer equipment. Another possible reason was that the class contained Stuart whose brother, Allen, was in the special school group, and several of the boys knew him. One group of boys became actively involved with a girl in a wheelchair when they saw how well she could control the movement of the 'buggy' using a joystick. Some of the 2RG girls were more diffident and awkward but by the end of the first session had become more relaxed and involved. It was noticeable that those who had visited the special school tended to adapt more quickly. In addition to discussions about the computer activities, School A pupils sometimes discussed with one another what special school children were trying to convey.

On a critical note, at least one teacher thought the School A groups were too large and as a consequence some children wandered aimlessly and were a nuisance at times. Ideally groups should have been smaller with more special school children in each group. From the pupils' point of view, the Computer Activity eventually became 'boring'. They would like to have participated in a variety of activities throughout the week. In the afternoon study sessions, 2RG were observed to work well in mixed groups in some sessions. The pupils offered ideas and were willing to discuss the Project and relate their experiences; although motivation and involvement varied throughout the week and was at a lower level in some sessions than in others. Pupils asked plenty of questions and shared their experiences. Some 'critical thinking' did seem to occur, although not all observers were in agreement on this point.

Post-module Group Interviews

During the second round of interviews, it soon became clear that the gender factor was not as salient as it had been previously. The girls mentioned the names of one or two boys in particular who would do the 'picking on' but their criticisms were less strident. As one girl put it:

> The boys would torment them most — well, those who are immature in our class would. They have a go at us, so they're bound to have a go at them. Some of the boys have got better. It's just a few who are like that, and they can change . . . you know, be all right some time but not others. Some of ours are right pains, though, but I don't think it's true of boys in other classes.

When asked to look back on the Module Week, none of the girls could give examples of any of the boys having behaved 'badly' towards pupils with mental handicaps. In fact, one group who had previously been the most critical of boys' 'picking on' behaviour said they felt the boys had enjoyed the week as much as the girls. They agreed with Julie who said:

> It's funny. I thought the boys would be right bored and not want
> to bother with them, but they played with them on the
> computers and that . . .

They no longer saw teasing pupils with mental handicaps as such a great problem. In neither boys' nor girls' groups did gender dominate the conversation as it had a year previously. Some of the boys thought 'girls would pick on girls and boys would pick on boys'. However most were adamant that *in general* the girls were more caring than boys, and that if any one picked on them it would be the boys rather than the girls.

The main concerns that emerged on this occasion were mostly to do with attitudes towards school. Some of them had become more complaining about the curriculum, teaching methods and teachers' attitudes generally. Complaints were that the work was too hard; that in some lessons they spent most of the time copying from books; there was too much homework; teachers were too strict; lessons were boring. Others were not as enthusiastic about school as they were last year, but had positive things to say about certain subjects. All pupils felt the work was much 'harder' and that more was expected of them. Generally, the pupils felt that teachers had an unfavourable image of their class as a whole. As one group of girls put it: 'The teachers think we are the worst class in the school.' The form teacher confirmed that the class was going through a particularly bad period.

It was because the work had become 'hard' that many of them felt less optimistic about integration. 'Picking on' was still an important factor, but the stress now was more on whether pupils with mental handicaps would be able to 'cope'. If they couldn't 'cope' it would not be fair on other pupils. Peter was particularly adamant on this point.

> It depends on whether they could cope with it — the work. If
> they could, it would be all right. But if someone could not cope,
> I'm not being selfish, but it wouldn't be fair on us. They need
> twice as much attention as us.

Another boy felt that he could hardly cope with the work himself, and so he didn't see how pupils with mental handicaps could be expected to do it. It seems that as more demands were being made on them academically, they began to give more priority to their own needs for teacher attention. Because they would need special help, pupils with mental handicaps would divert teacher attention from 'normal' pupils. These views tended to be voiced by boys rather than girls. Thus the situation at T2 was the reverse of what it was at T1. At that time it was the boys in this class rather than the girls who were more accepting of the integration idea.

One notable exception was Stuart, the boy who had a brother with a mental handicap. His views were similar to the ones he expressed previously.

> Allen wants to come to this school. He would find it hard to cope but it depends what he does. I think all the kids at the special school could cope in this school if they all had something to do like they do at the special school. It would be hard for some to get up steps but people could help them. Some people would torment them, not so much to their face but talking to friends about them . . .

All the pupils said they enjoyed the Module Week. They felt it was a change from normal lessons. Those who were most complaining about school at present were particularly enthusiastic! They could all remember the names of the special school pupils with whom they had come into contact and could describe what they looked like and some of their characteristics.

> X was in a wheelchair. She was older than she looked. She was brilliant on the computer. She couldn't talk very well but we got to know her.

> Y was a laugh! He kept playing about and swearing.

> Z looked smart. He seemed to enjoy himself.

Some of the girls kept in contact with these pupils on Wednesdays in Activities. In general they felt they had never done anything like that in school before and it had been a good experience. On a more critical note they felt they would have liked the opportunity to do other activities in addition to the Computer Activity with which they had become bored by the end of the week. They would also have liked to have taken the special school pupils out on 'trips' down town and round the park.

They all felt they had benefited from the module. Benefits mentioned were: an improved understanding of mentally handicapped persons' abilities (e.g. 'We used to think they were hopeless and they're not.'); a removal of fear (e.g. 'We learned not to be scared of them.'); the development of empathy (e.g. 'We learned what it feels like to be handicapped.'); more confidence in ability to relate to them (e.g. 'You learn how to cope with them.'); more awareness of what they had in common with them (e.g. 'They're different but not completely different. In some ways, they are the same as us.'); and more understanding of individual differences (e.g. 'I thought they were all the same but they're different from each other. Some were more friendly than others.').

Stuart again offered a point of view which differed from most of his peers. He felt that as a result of the module and pre-module activities attitudes had 'changed a bit, but soon went back to what they were like before'. He went on to explain that many pupils in the class still 'took the mickey' out of handicapped people. They still said things like 'He were a right spaz!' Admittedly it was only a small minority but he felt they influenced the others.

Most pupils, in fact, had heard peers using derogatory words both before and after the module had taken place and some even confessed to having said such words themselves. Words like 'spaz', 'Joey', 'mong', 'flid', 'spacker' were used regularly, but not all pupils felt the same about such language. One boy said:

> Joey. That one has been around for ages. I don't know where it came from. Another one is spaz. They'll say 'I went down town yesterday and I saw a right spaz.' They'll call each other spaz. It's not right because although it's harmless to us it's not to someone who really is handicapped.

But another made the point that since the module fewer people used slang terms and that when they did it was usually in an innocuous way (e.g. 'They're not being cruel — only a bit silly.'). In the interviews, most condemned such language but felt that it was the ways the words were used rather than the words themselves which were harmful.

For many pupils the language of discrimination against disability was usually considered to be part and parcel of nicknaming. Some of it was intended to be mildly derogatory and was applied to nearly everyone. It was 'a laugh' and a 'bit of fun', without much thought for the consequences or what it felt like to be on the receiving end. Anyone who objected ran the risk of being categorized as not able to 'take a joke'. Most derogatory nicknaming was directed at girls or at 'deviant' pupils (see Measor and Woods, 1984). Pupils who were 'too brainy' suffered equally with those who were considered 'thick'. In one interview, Anne said,

> There's a lad they call Tefal. He's always being picked on because he's brainy. He's got funny eyes. He's right nice to talk to. He's always helping people. They sit next to him and get all the

answers out of him and then move away and start tormenting him.

In general, pupils clearly did not think the consequences of having a 'bit of fun' were all that harmful, provided there was no intention to be cruel. Donald, who seemed in some ways more 'aware' than most other pupils, gave this account of a boy with moderate learning difficulties in the school:

> Probably a mentally handicapped pupil could come to this school. He would have to go to special maths with Peter Silver. He's another one who is a bit . . . you know, not right bright. In fact I think he'd get on as well as Peter to be quite honest. Peter talks funny, you know. He says 'I'm Pe-ter Sil-ver' [imitates slow, halting style and others in group laugh]. He looks funny under the eyes. Hair is odd and he never combs it. He gets in this taxi, do you remember [laughs] and he hasn't got no money so when he gets there he says 'Te-k me ba-ck' [imitates]. 'Where from?' 'I-don-n't-kn-ow!' [laughs]. He's been here since before Christmas. He's with Miss D. He's a good laugh. There are others in that class like him . . .

Most examples of this kind of talk came from boys, but girls also 'took the mickey' in what they regarded as a friendly way. Clare said there were a few pupils who were a 'bit slow' in Miss X's class.

> There's one called Karen who makes us laugh. Something happened in the corridor, and every time we see her we call her Doreen, even though her name is Karen. When we see her we say, 'Eh, up, its Dor-een' [laughs]. She answers to Doreen. She's all right but sometimes she kicks and thumps you . . .

Conclusion

From the foregoing it is evident that the most striking contrast between pre-module and post-module interview responses was in attitudes towards school. Pupils had many more negative things to say about school on the second occasion. This shift in attitude between the second year (i.e. *first* year at secondary school) and the third year is one with which most teachers are familiar. The enthusiastic, willing, extrovert 'junior' becomes a sulky, bored 'teenager'. The shift seems to coincide with the change to a more formal, academically oriented curriculum. Judging from what the pupils say, the changes in method and content heralded by the School Focused Secondment Programme (SFS) do not seem to have had much influence yet on the third year curriculum of this class.

What was the relationship of this phenomenon to attitudes to mental handicap? The attitude of the boys in particular seems to have become more negative. They were less supportive of the idea of integration and the reasons they gave were to do with concerns about the effect on their own educational progress. This feature showed up in both the interview and questionnaire data. There were no marked changes in attitudes amongst the girls, although their feelings about integration were now more mixed. If anything, they were as a group slightly more in favour than previously, but compared with some other classes, not strongly so.

The change in the boys' attitude does not seem to be linked with their experiences during the Module Week. There was no evidence that their reactions to special school pupils were particularly unfavourable: rather, the reverse was true. The revision of their attitudes to integration seems to have resulted from their changing perception of school work. Some still saw integration as providing a 'good experience' but their priorities had altered and they were now more worried about the diversion of teacher attention which 'mixing' would inevitably entail.

One suspects that the more competitive social climate in the class proved to be a fertile breeding ground for the language of discrimination. This was increasingly directed at 'brainy' as well as 'thick' kids. In the interviews pupils were more willing than they had been previously to admit to having used derogatory language, although some of them tended to think that it was usually 'harmless'. This is a graphic illustration of how the institutionalization of discrimination takes place.

The girls were now more likely to be uncertain about integration, whereas previously many of them had opposed it. They were perhaps less influenced in this respect by their negative attitudes to school than by changes in their perceptions of boys' behaviour and boys' potentialities for relating to pupils with mental handicaps. This was possibly a consequence of their experiences during the Module Week.

The gender issue, if not dominant, was still significant. Despite their experiences on the module there was still a tendency for girls to think that 'boys would torment them (i.e. mentally handicapped pupils) the most', and both sexes felt that girls would be more caring. This view was sustained perhaps by the girls' perceptions of the boys' current attitudes to integration and by the behaviour of one boy, Michael, in particular, who probably had the most prejudiced attitude of all second years. He was the only one to write derogatory words on his questionnaire and he openly confessed to disliking pupils with a mental handicap. He was influential in the classroom because of his association with the 'top dog', Ian. Girls did not like him because he 'irritated' them. The teacher noted that he tended to be anti-school and opposed anything which implied a recognition of teacher authority. On one occasion he had referred to other pupils as 'mugs' for participating in a particular project.

In the light of these findings, was the module a waste of time for these pupils? A year after it took place attitudes seemed more negative, particularly amongst the boys. In the previous chapter we discussed the importance of ascertaining the reasoning behind attitudes to integration, and in this respect, in comparison with boys in other classes, those in 2RG did not seem to have made much progress. However, they themselves would probably have disagreed with this. Like the girls, they felt they had learned a great deal about mental handicap, were more empathetic and more confident about relating to such pupils.

In the current period attitudes were clearly in part being determined by academic pressures. One would hope that in the future when such pressures are off the pupils may reconsider their views and at that time experiences prior to and during the Module Week may in retrospect prove to be a valuable reference point. One suspects that had the module taken place in the third year it would have been less successful. Some pupils would have regarded it as a welcome break, but the kind of resistance displayed by Michael might have become more generalized as pupils recognized the contradiction between the academic labelling processes in which they were enmeshed, and the 'common humanity' idea which guided teaching on the module.

Chapter 10

Teacher Commitment

In this chapter we return to School A for a closer look at the perspectives of teachers who became involved in the Project. The aim is to provide an account which will illuminate the complexities of teacher motivation and the nature of their commitment to the Project. But before doing so some further consideration of the context is necessary. In Chapter 4 reference was made to School A's involvement in the LEA's School Focused Secondment Programme whereby five teachers from each secondary school were commissioned to work in a coordinated programme to develop the curriculum. By the time the Project was under way in this school, the SFS group was already at work. Several themes had emerged — modularization, multi-disciplinary relationships, equal opportunities, pastoral structures and the learning process with particular reference to language. These themes were consistent with the way the curriculum had been developing prior to SFS.

Several years previously, the school began the process of developing an integrated studies approach, alternative organizational structures and child-centred teaching methods. There had been a number of innovations like the move to mixed ability teaching and the creation of new subject areas such as Social and Personal Education and the Activities Programme which required more emphasis on negotiated curricula. Many of these changes had been 'bolted on' to the existing curriculum and it was not until the mid 1980s that attempts were made to develop cross-curricular, 'whole school' strategies. SFS was the latest and most heavily funded move in this direction.

Paralleling these developments was the establishment of an integrated resource for children with moderate learning difficulties (MLD) who would formerly have been sent to special schools. From the beginning it was recognized that policies towards pupils with special needs could not be divorced from school-wide issues like mixed ability teaching and cross-curricular collaboration. This was an inevitable consequence of providing for the needs of pupils with moderate learning difficulties in the ordinary classroom and of establishing a resource rather than a unit.

The aims of the Project articulated with these developments in almost every detail. It was directly concerned with modularization; active, child-centred approaches to learning; language awareness; and the creation of teams of teachers from different subject areas who would work together on a 'new' theme. It also emphasized awareness-raising in relation to all forms of stereotyping, prejudice and discrimination which had been key topics in discussions on mixed ability teaching, equal opportunities, the integration of pupils with special needs and pastoral care policies.

The Interview Study

In the Spring Term of 1987 it appeared to the Research Team that most of the teachers who had volunteered for the Project were falling behind in their preparation for the Module Week. The Research Worker had spent some time linking each teacher with a member of the community who had some special experience of mental handicap, but not one teacher had so far contacted their community link. A few had visited the special schools, most had attended at least one meeting to discuss the module, some had talked to pupils about handicap and others had dealt with the issue in lessons, but the general impression was that the teachers were 'holding back'.

It was partly in order to explore the possible reasons for this that the Research Worker carried out semi-structured individual interviews with several teachers. Teachers were asked why they had become involved in the Project; about any worries they had regarding the community links, visits to the special schools or preparation of the module; about what they hoped they and pupils would get from the module, what problems the module might come up against, what training they required and what criticisms they had heard from other staff. These questions were asked in no particular order and were used essentially as stimuli for discussion.

It soon became clear that from the teachers' point of view the main reason for not having gone ahead with preparations was 'lack of time' at that particular point in the year rather than lack of commitment or 'fear of the unknown', as one of the Research Team put it. Most of them felt that it boiled down to the workload. All of them were involved in some way with new developments that were taking place in the school, including GCSE, SFS and revised curriculum planning. The Project was just 'another thing' they had to think about and because it was in the future, over a term away, many felt they could put it aside for a while. However, most were at pains to stress that the Project still appealed to them for various reasons.

For the Research Team this was not an unexpected finding. We felt that 'lack of time' was probably a manifestation in teacher consciousness of a whole host of social and material constraints (see Quicke, 1987) and we were prepared to live with the fact that at that time of the year it was virtually impossible for teachers to give the Project top priority. We were also prepared to acknowledge that even when they did become involved the teachers would probably be partly motivated by material or vested interests. Often, the aim is to maintain a favoured career self-image and we were not surprised therefore when one interviewee said that he felt the Project was being 'used by the organizers to channel ambition into promotion'.

It was also true that the Project could not avoid being tangled up with the micro-politics (Ball, 1987) of the school. Some teachers thought that the Senior Management Team were using the Project to outmanoeuvre staff whose views they regarded as traditional. Others were keenly aware that from the point of view of subject territorial interests their department had to be represented in the Project at all costs, even if this meant 'volunteering' for activities that none of the department were particularly keen on. This was graphically illustrated by one young teacher's explanation as to why she had become involved in the Project.

> I sat in the staff room at lunch time and somebody said that our department was not represented. And so I went to the meeting. I had no choice. I suppose I could have said no, but I didn't in the end. That's how I got involved! I just sat there and thought 'What am I letting myself in for?' The other members of my department don't want to do this, otherwise they would have gone along. I was a bit annoyed...

However, whilst accepting such features as an inevitable part of the reality of life in schools, we would have been extremely reluctant to continue with the Project had these pragmatic concerns become so dominant that they completely overshadowed 'paradigmatic' concerns, defined by Hammersley (1977) as relating to the ideal pedagogical aspects of the self-image and 'how teaching might be, how it would be in ideal circumstances' (p. 38). This aspect of the teacher perspective is derived from deep moral concerns and is indispensable to the development of 'good' educational practice.

Of course, we acknowledged that there would almost certainly be inconsistencies between teachers' paradigmatic orientations and their actual classroom practices; the notorious 'gap between words and deeds'. In practice, the situational constraints make compromises unavoidable. But we did expect those involved in the Project to have an underlying commitment to it at a paradigmatic level, to be aware, at least, of inconsistencies or contradictions and to accept that the compromises that had to be made were indeed compromises.

We hoped to obtain from the interviews a sense of teachers' commitment. This was more crucial from our viewpoint than any other aspect of our action research model. Provided we facilitated the development and deepening of this commitment we were not too concerned about maintaining our research orientation in all its purity. For instance, the perception of us as 'experts' existed at the beginning, lingered throughout and was evident to some degree even in the final stages of the evaluation process. However, we felt this in itself did not seriously impede the development of a sense of 'ownership'. As the interviews revealed, many teachers were prepared to take responsibility for the development of a 'new' curriculum and analyze their existing perceptions as a basis for further exploration, experimentation and evaluation. And nearly all those who volunteered for the Project, even those whose initial motivation was suspect, were eventually prepared to collaborate with colleagues and share their experiences.

For us the most striking feature was that whatever difficulties arose these teachers continued to be morally committed to the Project. That is, their involvement seemed to be values-driven. As Nias (1981) points out such commitment might involve ideals derived from religious or other philosophies, or might be expressed in more down to earth terms like 'caring for children'. In the interviews it was revealed in autobiographical accounts of childhood experiences of handicap, and in statements about political and religious identity. However, in contrast to Nias, we would argue that moral commitment was also evident in the teachers' professional concerns, i.e. their worries about doing a 'good professional job'. We do not think it is possible to distinguish such concerns from others which are said to reflect a different sort of commitment, one that is more morally or vocationally oriented. Thus moral commitment was revealed in the teachers' professionally located perceptions of the Project as

(a) a learning experience and a chance to develop 'good practice';
(b) part of a school-wide process of change;
(c) awareness-raising for pupils;
(d) the first step towards the integration of children with severe learning difficulties.

Finally, such commitment was also revealed in their general worries about what was necessary to make the Project a success. These themes will now be discussed in greater detail.

Childhood Experiences of Handicap

Most of the teachers who became involved in the Project could recall childhood experiences which they seemed to regard as an important reference point when offering explanations of their current views about handicap. Whilst not wishing to understate the amount of discrimination that took place — most admitted there was a good deal — they were usually at pains to stress that as far as they could recall, relationships they had personally made with such children were usually 'good humoured', 'mutually beneficial' and involved 'genuine friendship'. Within supportive relationships, they had even been able to joke about their friends' disabilities. For example, one said:

> I had a friend at school who was physically handicapped. We used to call him 'clank' because of his callipers. There was a lot of banter, but it was all in good fun and he accepted it. He was not bullied. It was just a boisterous boys' grammar school atmosphere of the 1960s. We did not even think about not accepting him as one of us... It would never have occurred to us.

Unsurprisingly, most acknowledged that the attitudes and beliefs of their parents played a crucial role in providing them with a moral starting point. Often, as the following quotation illustrates, there was not much room for negotiation on the question of discrimination.

> I was brought up in a home where things like prejudice against handicap were just 'no go' areas. Both my parents were strong socialists and tied to that political view was the moral belief that that sort of thing just wasn't on. So consequently, if that kind of prejudice was ever expressed it was crushed pretty quickly, and as a result you tend to learn your lesson. To be quite honest I would get a clip round the ear'ole if anything like that happened. I'm grateful for that; for being brought up in a mode of thinking that doesn't discriminate.

In all these accounts, when mental handicap was mentioned the relationships formed were clearly not as intimate as with other forms of handicap. One teacher remembered a 'pleasant relationship' with an 'ESN' hedge cutter in a rural setting but not all relationships remembered were as positive. Some recalled having gone along with a crowd of pupils who regularly expressed discriminatory attitudes, but in such cases alternative views were provided by their parents, thus stimulating critical reflection. The following quotation gives an indication of the kind of thing that some recalled having been caught up in as children. In this particular case the teacher concerned was able to discuss the experience with her mother who worked as a nurse in a 'mental home' and who had herself had to overcome fears about people with mental handicaps.

> This was when I was at primary school. The man was very tall. He was probably quite young but he seemed old to us, probably about 20 . . . and an old woman who used to move her lips about and charge up the road. It used to frighten me at first and my mother had to explain that they were a bit different. She was a nurse and worked in a mental home. She was also scared of them at first, but managed to get over this. Some children used to torment them. It was fun in a weird sort of way that they did chase us. Kids like being frightened! I wished I had known someone who was mentally handicapped because I'm sure the younger you are and the earlier you mix, they just become people like you, whereas if they're separate . . . its's the fear of the unknown really isn't it? I don't remember ever teasing one myself but you always forget things that were naughty don't you? I remember walking down a passage with the intention of bumping into them!

In this and in several other accounts it was evident that one of the main lessons perceived as having been learned from childhood experiences was that the best way to overcome the 'fear of the unknown' which is often at the root of prejudice is for children to 'mix' together in the early years. Thus, for many of these teachers, there was really no question but that 'integration' was the best policy to aim for. Whether or not they supported a particular strategy for integration in the here and now was another matter. The point is that many of them had a clear commitment — which they saw as rooted in childhood experiences and early socialization — to the idea that handicapped persons need not and should not be 'cut off from humanity' and treated as 'outsiders'.

Political and Religious Beliefs

Several teachers made an explicit connection between their political and religious beliefs and their involvement in the Project. One was a Roman Catholic and totally opposed to abortion. He described an argument he had used in discussions with pupils:

> I would argue that who is to say, even if a profoundly mentally and physically handicapped kid can't do much, that they can't feel much? Our kids [i.e. mainstream] were saying their life must be so horrible and so they must be so unhappy but how can you tell they're unhappy?

Another was a member of the Labour Party and a life-long socialist — 'Integration is a socialist philosophy.'

At first some members of the Research Team were doubtful about seeking the involvement of teachers who were so obviously 'ideologically' motivated in a political and/or religious way. One of us was acutely aware of the prejudice and discrimination against people with mental handicaps that had been practised in the name of religion and was worried that certain teachers would attempt to impose their own religiously motivated moral concerns on pupils. The following quotation from the Roman Catholic teacher provides a case in point:

> I was talking to my fourth years today, just saying I was doing a project on mental handicap with second years. The thing that they came up with straight away and what they were most interested in was 'death' and whether the profoundly handicapped people should be killed or allowed to live ... that was the thing they were most worried about. They were saying, you know, 'Could I take it if I lost both my legs? If I had no control over speech, or mind or body,' they said, 'I probably wouldn't want to live'. They said that I would want the support machine switched off if I was on one, and they were talking like this and they refused to budge on to any other subject; it was this issue of do we allow them to live ...

What may have been a preoccupation of fourth years was not necessarily uppermost in the minds of second years and yet the teacher was using this example from his practice to demonstrate the 'kind of issues that I'd like to focus on with second years'.

However, even this teacher, who appeared to be the most religiously motivated of all, saw his role as a facilitator of wide-ranging discussion and as someone who 'helped pupils make up their own minds'. In practice, he clearly did not adopt a didactic teaching style and pupils in his groups felt at ease enough to explore most of the issues they themselves saw as relevant, in addition to those that were of particular interest to the teacher.

The same was true of politically motivated teachers who on the whole were more concerned with the question of integration. Their practice was also characterized by open discussion and a non-directive teaching style and there was no question of them seeking to indoctrinate their pupils. They were willing to express the following views in their interviews with the Research Team but did not bring them up in this form in discussions with pupils.

> I have been in the Labour Party nearly all my adult life. I believe in integration because of the common humanity idea. I don't want to get political about it but the Tories seem to want to integrate every minority group of every sort into the community purely to save money; and any group, whether it be the aged, the handicapped . . . being integrated must be properly resourced. You can't do anything on a shoestring because otherwise you are just baby-minding and that's not what it is about.

Eventually, the Research Team, far from having qualms about the contribution of such teachers, positively encouraged it, as long as their practice was **guided** by progressive educational principles. An underpinning 'philosophy' that went beyond the boundaries of education seemed to deepen their commitment to the Project.

Perception of the Project as a Learning Experience and as a Chance to Develop Good Practice

Some teachers said they regarded the Project as an opportunity to develop new teaching strategies, try out new skills, explore new areas of experience and work collaboratively with colleagues. They saw it as potentially allowing them scope for creative involvement in the development of a 'living' curriculum. They felt that if teaching about mental handicap was perceived by pupils as 'just another lesson' and was taught in a didactic way using a transmission mode there was every danger that the whole exercise would be counter-productive. It was essential, therefore, that the pedagogy should be practical and child-centred, involve active learning and plenty of pupil participation. If possible, pupils should have experience of contact with peers who had mental handicaps. At every stage, the pupils themselves should be consulted about the best way forward and they should be encouraged to discuss issues in groups and critically reflect on their experiences. There was a concern that issues should be addressed at the affective level as well as the cognitive level. As one teacher put it, the aim should be

> to get inside the head of a mentally handicapped person and see life as they see it, and recognize its limitations and strengths and its satisfactions; what the quality of life is and how we can make that better for individuals. How you recognize joy and happiness, and so on. It's at those levels . . . a feelings approach more than specific and concrete aspects of handicap. It's about getting us and pupils to explore feelings, and learn things which could be applied to handicap and all relationships. Sometimes we are more sympathetic and caring to those who are overtly handicapped than to those, say, who are depressed or to kids in school who smell and often have bigger problems than a handicapped kid who gets a lot of time and attention in a one to one relationship.

This statement revealed another important aspect of the teachers' perspective. Most felt that if they were going to teach well they should begin by analyzing their own feelings about mental handicap. They recognized that they couldn't take it for granted that their own reactions to handicap would be unproblematic, because they suspected that people who were otherwise caring and sympathetic might have a block when it came to mental handicap. Thus they felt it was imperative that before they worked with pupils they should themselves have experience of relating to pupils with mental handicaps. Only in this way could they get rid of preconceived ideas and learn how they would deal with their own emotions when faced with this particular form of handicap. They saw pre-module contact with children with severe learning difficulties as essential for themselves as well as the pupils. Apart from self-analysis, on a practical level they would need to know 'what such children could do' so that they could devise joint activities, which they regarded as indispensable for the success of the module.

Those who referred to these matters clearly relished the thought of broadening their experience and developing their competence as professionals. Their enthusiasm for the venture comes through in this teacher's account of her visit to the special school.

Before we went I was apprehensive about what I would find and how I would react. When we first got there, straight away the appearance impressed; lots of space and colourful displays, like an infant and junior school. The general impression was very encouraging. After about ten minutes, I was sent to a unit for the profoundly handicapped, and I must admit when just seeing that it took half an hour to get their coats off I was surprised. Rather than just watching, I tried to help a bit, but just felt inadequate. When I saw that some of them were just going to sit or lie there I must admit . . . it upset me to be quite honest. I bucked up when the physiotherapist told me that I'd get the wrong impression in an hour and a half. 'You have to be here for years to see the positive side.' When I began to help one or two put shoes, socks on, etcetera, it helped me to be more objective. It takes your mind off just looking . . . if you get on and do something, it helps. I learned a lot in there. I felt no revulsion or pity. Didn't bother me when one girl was sick all over her coat. I don't think they could join the module, but it would be good for one of our kids to go down and see them; just go in and do what I did, you know, help in a very small way.

When she moved from the unit to a less severely handicapped class she realized what a range of ability there was amongst these pupils. She was more optimistic about their participation in the module.

Most were walking around. It was wonderful to see children who were communicating with each other, moving around the room. As soon as I went in there, they instantly wanted to know who you were, and got to know your name. They poked and prodded you. As soon as we moved off to do drama, two of them grabbed my hands straight away, showed me the way. Some were talking, although most of it was just odd words. You could understand them . . . I was surprised at the level of discipline that was imposed; I'm not criticizing it, but I was surprised at how they achieved that . . .

She felt the visit had been constructive. Gradually she ceased to be pre-occupied with her own fears, and after the initial shock tried to approach it in a professional way. The issues that concerned her were mainly to do with teaching methods. How could she adapt what she did with School A pupils so that special school pupils could join in, whilst at the same time making it an interesting and educational activity for all pupils? What learning would take place? What would all pupils get out of it?

Perception of the Project as Part of a School-wide Process of Change

For some of the more senior teachers commitment to the Project took a somewhat different form. Although 'change' was the operative word it was more to do with 'whole school' change than just their own personal and professional development. Thus they were more interested in the Project as a vehicle for the development of cross-curricular collaborative inquiry and a shared view of the purpose of change. Although senior management had given their support to the Project, they saw the philosophy behind it as essentially one which valued a 'bottom up' rather than 'top down' model of change, and thus encouraged genuine negotiations between staff and senior management and the facilitation of staff involvement and staff ownership of curriculum change.

One such teacher was a member of the SFS group and his main preoccupation at this time was the whole process of staff consultation, and staff ownership of curriculum change. He felt that previously in this school staff had been consulted and negotiations had allegedly taken place but they were a 'sham'. He thought it was pointless not to involve teachers in innovation because 'if they felt it did not belong to them there were so many ways they could prevent it happening'. Thus he was interested in how the Project was perceived by the staff and in understanding the processes whereby they did or did not become fully involved.

At least one of these teachers tended to see himself as operating at what he described as the 'structural level'; that is to say, as an organizer and facilitator rather than as a someone who 'got involved with the "nitty gritty" of "face to face" communication with handicapped kids'. It was quite clear to him, as to other senior teachers, that they perceived their role as essentially that of providing a framework of support for younger, inexperienced or non-promoted colleagues. The Research Team felt that this form of commitment was equally valid in its own way. Even if it did not involve these teachers in exploring their own feelings, they were still performing a necessary task and one which they could easily have shirked had they not thought the Project was worthwhile. In fact we felt that the organizational contribution of one teacher was valuable even though it was clear that he had doubts about becoming involved in the Project because of his own emotional response to mental handicap and his inability to make relationships with youngsters with this form of handicap. Although he felt he would 'cope' and 'see it through', it was at *that* level he would function, and 'not with real warmth and genuineness', as he put it.

Perceptions of the Project as Awareness-raising for Pupils

When certain teachers spoke about their pupils, it was clear that they anticipated the latter's views about handicap would be influenced by stereotypes and their experiences of handicap would be limited. In fact, as the pupil questionnaire and interview data shows, there was a wide range of beliefs, attitudes and experiences of handicap amongst this particular group of pupils. Some pupils had regular contact with children and adults with mental handicaps, and others, even if they had no first hand experience, were fairly broad-minded and empathetic in their approach, or at least appeared so during the interviews.

However, although pupils' pre-module awareness was to some extent underestimated, we did not have the impression that teachers who made comments about pupils' restricted experience held views which they were unwilling to revise in the light of evidence of pupil knowledge of handicap. The teacher quoted below was clearly using a deficit model but she was optimistic that pupils could benefit from further experience and that perhaps their understanding was not as limited as she had at first thought.

> Kids in my class are very narrow-minded and very insular. I'm doing an outsider's project with them at the moment — about people who are outside society — gypsies, religious groups, etc. They really just regurgitate the thoughts of their parents. They're very cosy, I find; not all of them, but most live in their own little worlds. They call each other things like spazzy and flid. But they don't know what flid means. When I explained to one boy what it meant, he said, 'That's not very nice, is it?' And I said, 'If you had a brother or a sister who was spastic, would you like it then?' 'No,' they say, 'it's a term of abuse!' A lot of that in my class. They can be very aggressive to each other — over many things, like borrowing a pencil without asking. But they don't say 'You coon' or 'You nigger' to each other ... but they all use 'spaz' and 'flid'. They're very competitive, my kids, even though we try not to encourage this. But they're not all the same. They use stereotypes but it's easy to stereotype them! Sometimes they surprise you. I must admit I didn't know that so many of them actually knew someone who was handicapped.

Perception of the Project as a First Step Towards Integration

As mentioned above, several teachers supported the general principle of integration even if they did not necessarily see the present Project as part of a clearly defined integration policy. There were some, however, who perceived it as the first step towards the integration of pupils with severe learning difficulties into the mainstream. Most of these were designated Special Needs teachers. We felt that their attitudes in general contained many contradictions. For example, one in casual conversation said of pupils attached to the MLD resource that it was unlikely that such children would ever be fully integrated because they were 'too far behind to catch up'. Another spoke about how he was happier working in a comprehensive rather than a special school, but in fact was prepared to go back into special school if it meant promotion.

Yet it would be wrong to suggest that these contradictions, perhaps reflecting uncertainties about career interests, somehow invalidated what appeared to be a genuine commitment to the Project. More than any other group, they had doubts about what could be achieved in the Module Week. One of them felt that it would not necessarily answer the problem of discrimination against pupils with special needs generally, but he thought it was one way of getting things started. Others opined that in an ideal world children with severe learning difficulties would be integrated in the same way as children with moderate learning difficulties, but this was a long way off.

There was also a view expressed that the Project was all part of a gradualist approach to integration. As one put it:

> We're starting integrating MLD children into this school and there would come a point, if that's successful, you would gradually move further and further along the spectrum and might start considering integrating children who for the moment are being kept in special schools. The Project would be a start. It's a progression. I don't think you can do it just like that. It would be nice to think that you could just wave a wand and change things overnight. It takes people a long time to adjust and as you move the boundaries then the possibilities become greater.

Teacher Worries

Projects like this have to be thought out carefully and many teachers were worried that they just would not be able to put the time in to do a 'good professional job'. There were so many things that could go wrong and many of these were beyond their control. One teacher was concerned that if things did go wrong they would all start blaming each other and this could have an effect on other projects that were taking place. He felt it was important for them all to understand the need for an 'experimental attitude' within a supportive framework, so that if mistakes were made they could be laughed off and they could go back to square one without recrimination. Only in this way could a climate be created where teachers were willing to take risks, lose their inhibitions, overcome any embarrassment and adopt a flexible and imaginative approach to teaching.

The Research Team felt that provided it did not become crippling a certain amount of worry was positive because, to put it simply, at least it showed the teachers cared. But there were different kinds of worries, and some were more difficult than others for us to come to terms with because they seemed to reflect a deep-rooted cynicism. Even here, however, we felt it important to distinguish between cynicism and realism. A cynical attitude was displayed by one or two teachers who ultimately did not contribute to the Project. One seemed to adopt the view that such projects were nothing but 'political games' conjured up by people bent on asserting their own influence. Another felt that pupils in the school were 'too far gone' to be capable of responding 'humanely' to a group of 'handicapped pupils'.

A realistic view often appeared pessimistic but differed from a purely cynical view in that there was no condemnation of pupils, and simplistic analyses of teacher motivation were avoided. There was a continuing 'belief in people' but a recognition that the chances of genuinely progressive changes within the current framework were minimal.

The Research Team sympathized with this view because we largely agreed with the analysis of schools which underpinned it. But we did not think holding such a view should necessarily lead to a permanent state of bitterness or a complete withdrawal from schools. We felt that teachers who were critically analytical in this way were in short supply and at the present time it was more important than ever that they should participate in educational debates. Out of the two or three teachers who could be said to have a critical grasp of current processes and the nature of schooling generally, only one was interviewed. The following summary of his views illustrates his vision and his pessimism in the current period.

He was a member of the English Department and had been teaching for twelve years. He was committed to the integrated curriculum and saw the Project as one way to explore this. He felt that a whole-school approach was something quite exciting to get involved in. His initial concern was not primarily with teaching pupils about mental handicap but with the processes involved. He supported any development which challenged the way things were organized at present. There were two sorts of obstacles to changing to an integrated curriculum. The first was personal and mainly to do with lack of time. The second was organizational and to do with the nature of subject departments and the nature of the existing structure of schools. What needed to be challenged were the vested interests of subjects and of hierarchies. To break that down one had to break the organization down, and that was why at the moment he was pessimistic because he felt the vested interests were too powerful. SFS had not yet come to grips with the essential tasks of identifying the existing curriculum or exploring what all teachers might contribute to an integrated curriculum. He felt the curriculum debate that had been begun in the school was essentially uninformed and that teachers on SFS had been selected on the wrong basis. He hoped the Project would be a genuine attempt at a whole-school approach but it was difficult to judge until he saw it in action.

At present all his spare thinking time was taken up with other matters. There was never enough time to do everything. If teachers didn't prioritize 'they'd be dead before they were 40'. He thought that one of the great ironies of teaching was that if you got involved in curriculum change and development the first thing to suffer was your teaching, but if you didn't get involved your career suffered. It was a Catch 22 situation!

Although he supported the Project, given unlimited time and resources his priority would be to explore something on a larger scale that would last for years. But he thought the task was enormous because there were so many things wrong with schools.

> On a physical level, the design of a lot of school buildings is wrong. On a materials level the amount of money for spending on new materials is limited. On an educational level the time and opportunity you have to develop new curricula is restricted. And all these things seem to point to one thing in the end, and that is lack of resources. The fundamental problem is lack of money in education. Not that money is the answer to everything, but schools need to be re-equipped and designed better and teachers need to have time off to think about what they are doing, rather than just rattling it off day in and day out.

Concluding Comment

Since professional concerns differ amongst individuals variously located in school structures, we would expect teachers to have different priorities with respect to *how* the goals of the Project might be achieved. For some, teaching methods would be all important whilst for others the emphasis would be more on conceptual frameworks and organization. We would also expect to find differences in their perspectives on change. There was some suggestion that the older, more experienced teachers were more cautious about the possibilities of change than their younger colleagues, many of whom were in their first year of teaching. However, whether or not there were two subcultures operating, one a 'veteran', the other a 'novitiate' subculture (see Riseborough, 1986; Poppleton, 1988), is open to doubt because clearly those who volunteered for the Project all had a great deal in common.

What is revealed in the interviews is not the orientation of a group of technicians 'going through the motions', but the approach of self-motivated professionals who are concerned about 'getting it right' in terms of their own needs and values. We were impressed with the way they were prepared to talk about their personal experiences and worries, and the difficulties they envisaged. In fact, it was the memory of these stories, confessions and statements of belief that kept hope alive in the more frustrating and unproductive phases of the Project. The fact that this commitment was sustained throughout the period is, in our view, a mark of the Project's success in this school.

However, getting within the skin of teachers also brings researcher *Angst*! After the interviews it was easier to appreciate the exact nature of the burden we as external researchers were placing on them. We were in effect asking teachers to become more extended professionally in a situation where they were already being stretched to the limit. Hoyle (1980) has defined extended professionality as a perspective which takes account of a broader educational context and wider range of professional activities, in comparison with restricted professionality which is largely intuitive and classroom-based. Most of the teachers clearly saw us as pushing them in the direction of the former, which is where most of them wanted to go but probably not at the pace we were demanding. As Poppleton *et al.* (1987) have pointed out the process of extending professionality can go too far, leading to mental and physical exhaustion, i.e. burn out, particularly if resources and other forms of support are not forthcoming.

Chapter 11

Summary and Evaluation

We conceived the Project as a piece of action research in which the Research Team was involved in both curriculum development and evaluation. Evaluation was formative and ongoing and could not be separated from development. Our discussions and judgments about materials, lesson plans, activities and organization provided constant feedback to teachers. The findings from interview and questionnaire studies were also fed back as soon as they had been collated. From a data gathering viewpoint the whole process was inevitably haphazard. The main focus of our efforts was constantly shifting and we were always in a position of not having time to monitor developments in sufficient detail. Inevitably, therefore, there are gaps in the data and some of our judgments are based on limited evidence.

When writing up the Project our overall aim was to produce an account which would convey the full complexities of the experience and illuminate 'processes' (see Parlett and Hamilton, 1972). This model of evaluation is often considered to be in tension with another which stresses pre-specified objectives and pupil learning outcomes (McCormick and James, 1983), and in this respect our approach might be characterized as eclectic because we were concerned in part with pupil learning outcomes. Although, as we explained in Chapter 8, the questionnaire was not primarily for use in assessing outcomes, it did provide an indication of what pupils may have gained or lost from participating in the Project. Progress was defined in terms of the achievement of Project aims which were formulated at an early stage and therefore our evaluation was concerned with the attainment of pre-specified objectives.

But if this was the only aspect of evaluation we had considered it would have been of limited value for two reasons. First, there were other outcomes which were not measurable or pre-specified but in many ways just as significant; for instance, the pleasure many pupils obtained from just participating in the various activities and the changes that took place in teacher motivation. Second, a consideration of outcomes only would not have helped us to diagnose the reasons for the results obtained. For this we needed to look at 'processes', at social action and other aspects of the social milieu that might have contributed to the results. The task involved identifying relevant processes because clearly not everything that happened during the course of the Project was equally significant. We proceeded by theorizing about processes and seeking data to confirm or disconfirm our theories. Thus we theorized that teacher 'ownership' and pupil culture would be important features and sought data on how these were enacted in processes. In this way we hoped to readily identify and then describe those processes which were the most important influences on our results. These accounts make up the content of most of the foregoing chapters. Now, by way of summary, we intend to pull this material together in commenting on twelve criticisms which were voiced by teachers, members of the Research Team and other workers, as well as teachers not involved in the Project.

1. *The most favourable circumstances for successful inter-group contact were not established.*

It will be recalled that School A was the only school to opt for an inter-group contact model. As indicated in Chapter 3, for such a model to work the circumstances in which contact takes place have to be favourable. Using Stephan and Brigham's (1985) criteria, we can assess the circumstances in School A. Although an effort was made to put special school pupils on an equal footing with School A pupils, the mere fact that the former arrived and left in a special vehicle and were perceived as coming from and returning to a non-normal setting militated against this. Also, although there were opportunities for School A pupils to relate to special school pupils as individuals, the context was such that the identity of the latter as persons from a special institution rather than as, say, members of a family or neighbourhood, was always dominant.

However, two of Stephan and Brigham's criteria were met. The Project had the support of authority figures, and involved activities characterized by cooperative interdependence. In fact these two positive aspects were linked, making their impact even more powerful. It was a member of the Senior Management Team who suggested that the title of the Project in School A should be changed from 'Teaching About Mental Handicap' to 'Working Together' and who was mainly instrumental in establishing it as a community project. In the Module Week there was a great sense of everyone's contribution being valued. In our judgment this largely compensated for the weaknesses in the design of the Project in this school.

Finally, it is worth noting that in all three schools the question of inter-group contact was discussed at some length. There was general agreement that such contact would have to be carefully structured and visits to special schools would have to involve small numbers of pupils who would participate rather than just 'look'. All recognized the pitfalls but they felt strongly that some form of contact at some stage was essential both for staff and pupils.

Within the lifespan of the Project only School A managed to arrange this. Why? One reason was that as the pilot school they were the first to make contact with the special schools and the first to arrange visits and participation in joint activities. The same process could not realistically have been repeated next year in the other schools, because this would have been too disruptive for the special schools. However, other forms of contact in the community might have been arranged.

In School B the notion of contact was discussed, but it was felt that arranging contact with a special school was not the most appropriate starting point. For the First Year Team the experiences of the pupils in School B was the main focus initially. It will be recalled that in School B's child-centred approach the aim was to develop a more mature attitude to learning which hopefully would be a natural consequence of the commitment to a pupil–staff team approach to curriculum planning and development. The emphasis was on pupils' existing experience, rather than with providing pupils with experiences, which seemed to be stressed more by School A. There was much more concern, therefore, in School B to find out which pupils already had some knowledge of handicap, and then to work with them to provide a core of expertise which could then be used to enrich discussions in the rest of the year group. Contact with special school pupils at a later date was not ruled out, but it certainly was not given priority.

> 2. *All teaching approaches which did not involve contact with mentally handicapped children or adults were of limited value. Contact is the most important aspect of this kind of project and without it prejudice in real life cannot be tackled properly.*

One critic of the Project thought our suggestion in one school that contact was not necessarily essential would lead to a 'sterile curriculum'. Our own view was that good quality contact would be beneficial but that even if it was achieved, it would still be necessary to have teaching sessions devoted to critical reflection on the experience of contact. Moreover, we felt that a lengthy preparatory phase which did not involve contact was essential. In the absence of any prospect of contact, we also believed that the topic could still be dealt with in school in a way that was not 'sterile'.

This belief was borne out in School B and School C. In School B we observed teaching strategies which did not involve contact but which excited and captured the imagination of pupils. From being reluctant to participate at first, pupils eventually lost their inhibitions and were able to discuss issues more confidently. At School C pupils said they enjoyed the module and felt that it was different from other Humanities lessons. The topic seems to have been brought alive by creative teaching methods and the involvement of pupils in non-traditional lessons.

A point to note is that at School B, although no contact with special schools was arranged, pupils' previous experiences of contact were used as a basis for curriculum development. However, since this was unsupervised, we did not regard it as part of the teaching programme. It was an important resource, but only one amongst many resources that pupils brought with them to the learning situation.

> 3. *Although the aim was to encourage a child-centred approach to learning about mental handicap, this was never realized. All that happened was that the values of the teachers were imposed on pupils, albeit in more subtle ways than by traditional teaching methods.*

One worker commented that in the simulation exercises pupils were being manipulated and the child-centredness of the exercises was an illusion. Children did not in fact negotiate their own learning.

We had some sympathy with this view. We observed one or two instances where child-centred rhetoric was used to mask what was in effect a directive teaching approach. In some ways the more overtly directive approaches adopted in some of the study sessions in School A were more honest in that there was no attempt to hide the fact that pupils were being inducted.

However, in School B in particular, we felt that a genuine attempt was made to involve the pupils right from the start. Clearly, some directiveness and manipulation were employed, but ultimately the aim was to facilitate pupils' critical reflection on their own experiences and this was by and large achieved. In any case, words like manipulation are emotive and do not reflect the teachers' own interpretation of the aims of the teaching programme or their views of the nature of the relationships they established with pupils. Most would admit to 'steering' discussions and 'guiding' pupils but would distinguish these activities from 'manipulation'. In conversation, some teachers were fully aware of the danger of playing on pupils' emotions when dealing with sensitive topics like handicap.

> 4. *Mental handicap is not an appropriate topic for the curriculum of second year pupils. They have not had sufficient experience of handicap and it has little relevance for them.*

We felt strongly that this criticism was misconceived. The questionnaire responses showed that there was an enormously wide range of views, knowledge and experiences amongst pupils in relation to handicap in general. Many pupils already knew someone who was handicapped and a substantial number had had first hand experience of mental handicap. The majority of pupils' views, if not always correct, were sensible, and there were very few bizarre or derogatory statements. We felt there was a diversity of views on which to base discussion and a richness of ideas which could be worked with.

In the teaching sessions pupils showed that they could think critically about most issues to do with handicap. Not all pupils were equally sensitive, but we would not have expected this. The topic was as relevant to them as other topics involving controversial and sensitive issues.

In one school (School C) some of the staff felt that the Project did not go far enough and considered that pupils at this age were capable of handling complicated philosophical issues like the 'right to live' and the 'quality of life' for people with mental handicaps and their families. In our view, although such issues are important, they are not as relevant for these pupils as issues like 'integration' which have implications for their own education and day to day lives in school.

> 5. *The aim that teachers should 'own' the Project was not realized.*

There is a germ of truth in this assertion. As we pointed out in Chapter 4, organizational issues did become disproportionately onerous in School A and teachers did not have the time to participate in all decision-making processes. It was also true that many of them never felt confident enough to articulate their interpretations of the aims of the Project. These aims were, in the main, formulated by the Research Team. However, there is no doubt that efforts were made to encourage a sense of 'ownership'. Planning meetings were held regularly and most teachers attended at least one of these. The Research Team discussed all aspects of the Project with teachers individually and no decisions were taken without involving all teachers in the process at some stage. Some of the immediate objectives were modified in the light of teachers' comments. There was immediate feedback of information about pupils' attitudes obtained from questionnaires and interviews, so that staff did not feel the Research Team knew something which they didn't. The school coordinator and members of the Senior Management Team operated a genuinely democratic style of leadership.

In School B the question of 'ownership' was not discussed at any great length, perhaps because the Second Year Team took it for granted that having agreed the Project fitted in with the overall plan for the curriculum they would be obliged to take responsibility for it. It was evident, however, that not all members of the Team were equally willing to take initiatives and the Project was clearly higher on the personal agendas of some than others. In School C most of the staff when interviewed said they would have liked more involvement in the developmental stage of the Project. They certainly felt they had not 'owned' the Project, although this did not mean to say that commitment was therefore lacking.

> 6. *Teachers became involved in the Project but their motivation was mixed and for most of them mental handicap was a side issue.*

Even if this were true, from our viewpoint, it would not have mattered. We had no objections to teachers using the Project to develop progressive teaching programmes on any aspect of handicap broadly defined. We took the view that such programmes, even if only marginally concerned with mental handicap, would produce citizens who were less prejudiced in their general approach to life and this would ultimately be beneficial to people with mental handicaps. Thus some programmes formulated under the auspices of the Project were only loosely connected to the major theme.

However, we hoped that at least some of the teachers would develop a specific interest in mental handicap and that the Project as a whole in the school concerned would be informed by this particular theme. And this did occur. Some who were only vaguely interested at first became more committed to developing an understanding of mental handicap after visiting special schools.

As pointed out in Chapter 10, we were impressed with the way teachers' commitment to the Project seemed to be values-driven. This commitment is revealed in the accounts provided in that chapter. If teachers had not been morally or vocationally committed we would not have pursued the Project further in their schools.

> 7. *Although everyone concerned was committed to the Project, it was just unrealistic to expect teachers to do a 'good professional job' burdened as they were with a workload that was already too heavy. In short, the Project was impractical.*

We sympathized with this view and felt it was remarkable that despite the difficulties teachers did manage to take the Project on board. These difficulties should not be underestimated. Some were common to all schools. Most staff were involved in the implementation of GCSE and involved in in-service activities attendant upon School Focused Secondment Programmes. All three schools were committed to using a team approach in developing the curriculum and this meant participation in many lunch-time and after school meetings. Most teachers had heavy teaching timetables. There were anxieties about resources, redeployment and, in the case of School C, amalgamation with another school. A few teachers were worried about the proposed National Curriculum and Assessment which they felt contradicted the kind of educational reforms that the Project exemplified.

As mentioned in Chapter 8, from our point of view there were certainly many disadvantages in embarking upon the Project in the schools at this particular point in time. On the other hand we knew from our experience that for an outside research team making an intervention in a school there was never a 'best time'. At least all three schools were involved in changing their curricula in some way and this was a helpful state of affairs from the Project's viewpoint because it meant links could be made with ongoing change processes. We were also fortunate to have the support of certain key personnel in each school. The fact that we were swimming with the tide made the implementation of the Project a practical possibility. When we sensed that this was not so we did not pursue the Project further in that school, as in the cases of Schools E and F.

> 8. *It would have been a better use of resources to have concentrated on 'awareness' courses for teachers in the first year of the Project and postponed teaching pupils about mental handicap until the second year.*

We were undecided about this. On the one hand it was evident that things were carried out in a rush in all three schools. We would have liked more time to explore issues in greater depth with individual teachers. Some of the work was superficial. We observed teachers not picking up on important points raised in discussions with pupils. Even the most confident and enthusiastic teachers said they would have liked to have known much more about mental handicap. Some teachers needed more support than we could provide in working through their own feelings about mental handicap.

On the one hand, as pointed out at the end of Chapter 6, it could be argued that staff needed some experience of teaching about mental handicap before training courses could be effective. In School A there was a feeling amongst staff that it was better to get involved in the teaching process as soon as possible because otherwise the enthusiasm generated at the start of the Project would not be capitalized upon. A member of the Senior Management Team also expressed the view that it was impractical to plan a Project of this nature too far ahead. In School C it was felt that if the aim was that staff and pupils should learn together there was no reason to postpone implementation of a teaching programme until staff were 'ready', even though a certain amount of planning was essential. In School B the Research Team felt that the modular approach had been vindicated, since staff seemed more enthusiastic and committed after the Project had taken place.

> 9. *Despite the aim to 'cogwheel' with ongoing change processes, the Project was in fact 'bolted on' rather than integral to curriculum development in each school and made very little impact on this development.*

This was a criticism which tended to be voiced by those not involved in the Project. Teachers who were involved usually recognized the connection between the Project's aims and their own values and concerns. There are some graphic illustrations of this in the accounts presented in Chapter 10. Many saw the Project as providing them with experience of different ways of teaching. Nearly all the aims-in-practice were similar to those proposed by the teachers themselves and by the local authority in its recommendations for curriculum initiatives.

However, we doubt if the Project made a major impact on any of the schools, nor did we expect it to. We thought that it could do little more than help to 'nudge' schools in the right direction. We also wanted to avoid putting the clock back! That is, we wanted to avoid falling into the same trap as many other projects dealing with controversial issues, and introduce practices which were ultimately counter-productive. In this respect the programmes in Schools A and C were high risk strategies — the former because we were in the dangerous territory of unequal inter-group contact, the latter because the Project was set up in such a way that teachers did not feel that they 'owned' it. We were more comfortable with the way the Project was taken up in School B.

> 10. *Team work was spoken about a great deal but in practice teachers worked as individuals with little meaningful contact across the subject or the school–community divide.*

Whilst the extent of team work was more limited than hoped for originally, there is no doubt that some of it took place. In School A teachers were adamant that one of the things they had really enjoyed was the positive interactions which took place between staff from different disciplines. After a slow start, fruitful contacts were also made with community links. In the Module Week, of several adults involved with each class, usually one or two were teachers and the others were parents or non-teacher-trained adults from the community.

Not all went smoothly. There was a certain amount of tension between some of the special school teachers and School A teachers. There were several possible reasons for this. Differing perceptions of the 'nature of learning' in the Module Week played a part. Teachers differed about whether any useful learning had taken place for special school pupils. Also, because of the way the Project had been set up, the special schools were not involved in the initial planning. When they did become involved, there was a problem of communication with one school which was difficult to resolve due mainly to time constraints. Some special school teachers clearly underestimated the complexities of the process of innovation in a large comprehensive school. Nevertheless, some teachers clearly valued contact with teachers in the comprehensive school and welcomed a continuation of the links established.

In School C some team work was required to get the Project off the ground but not much team teaching took place and there were few opportunities for staff to discuss materials with colleagues. However, the staff in this school cooperated well with outside community links. They had the opportunity of becoming observers or active participants in lessons in which the 'outsider' took the lead. Either way the teaching staff seemed to benefit greatly from the experience.

In School B the teachers were already working together in a team and so the appropriate structure already existed. In this situation, the Project provided a suitable focus for the development of team work. As in the other schools, the involvement of an outsider, in this case the actor in residence, was welcomed and much appreciated.

> 11. *Pupils imbibe attitudes to mental handicap from their communities and these are basic to their identities and therefore difficult to change. A Project confined largely to fostering change within the school setting only is bound to have a limited impact.*

In particular we felt that gender role identity was particularly resistant to change. We have argued elsewhere (Quicke, 1989) that identities based on male domination and female passivity produce a social and emotional climate which is not conducive to positive attitudes to mental handicap. These identities can be influenced by school experiences but they are deeply rooted in early childhood socialization. By the time pupils enter secondary school it is usually the case that traditional gender stereotyping has been established and is continually reinforced by influences from the media, the family and the job market.

Bearing this in mind, we were encouraged by the development of girls' attitudes in School A. At T1 girls tended to be perceived and to perceive themselves as more 'caring' than boys. We were concerned that this might have represented a show of caring behaviour out of conformity to type. However, the analysis of responses on the questionnaires indicated that many girls had begun to think about the issues in a way which was less influenced by a stereotyped reaction. The interviews with 2RG revealed that whereas previously many of them had referred to the need for special provision, they were now more concerned with the possibilities of integration. This could have been a direct consequence of their experiences during the Module Week when they saw boys interacting positively with pupils with mental handicaps. Prior to this they felt that, unlike themselves, boys were uncaring and would 'pick on' pupils with mental handicaps in an integrated setting.

Boys' development was more disappointing but we felt that this was mainly due to the fact that the changes heralded by SFS and by curriculum initiatives like the Project had not yet had a chance to counter the divisive effects of traditional curricula. Boys' perceptions of the nature of the classroom as a learning environment made them less enthusiastic about integration.

12. *Although pupils made many perceptive and sensitive observations and exhibited positive behaviours when in contact with mentally handicapped pupils, on the whole these features did not reflect what they really felt. When away from 'official' situations and unconstrained by the need to 'please the teacher' or present themselves in a good light, they tended to revert to more negative attitudes and behaviours.*

There is no doubt that pupils' views/behaviours expressed in interviews and official settings often do not match those expressed in the informal setting of the peer group. In her diary one girl wrote of her friend:

> ...she shouted, 'Oh, they're just going to the Crucible Theatre to see a lot of stupid spazzies', which I thought was cruel, so I asked her why she had said it but she just laughed.

The girl in question had made a good impression on teachers during the Module Week at School A. She appeared to be a very sensible, perceptive, mature young person. But the intriguing question is, was the language used by this girl when shouting after her peers an expression of what she really felt? And if so, were her allegedly positive views and behaviours merely conjured up to please the teachers? Or was it the other way round? Was she expressing her real views when talking to teachers and being insincere when talking to peers? Or maybe neither of these descriptions is correct.

It could be that the girl was being insincere in both settings or being sincere in both settings. Our judgment was that the latter better fitted the facts as we knew them. Many pupils were indeed inconsistent. We felt the quality of their responses on the questionnaire and in the interviews often reflected genuine empathy, but we also felt that negative comments in the peer group were more than just a reflection of going along with the crowd for the sake of a quiet life. We interpreted this inconsistency as an expression of their experiences of a moral conflict. They were not just articulating views of which they had no real understanding, but were 'living out' two sides of an argument.

Of course, not all pupils were aware of this conflict to the same degree. And this brings us back to one of the main aims of the Project which was to make pupils more aware of value dilemmas and to help them clarify their thoughts and recognize inconsistencies. It was important to encourage them to bring views expressed in the peer group out into the open, so that they could be compared with alternative views. This could only happen if the barriers between the formal culture of the school and the informal culture of the peer group were broken down. And so the important question is: Did the Project achieve this?

In School A we had insufficient data to be able to draw any conclusions on this point, but we had the impression that pupils were less reluctant to speak about informal culture at T2 than they had been at T1. In the interviews at T2 they were prepared to talk more about their own behaviour towards different categories of pupils. In School B, developments were even more encouraging. In small group tutorial sessions pupils challenged each other's language. The Research Worker observed that most of those who did the challenging tended to have had greater contact with people with mental handicaps. They were not merely being compliant with teachers' views and values but genuinely considered that derogatory terms devalued the people they knew and were 'unfair'. However, these were only small beginnings. We felt that a great deal more needed to be done if pupils were to become more aware of how their views on handicap reflected moral conflicts and how these were related to cultural experiences.

Retrospect and Prospect

We began this report with an overview of the evidence on attitudes to mental handicap in our society. This demonstrated that prejudice was still widespread despite the alleged change to a more humane approach in recent years, and that faulty attitudes were often unacknowledged as such because they were institutionalized and taken for granted. By institutionalized we meant that prejudice was continually being generated and reinforced by the way institutions worked. Sometimes discrimination was overt, but mostly the processes which produced prejudice were more subtle and covert. School was one such institution. Via the covert and the hidden curriculum a competitive climate was created which was basically unfavourable for the development of genuinely positive attitudes; a climate which was underpinned by a definition of achievement productive of status hierarchies relegating people with mental handicaps to the bottom of a large, multi-layered heap.

However, there are countervailing tendencies. For instance, in some schools attempts have been made to develop curricula, organization and pedagogy devoted to the notion of 'education for all'. This has entailed, amongst other things, re-vamping the curriculum so that material is more accessible to pupils of all abilities and from all types of background; altering teaching approaches so that all pupils feel their contribution is valued; and changing from a streamed to a mixed ability organization. We felt that these changes were in tune with the philosophy and aims of the TAMH Project and therefore we were quite happy to align ourselves with those elements in schools which were pushing in this direction. We envisaged the Project cogwheeling with progressive developments, contributing to them and at the same time gaining strength from them.

In the long term the success of the Project, therefore, was tied in with the success of wider changes in the curriculum of the schools concerned. At the beginning we were hopeful that such changes would occur. They were supported by the LEA's Curriculum Initiative which received central government funding in the form of monies from TVEI, TRIST and LAPP. The latter were interpreted and taken up in a non-divisive way by the LEA. A letter from the Chief Education Officer in December 1985 outlined proposals for broadening and restructuring the whole curriculum. Rather than traditional, didactic methods and a subject-centred approach the need was for more emphasis on skills, competencies and understanding in an integrated curriculum context. The main plank of reform was to be modularization of the curriculum whereby courses were to be broken down into smaller units. From the Research Team's point of view this context was a particularly favourable one. Rather than being bolted on to the traditional curriculum as an optional extra there was every chance that 'mental handicap' could be incorporated into a module alongside and of equal status with other modules, perhaps even accredited, and thus firmly embedded in the curriculum.

By the end of the Project we were still hopeful but were concerned about the possible effects of the proposed National Curriculum first outlined in a consultative document in 1987 and now the centre-piece of the Education Reform Act of 1988. We felt that in many ways this 'reform' was derived from a markedly different educational philosophy from the one that we espoused. It also seemed to contradict the thinking behind other Government initiatives like TVEI. However, we understand that it will still be possible to develop cross-curricular themes and that at local level, for the time being at any rate, existing policy objectives will continue to be pursued.

In the final analysis our optimism is sustained by what we discovered about pupils and teachers during the Project. Children's views inevitably reflect the wider adult culture where prejudice is deeply embedded. We expected to find attitudes determined by stereotypal thinking and ignorance, but were pleased to discover that many children already had some knowledge of handicap and were morally sensitive and responsive. A substantial minority had had personal experience of handicap in the family

family or neighbourhood. These were definite strengths on which the Project could build. Likewise, we were encouraged by the degree of teacher commitment which was sustained against all the odds.

Chapter 12

A New ERA of Prejudice?

As indicated at the end of the last chapter, we became increasingly concerned about the possible impact of the Education Reform Act (1988) on progressive curriculum development in schools. The Project was premised on the belief that whilst prejudice could be challenged through education this would only happen if schooling was reformed in the direction of greater comprehensiveness. We regarded the various local curriculum initiatives as potentially capable of delivering this kind of reform in schools; that is, a reform guided by principles of equality and respect for persons and seeking the enhancement of a curriculum which, whilst catering for individual diversity, was an essentially integrative rather than a divisive force. We saw the Project itself as an example of these principles in action, and as one of several projects which were contributing to the development of progressive structures and processes throughout the local authority.

The National Curriculum (NC) and its associated assessment system seemed to threaten these changes. It prescribed a curriculum content which was strikingly traditional. With the exception of technology, the range of subjects proposed — the core and foundation subjects — read very much like a late nineteenth-/early twentieth-century timetable. In comparing the curriculum prescribed by the Board of Education regulations of 1904 with that proposed in the 1987 consultative document, Aldrich (1988) comments that 'there is such a striking similarity between the two lists that it appears that one was simply copied from the other . . .' (p. 22).

The local initiatives to which we related were based on an explicit critique of the traditional curriculum. There was a focus on breaking down the barriers between the practical and the academic curriculum, and on the construction of 'new' subjects built around particular themes and modular in structure. The underpinning philosophy of this 'new learning' is familiar to most liberal progressive educators and has guided 'good practice' in primary and secondary schools for many years. Interestingly, it was also incorporated, at least at the level of rhetoric, into the thinking behind Government initiatives like TVEI. There were, of course, as Pat Broadfoot (1986) points out, many other strands of ideology at work within this initiative, but the local interpretation and take up of TVEI seemed to us to involve changes with which we could identify and which would provide a favourable context for the Project.

The National Curriculum conveys virtually nothing of the radical and innovative rhetoric of TVEI as expressed, for instance, in the DES/DOE Joint White Paper *Working Together — Education and Training* (1986). The recommendations for the allocation of time for the foundation and core subjects impose an inflexibility which is likely to place severe restrictions on possibilities for the creation of alternative curriculum structures. The Government response has been to suggest that the arrangements for the delivery of the National Curriculum can include cross-curricular themes. In a speech at the University of Manchester in September 1987, Kenneth Baker acknowledged the importance of study skills and attitudes which schools should promote, like self-reliance and self-discipline, a spirit of enterprise, a sense of social responsibility, the ability to work harmoniously with others, and to apply knowledge to solve real problems. He also considered that areas like moral teaching, social responsibility and understanding the structures necessary for democracy should also be included in the curriculum and went on to point out that 'describing the curriculum in terms of subjects will not exclude those desirable areas of learning and experience'.

However, doubts have been expressed by no less a figure than Sir Bryan Nicholson, former chairman of the MSC, who was reported as having warned the Education Secretary that the rigid subject timetable would make it impossible to run TVEI-type practical courses, a high proportion of which were modular and cross-curricular, and needed to involve 'intensive spells of concentrating on a single project without time for other subject studies' (*TES*, 1987). The delivery of cross-curricular themes is premised on there being scope for this kind of flexibility. The point was reinforced by David Hargreaves (1987) in his critique of DES guidance on the National Curriculum:

> The guidance is largely couched in terms of the conventional disciplines or subjects and potentially opens up a fierce battle for time (and resources) especially in secondary schools and in consequence a perceived hierarchy of importance. This may well

weaken some of the most recent imaginative curriculum development, mainly school-based on modular structures with their potential for cross-disciplinary work and for movement away from the conventional secondary school timetable (p. 4).

These statements were made over a year before the passing of the Education Reform Act. They point up the tension between two rival curriculum approaches which seem to co-exist in Government thinking: on the one hand, the forward march of the 'new vocationalism' represented by TVEI; and on the other the restoration of traditional curricula reflected in the National Curriculum. The tension seems to have been resolved by interpreting TVEI as having a role to play but one which is subsidiary. It seems likely for example that TVEI extension will become a lever to help the implementation of the National Curriculum by structuring some of the cross-curricular themes.

Two such cross-curricular themes are of major concern to us — Personal and Social Education (PSE) and special educational needs. PSE is important because its rationale makes explicit the aims and objectives which we regard as central to the achievement of sociality and community in schools. According to HMI Document No. 14 of their series on Curriculum Matters (1989), PSE is concerned with the development of pupils as mature, moral and socially responsible persons and refers to the need for teachers to attend to the processes of learning as well as to the content of what is learnt. The aims include references to 'having ideas on such social values as fairness in pupils' everyday lives', and to ensure the implementation of such aims, the development of 'new' teaching and learning strategies such as cooperative group work is recommended. It is evident that PSE's focal concerns are almost identical to those of the Project.

Of course, it is recognized that such aims should infuse practice in all subjects in all classrooms and characterize 'good practice' in schools. In this sense, it seems entirely appropriate for PSE to be a cross-curricular theme. The problem is that the curriculum itself may be organized in a way which precludes the aims of PSE ever being realized. The reinforcement of old subject divisions is likely to be accompanied by the old stratification of school knowledge into high and low status subjects with the consequent stratification of both teachers and pupils (see Meighan, 1981). If perceptions of worth are determined by what subject you teach and how well you achieve in that subject, and teachers and pupils are hierarchically ordered, then the values of PSE will be undermined. This outcome is not inevitable because theoretically cross-curricular strategies and 'pastoral' work could involve a deliberate emphasis on countering the potentially divisive effects of the subject-based curriculum. However, the chance of such strategies being successful are slim, in our view. Under the new arrangements there will be very little time for teachers to do anything other than to become preoccupied with attainment targets and assessment. Primary school teachers are already finding that there are just not enough hours in the school day to cover all the ground in core and foundation subjects, even if subjects are integrated. Also, the two subjects — Maths and Science — which have traditionally been amongst the most prestigious, and retain this status as part of the 'core' of the National Curriculum, are precisely those subjects which lend themselves to a seemingly unavoidable differentiation of pupils according to 'ability', and have a track record of doing so in a way which is both demeaning and de-motivating for pupils. Whilst it is true that progressive practices are possible in these subjects, such practices have not actually been implemented to anything like the extent anti-progressives imagine. Progressive education is hostile to differentiation when it becomes central to the pupil experience and when it reinforces status hierarchies.

The other cross curricular theme of interest to us is special educational needs, which brings us back to the topic of integration. From an integrationist point of view the emphasis on pre-specified, hierarchically ordered objectives and regular, rigorous, formal and informal assessment procedures has predictable consequences. ERA prescribes a system of assessment in the various core and foundation subjects at 7, 11, 14 and 16 which will be based on the knowledge, skills and understanding expected of pupils at each stage and specified in some detail in statements of attainment defining up to ten levels of attainment, each level representing on average up to two years of progress. This will mean that children in the same class will be formally assessed as being at several different levels and progressing at different rates. Those classes in which pupils with special needs have been integrated will contain an even wider range of attainment levels. There is of course nothing new in this and schools have always accommodated by using flexible groupings and support teaching. But as Wedell (1988) suggests these forms of 'good practice' are likely to be curtailed by the way the requirements of the National Curriculum and its assessment are formulated. Given the new emphasis on publicly available information about a pupil's level of attainment and given the sheer amount of assessment that will have to be done, it seems likely that the most logical 'managerial' solution would be a return to some form of streaming (see Gipps, 1988; Swann, 1987), and possibly even to a situation where more children are placed in special schools. It seems almost inevitable that the integration policies heralded by the Warnock Report and the Education Act 1981 will be reversed.

However, the National Curriculum Council (NCC) has given its full support to the principle of maximum participation in the National Curriculum by all pupils with special educational needs and the minimal use of disapplication arrangements. Theoretically, therefore, the new curriculum could facilitate integrationist policies because pupils with special needs will be pursuing the same curricular objectives as all other children. Even special schools will have to review their curriculum to see to what extent they can deliver elements of the National Curriculum, and pupils in those schools being considered for integration will have a detailed record of attainment in the core and foundation subjects which will give a clear indication of their strengths and weaknesses and exactly where they could or could not fit into the curriculum in mainstream classes.

But even when the NC is not disapplied, pupils with special needs may find themselves in an 'integrated' school environment where there is in fact very little in the way of functional integration either for themselves or for other 'low ability' pupils or, for that matter, for any pupil. The NCC's definition of 'good practice' recognizes the necessity of meeting a diverse range of needs (see Circular No. 5), but these needs are defined in terms of the National Curriculum, thus involving an emphasis on categorization by level of attainment and rate of progress in the system. Many other pupils will therefore be in a similar position to those with special needs — on rungs of the attainment ladder 'looking up' to those just above — but there is not much consolation here for those who at the end of the day are going to end up permanently on the lowest rung.

As argued earlier, a 'whole school' policy towards integration requires the establishment of a climate that fosters sociality as well as catering for individual differences. Such a policy is not therefore solely concerned with the individualization of learning programmes enabling each pupil to progress at his or her own rate, but also with creating the conditions in which pupils recognize the value of working together with pupils of all abilities in all areas of the curriculum. The danger is that only lip service will be paid to the desirability of cooperative mixed ability group work, while the main thrust of policy implementation will be in the direction of making sure that individuals have the 'correct' programme, and where group work does occur it will involve grouping pupils by levels of attainment. According to the NCC in their circular (No. 3) on implementing the NC in primary schools, the fact that pupils will be working at several different levels within different subjects is such an important consideration when it comes to the organization of teaching and learning that 'the usual arrangement of classes needs to be re-examined'. It goes on rather ominously to suggest that although the issues are complex, 'the organization of classes by age may not in all circumstances be the most effective'. Not that this implies a move to vertical grouping as a progressive educator would understand it. The next sentence reads: 'Most teachers currently group pupils by levels of attainment for all or some parts of their work, particularly in mixed age classes as currently constituted.' Is an alternative constitution of classes by attainment level rather than age being envisaged, or some compromise involving a consideration of age and attainment level? Either way there is clearly a preoccupation with attainment level as the basis for the organization of teaching and learning under the new arrangements.

It is possible, of course, to argue that even without an emphasis on group work the assessment system could in theory be operated in a way that will make all pupils feel they are valued members of the school community. Thus an assessment system might be devised which differentiates children but which is not divisive. Such a system is difficult to create in the context of a National Curriculum where there is clearly not going to be parity of esteem between different forms of achievement. Nevertheless, if assessment were used to provide the feedback pupils require to help them learn, and if it were not always seen as a means of comparing them with other pupils, then pupils might retain confidence in their abilities even in relation to those forms of achievement where they recognize their own lack of talent.

It might be possible to establish such a system if all the recommendations of the TGAT report (1988) were implemented. It is widely known that this report places an emphasis on formative and criterion-referenced assessment and recommends that teacher assessment should be used as a fundamental component of the system. Overall assessment would be based on a combination of moderated teachers' ratings and 'standardized assessment tasks' (SATs: see Recommendations 11 and 14). The tasks themselves would involve a wide range of practical, oral and written tasks administered in a way that pupils would not regard as markedly different from normal classroom activities. Moreover, it is envisaged that the role of SATs will not be separate from the role of teacher assessment (TA). The TGAT report (para. 49) points out that the 'discontinuity between teachers' own assessments of normal classroom work and the use by them of externally provided tests need not be a sharp one'. Thus, material or tasks which are suitable for and proper to a SAT may well be useful within TA. Both must be designed to be used formatively and will be combined to provide each pupil with an overall assessment. It is possible that a SAT having been used as a formal test may become a resource for teaching, learning and assessing within TA. This incorporation of teachers into the process of developing assessment procedures and materials might enable the national assessment system to remain genuinely formative, but this would only happen if the teachers themselves had the time to implement it or were not continually under pressure to arrange pupils formally into a 'pecking order' for reasons of public communication.

Ideally, perhaps, teachers should have the time to consider how an assessment system might be developed which fitted in with a broader philosophy of education which emphasized pupils' successes rather than their failures and which took into account other forms of achievement in addition to those prescribed by the National Curriculum. Thus, perhaps, the kinds of practices developed in relation to Records of Achievement could form the basis for the national assessment system. An acceptable compromise may be Moon and Mortimore's (1989) proposal of a system of graded assessments which along with a personal statement, a school statement and examples of good work would make up the pupil's Record of Achievement.

However, doubts have been expressed as to whether a progressive form of assessment can ever be operated in a curriculum context where objectives are prescribed in such detail and which is so inflexible. Even before the days of the National Curriculum, there were problems about establishing 'good practice' in contexts where organizational constraints meant that pupils often ended up taking a test at a time and in a manner (e.g. group pencil and paper tests) which was convenient for the school rather than appropriate for them. We are inclined to agree with Broadfoot (1986) that innovations in assessment can only be successful if they are accompanied by radical changes in the organizational structures and underpinning cultural assumptions. Her conclusion is that even initiatives like graded assessment may well reinforce social divisions rather than reduce them in a situation where 'social justice [is] devalued into an associated rather than a prime goal' (*ibid.*, p. 222). Ultimately, therefore, teacher 'ownership' of assessment is not a sufficient guarantee of progressive practice. It is important that teachers themselves should recognize the importance of establishing an assessment system that is compatible with the notion that children should have an equal opportunity to receive a broad education based on a broader definition of achievement with different forms of achievement being recognized as of equal status.

However, there is a very real danger that a narrow testing programme establishing a 'pecking order' amongst pupils is what will eventually emerge. The difficulties posed by alternative approaches would be too problematical. According to Nuttall (1989) teachers will be under so much pressure there will not be the motivation to get the best out of the pupil. He describes the emergence of a 'monster of an external assessment system' where the progressive aspects like teacher assessment and moderation are increasingly de-emphasized because they are too complex to take into account. It is likely that aims like 'respect for persons' will be undermined by a national assessment policy which as Pring (1989) points out will 'in practice feed into the political arena in a manner which undermines the efforts to enhance the dignity of schools and of the children within them'. Experiences of testing using bench marks in a single national assessment in the United States have not been a success. The likelihood of misinformation is great because of the inherent problems of reliability and validity. Couple this with the inevitability of certain levels of performance being perceived as 'failure', and you have a recipe for deepening the alienation of pupils in schools.

The Education Reform Act seems unlikely to reform the structures and processes which create all the negative aspects of school life with which we have long been familiar: teachers who have low expectations of pupils, who 'explain' failure in terms of 'ability' or 'cultural deprivation' and who see no effective alternative to streaming pupils; and pupils who regard themselves as poor learners, who 'switch off', who are divided from their peers along 'ability' and also class, race and gender lines. It is more likely that we will witness the reproduction of a social and educational climate which exerts 'on many pupils, particularly but by no means exclusively from the working class, a destruction of their dignity which is so massive and pervasive that few subsequently recover from it' (Hargreaves, 1982, p. 17). Prejudice will not be challenged because genuine education will no longer be possible in schools. The latter could in fact become more than ever before a breeding ground for prejudice. We hope that this will not happen. As indicated earlier, the moral commitment of teachers and pupils gave us some hope for the future.

References

AINSCOW, M. and TWEDDLE, D. (1979) *Preventing Classroom Failure: An Objectives Approach*, London, Wiley.

ALDRICH, R. (1988) 'The National Curriculum: An Historical Perspective', in LAWTON, D. and CHITTY, C. *The National Curriculum*, Bedford Way, Papers 33, Institute of Education, University of London.

APPLE, M. W. (1983) 'Work, Class and Teaching', in WALKER, S. and BARTON, L. (Eds) *Gender, Class and Education*, Lewes, Falmer Press.

ARMISTED, N. (1974) *Reconstructing Social Psychology*, Harmondsworth, Penguin.

BAKER, K. (1987) *The National Curriculum: Key to Better Standards*, transcript of speech delivered at Manchester University on 17 September 1987, DES.

BAKER, J. L. and GOTTLIEB, J. (1980) 'Attitudes of Teachers Toward Mainstreaming Retarded Children', in GOTTLIEB, J. (Ed.) *Educating Mentally Retarded Persons in the Mainstream*, Baltimore, University Park Press.

BALCH, P. and PAULSEN, K. (1979) *Strategies for the Modification and Prevention of Racial Prejudice: A Review*, paper presented at the Annual Meeting of the Western Psychological Association, San Diego, California.

BALL, S. J. (1987) *The Micro-Politics of the School*, London, Methuen.

BANKS, J. A. (1981) *Education in the 80s: Multi-ethnic Education*, Washington, National Education Association.

BANKS, J. A. (1985) 'Reducing Prejudice in Students: Theory, Research and Strategies', in MOODLEY, K. (Ed.) *Race Relations and Multicultural Education*, Vancouver, BC: Centre for the Study of Curriculum and Instruction, University of British Columbia.

BARDSLEY, P. (1987) *The Perceptions of Some White Working Class Pupils in a School with an Anti-Racist Policy*, unpublished paper, presented at St Hilda's Conference on Equality and Ethnography.

BARTON, L. and TOMLINSON, S. (Eds) (1984) *Special Education and Social Interests*, Beckenham, Croom Helm.

BAYLEY, M. J. (1973) *Mental Handicap and Community Care*, London, Routledge and Kegan Paul.

BELL, L. A. (1980) 'The School as an Organization: a Re-appraisal', *British Journal of the Sociology of Education*, 1, 2, pp. 183–92.

BELL, R. E. and GRANT, N. (1974) *A Mythology of British Education*, London, Panther.

BENN, S. I. (1967) 'Egalitarianism and the Equal Consideration of Interests', in PENNOCK, J. R. and CHAPMAN, J. W. (Eds) *Nomos IX: Equality*, New York, Atherton Press.

BENNETT, C. (1984) 'Paints, Pots or Promotion', in BALL, S. J. and GOODSON, I. F. (Eds) *Teachers' Lives and Careers*, Lewes, Falmer Press.

BIDWELL, C. (1965) 'The School as a Formal Organization', in MARCH, J. F. (Ed.) *Handbook of Organizations*, Chicago, Rand-McNally.

BINES, H. (1988) 'Equality, Community and Individualism: The Development and Implementation of the "Whole School Approach" to Special Educational Needs', in BARTON, L. (Ed.) *The Politics of Special Educational Needs*, Lewes, Falmer Press.

BIOTT, C., LYNCH, J. and ROBERTSON, W. (1984) 'Supporting Teachers' Own Progress Towards Multicultural Education', *Multicultural Education*, 11, 2, pp. 39–41.

BOOTH, T. (1988) 'Challenging Conceptions of Integration', in BARTON, L. (Ed.) *The Politics of Special Educational Needs*, Lewes, Falmer Press.

BROADFOOT, P. (1986) 'Assessment Policy and Inequality: the United Kingdom Experience', *British Journal of Sociology of Education*, 7, 2, pp. 205–24.

BRUININKS, R. A., RYNDERS, J. E. and GROSS, J. A. (1974) 'Social Acceptance of Mildly Retarded Pupils in Resource Rooms and Regular Classes', *American Journal of Mental Deficiency*, 78, pp. 377–83.

BUDOFF, M. and SIPERSTEIN, G. N. (1978) 'Low Income Children's Attitudes Towards Mentally Retarded Children', *American Journal of Mental Deficiency*, 82, pp. 474–9.

BURGESS, R. (1984) *In the Field*, London, George, Allen and Unwin.

BURTON, T. A. and HIRSHOREN, A. (1979) 'The Education of Severely and Profoundly Retarded Children: Are We Sacrificing the Child to the Concept?' *Exceptional Children*, 45, pp. 598–602.

CARPENTER, B., FATHERS, J., LEWIS, A., and PRIVETT, R. (1988) 'Integration: The Coleshill Experience', *British Journal of Special Education*, 15, 3, pp. 119–21.

CARR, W. (1987) 'What Is an Educational Practice?', *Journal of Philosophy of Education*, 21, 2, pp. 163–75.

CARRINGTON, B. and SHORT, G. (1989) 'Policy or Presentation? The Psychology of Anti-racist Education', *New Community*, 15, 2, pp. 227–40.

CLARRICOATES, K. (1980) 'The Importance of Being Ernest...Emma... Tom...Jane. The Perception of Categorization of Gender Conformity and Gender Deviation in Primary Schools', in DEEM, R. *Schooling for Women's Work*, London, Routledge and Kegan Paul.

CLOUGH, P. (1988) 'Bridging the Gap between Mainstream and Special Provision: a Curricular Problem', *Journal of Curriculum Studies*, 20, 4.

COHEN, E. G. (1980) *A Multi-Ability Approach to the Integrated Classroom*, paper presented at the American Psychological Association, Montreal, Canada.

COHEN, P. and BAINS, H. (1988) *Multi-Racist Britain*, Basingstoke, MacMillan.

CURTIS, B. M. (1981) *The Need for Full Integration of Disabled Persons in Their Society*, in Report of the Fifth Schweitzer Memorial Seminar: International Aspects of Rehabilitation, Virginia, USA.

DALE, R. (1979) 'The Politicization of School Deviance: Reactions to William Tyndale', in BARTON, L. and MEIGHAN, R. (Eds) *Schools, Pupils and Deviance*, Driffield, Nafferton.

DALE, R. (1983) *Education, Training and Employment*, Milton Keynes, Open University Press.

DES/DEPARTMENT OF EMPLOYMENT (1986) *Joint White Paper: Working together — Education and Training* (Cmnd. 9823), London, HMSO.

DEPARTMENT OF EDUCATION AND SCIENCE (1989) *A Survey of Support Services for Special Educational Needs*, DES.

DHSS (1971) *Better Services for the Mentally Handicapped* (Cmnd. 4683) London, HMSO.

DOWNIE, R. S. (1985) 'Ambivalence of Attitude to the Mentally Retarded', in LAURA, R. S. and ASHMAN, A. *Moral Issues in Mental Retardation*, London, Croom Helm.

DUNN, L. M. (1968) 'Special Education for the Mildly Retarded: Is Much of it Justifiable?', *Exceptional Children*, 34, pp. 5–22.

EDGERTON, R. (1967) *The Cloak of Competence*, Berkeley, University of California Press.

EFRON, R. E. and EFRON, H. U. (1967) 'Measurement of Attitudes Towards the Retarded and an Application with Educators', *American Journal of Mental Deficiency*, 72, pp. 100–7.

ENTWISTLE, H. (1970) *Child-centred Education*, Methuen.

EVANS, B. and SIMMONS, K. (1987) 'Exercises in Integration', *British Journal of Special Education*, 14, 3, pp. 115–17.

EVERHART, R. (1983) *Reading, Writing and Resistance*, London, Routledge and Kegan Paul.

FROMM, E. (1949) *Man for Himself* (1971) London, Routledge and Kegan Paul.

FULLER, M. (1980) 'Black Girls in a London Comprehensive School', in DEEM, R. (Ed.) *Schooling for Women's Work*, London, Routledge and Kegan Paul.

GARRETT, H. E. (1963) *Statistics in Psychology and Education*, London, Longmans, Green and Co.

GIPPS, C. (1988) 'Marks out of 10', *The Times Educational Supplement*, 1 April, p. 18.

GOFFMAN, E. (1968) *Stigma*, Harmondsworth, Penguin.

GOODMAN, H. *et al.* (1972) 'Social Acceptance of EMRs Integrated into Non-graded Elementary School', *American Journal of Mental Deficiency* 76, pp. 412–17.

GOTTLIEB, J. (1974) 'Attitudes Toward Retarded Children: Effects of Labelling and Academic Performance', *American Journal of Mental Deficiency*, 79, pp. 268–73.

GOTTLIEB, J. (1975) 'Public, Peer and Professional Attitudes Toward Mentally Retarded Persons', in BEGAB, M. J. and RICHARDSON, S. A. (Ed.) *The Mentally Retarded and Society*, Baltimore University Press.

HAMMERSLEY, M. (1977) *Teacher Perspectives E202: Schooling and Society* (Units 9 and 10), Milton Keynes, Open University Press.

HARGREAVES, A. (1989) *Curriculum and Assessment Reform*, Milton Keynes, Open University Press.

HARGREAVES, D., HESTER, S. K. and MELLOR, F. J. (1975) *Deviance in Classrooms*, London, Routledge and Kegan Paul.

HARGREAVES, D. (1982) *The Challenge for the Comprehensive School*, London, Routledge and Kegan Paul.

HARGREAVES, D. (1987) 'Getting the Mixture Right', *The Times Educational Supplement*, 11 September, p. 4.

HATTON, E. J. (1989) 'Equality, Class and Power: A Case Study', *British Journal of Sociology of Education*, 6, 3, pp. 255–72.

HEGARTY, S. and POCKLINGTON, K. (1981) *Educating Pupils with Special Needs in the Ordinary School*, Slough, NFER-Nelson.

HOLT, M. (1987) *Judgement, Planning and Educational Change*, London, Harper and Row.

HORNE, M. D. (1985) *Attitudes Toward Handicapped Students*, New Jersey, Lawrence Erlbaum Associates Inc.

HOYLE, E. (1980) 'Professionalization and Deprofessionalization in Education', in HOYLE, E. and MEGARRY, J. (Eds) *World Yearbook of Education, 1980: Professional Development of Teachers*, London, Kogan Page.

JACKSON, M. (1987) 'Core Studies "Must Allow for TVEI"', *The Times Educational Supplement*, 16 October, p. 15.

JEFFCOATE, R. (1979) *Positive Image: Towards a Multicultural Curriculum*, London, Writers and Readers Cooperative.

JOHNSON, D. W. (1981), 'Student–Student Interaction: The Neglected Variable in Education', *Educational Researcher*, 10, pp. 5–10.

JONES, R. L. (1972) 'Labels and Stigma in Special Education', *Exceptional Children*, 38, pp. 553–64.

KEHOE, J. (1984) *Achieving Cultural Diversity in Canadian Schools*, Cornwall, Ontario, Vesta Publications.

KLEIN, G. (1982) *Resources for Multicultural Education: An Introduction*, London, Longman/Schools Council.

KLEINIG, J. (1982) *Philosophical Issues in Education*, London, Croom Helm.

KRACHAI, J. (1987) 'Towards a Modularized Curriculum' in NIXON, J. (Ed.) *Curriculum Change: The Sheffield Experience*, University of Sheffield, Division of Education.

KUTNER, B. (1971) 'The Social Psychology of Disability', in NEFF, W. S. (Ed.) *Rehabilitation Psychology*, Washington, American Psychological Association.

LAIR, C. V. and SAUSER, W. I. (1981) 'Attitudes of Ordinary Pupils Towards Those with Special Needs', in HEGARTY and POCKLINGTON, *op. cit.*

LAMBART, A. M. (1976) 'The Sisterhood', in HAMMERSLEY, M. and WOODS, P. (Eds) *The Process of Schooling*, London, Routledge and Kegan Paul.

LEIGHTON, A. (1988) *Mental Handicap in the Community*, Cambridge, Woodhead-Faulkner.

LYNCH, J. (1987) *Prejudice Reduction and the Schools*, London, Cassell.

McCORMACK, M. (1978) *A Mentally Handicapped Child in the Family: a guide for parents*, London, Constable.

McCORMICK, R. and JAMES, M. (1983) *Curriculum Evaluation in Schools*, London, Croom Helm.

MacINTYRE, A. C. (1981) *After Virtue: A Study in Moral Theory*, London, Duckworth.

MARSH, P., ROSSER, E. and HARRE, R. (1978) *The Rules of Disorder*, London, Routledge and Kegan Paul.

MEASOR, L. and WOODS, P. (1984) *Changing Schools*, Milton Keynes, Open University Press.

MEIGHAN, R. (1981) *A Sociology of Educating*, London, Holt, Rinehart and Winston.

MENCAP (1982) *Public Attitudes Towards the Mentally Handicapped*, London, MENCAP.

MILES, M. (1981) *Attitudes Towards Persons with Disabilities*, Peshawar (Pakistan), Mental Health Centre.

MOON, B. and MORTIMORE, P. (1989) *The National Curriculum: Straitjacket or Safety Net*, London, Education Reform Group, Ginger Paper Five.

MOORE, J. and FINE, M. J. (1978) 'Regular and Special Class Teachers' Perceptions of Normal and Exceptional Children and Their Attitudes Towards Mainstreaming', *Psychology in the Schools*, 15, 2, pp. 253–9.

NATIONAL CURRICULUM COUNCIL (1989) *Implementing the National Curriculum in Primary Schools*, Circular No. 3.

NATIONAL CURRICULUM COUNCIL (1989) *Implementing the National Curriculum — Participation by Pupils with Special Educational Needs*, Circular No. 5.

NEWMAN, F. M. and RUTTER, R. A. (1983) *Effects of High Street Community Service Programmes on Students' Social Development*, Washington DC, National Institute of Education (Research Report).

NIAS, J. (1981) 'Teacher Satisfaction and Dissatisfaction: Herzbeg's Two-Factor Hypothesis Revisited', *British Journal of Sociology of Education*, 3, pp. 235–46.

NIXON, J. (1989) 'What is Evaluation after the MSC?', *British Journal of Education Studies*, 37, 2, pp. 125–35.

NUTTALL, D. (1989) 'Test "Monster" Must be Killed', *The Times Educational Supplement*, 10 April.

OLIVER, M. (1985) 'The Integration–Segregation Debate: Some Sociological Considerations', *British Journal of the Sociology of Education*, 6, 1, pp. 75–92.

PAGE, A. and THOMAS, K. (1984) *Multicultural Education and the All-White School*, Nottingham, University of Nottingham, School of Education.

PARLETT, M. and HAMILTON, D. (1972) *Evaluation as Illumination: A New Approach to the Study of Innovatory Programmes*, Occasional Paper 9, Centre for Research in the Educational Services, University of Edinburgh.

PHILLIPS, D. C. and KELLY, M. E. (1975) 'Hierarchical Theories of Development in Education and Psychology', *Harvard Education Review*, 45, pp. 351–75.

POLLARD, A., PURVIS, J. and WALFORD, G. (1988) *Education Training and the New Vocationalism*, Milton Keynes, Open University Press.

POPPLETON, P., DEAS, R., PULLIN, R. and THOMPSON, D. (1987) 'The Experience of Teaching in "Disadvantaged" Areas in the United Kingdom and the USA', *Comparative Education*, 23, 3, pp. 303–15.

POPPLETON, P. (1988) 'Teacher Professional Satisfaction: Its Implications for Secondary Education and Teacher Education', *Cambridge Journal of Education*, 18, 1, pp. 5–16.

PRING, R. (1989) 'Social Economics', *The Times Educational Supplement*, 2, June, p. B13.

QUICKE, J. C. (1985) 'Teaching About Disability in Secondary Schools', *British Journal of Special Education*, 12, pp. 121–2.

QUICKE, J. C. (1985) *Disability in Modern Children's Fiction*, London, Croom Helm.

QUICKE, J. C. (1986) 'Pupil Culture, Peer Tutoring and Special Educational Needs', *Disability, Handicap and Society*, 1, 2, pp. 147–64.

QUICKE, J. C. (1987) 'The Disability Curriculum', *Pastoral Care in Education*, 5, 2, pp. 114–22.

QUICKE, J. C. (1987) 'Who's Inside the Wooden Horse? The Role of Pastoral Care in Curriculum Change', in BOOTH, T. and COULBY, D. *Producing and Reducing Disaffection*, Milton Keynes, Open University Press.

QUICKE, J. C. (1989) 'Mental Handicap Awareness and Gender Relations in a Comprehensive School', in BINES, H. and ROAF, C., *Needs, Rights and Opportunities: Developing Approaches to Special Education*, Lewes, Falmer Press.

QUICKE, J. C., BEASLEY, K. and ALLEN, C. (1989) *Challenging Prejudice through Education*, unpublished report.

RAWLS, J. (1971) *Theory of Justice*, Cambridge, Mass, Harvard University Press.

RISEBOROUGH, G. F. (1986) *'Know-alls', 'Whizz Kids', 'Dead Wood' and the Crisis of School*, paper presented at BERA Annual Conference.

ROSE, C. D. (1981) 'Social Integration of School Age ESN(S) Children in a Regular School', *Special Education: Forward Trends*, 8, 4 (Research Supplement), pp. 17–22.

ROTH, J. (1977) 'A Yank in the NHS', in DAVIS, A. and HOROBIN, G. (Eds) *Medical Encounters*, London, Croom Helm, pp. 96–7.

RUDDUCK, J. (1979) *Learning to Teach Through Group Discussion*, Norwich, Centre for Applied Research in Education.

RUDDUCK, J. and WILCOX, B. (1988) 'Issues of Ownership and Partnership in School-centred Innovation: the Sheffield Experience', *Research Papers in Education*, 3, 3, pp. 157–79.

RYAN, J. and THOMAS, F. (1980) *The Politics of Mental Handicap*, Harmondsworth, Penguin.

SALMON, P. and CLAIRE, H. (1984) *Classroom Collaboration*, London, Routledge and Kegan Paul.

SANDBERG, L. D. (1982) 'Attitudes of Nonhandicapped Elementary School Students Toward School-aged Trainable Mentally Retarded Students', *Education and Training of the Mentally Retarded*, 17, pp. 30–34.

SCHWAB, J. J. (1978) in WESTBURY, I. and WILKOF, N. (Eds) *Science, Community and Liberal Education*, University of Chicago Press.

SCULL, A. (1977) *Decarceration: Community Treatment and the Deviant*, Englewood Cliffs, NJ, Prentice Hall.

SCULL, A. T. (1979) *Museums of Madness*, Harmondsworth, Penguin.

SHARP, R. and GREEN, A. (1975) *Education and Social Control*, London, Routledge and Kegan Paul.

SHEARER, A. (1981) *Disability: Whose Handicap?*, Oxford, Basil Blackwell.

STENHOUSE, L., VERMA, G. and WILD, R. (Eds) (1982) *Teaching About Race Relations: Problems and Effects*, London, Routledge and Kegan Paul.

STEPHAN, W. G. and BRIGHAM, J. C. (1985) 'Intergroup Contact: Introduction', *Journal of Social Issues*, 41, 3, pp. 1–8.

STEPHAN, W. G. (1985) 'Intergroup Relations', in LINDSEY, G. and ARONSON, E. (Eds) *The Handbook of Social Psychology*, New York, Random House.

SUTHERLAND, G. (1981) 'The Origins of Special Education', in SWANN, W. (Ed.) *The Practice of Special Education*, Milton Keynes, Open University Press.

SWANN, W. (1987) 'The Educational Consequences of Mr Baker', *Special Children*, 13, pp. 18–19.

SWANN, W. (1989) *Integration Statistics — LEA, Reveal local variations*, London, Centre for Studies on Integration in Education.

TASK GROUP ON ASSESSMENT AND TESTING (TGAT) (1988), DES.

TATTUM, D. (1982) *Disruptive Pupils in Schools and Units*, Chichester, Wiley.

TAYLOR, S. J. and BOGDAN, R. (1989) 'On Accepting Relationships between People with Mental Retardation and Non-disabled People: Towards an Understanding of Acceptance', *Disability, Handicap and Society*, 4, 1, pp. 21–36.

THOMAS, D. (1978) *The Social Psychology of Childhood Disability*, London, Methuen.

THOMAS, D. (1982) *The Experience of Handicap*, London, Methuen.

TOMLINSON, S. (1982) *The Sociology of Special Education*, London, Routledge and Kegan Paul.

TRINGO, J. L. (1970) 'The Hierarchy of Preference Towards Disability Groups', *Journal of Special Education*, 4, 3, p. 295.

TURNER, G. (1983) *The Social World of the Comprehensive School*, London, Croom Helm.

TWITCHEN, J. and DEMUTH, S. (1985) *Multicultural Education* (2nd edn), London, British Broadcasting Corporation.

VOELTZ, L. M. (1980) 'Children's Attitudes Toward Handicapped Peers', *American Journal of Mental Deficiency*, 84, 5, pp. 455–64.

WARNOCK REPORT (1978) *Report of the Committee of Enquiry into the Education of Handicapped Children and Young People*, London, HMSO.

WEDELL, K. (1988) 'The New Act: A Special Need for Vigilance', *British Journal of Special Education*, 15, 3, pp. 98–101.

WEIR, S. (1981) 'Our Image of the Disabled and How Ready We Are to Help', *New Society*, 1 January, pp. 7–9.

WILLIAMSON, D. (1979) 'Integration and PE', in GROVES, I. (Ed.) *PE for Special Needs*, Cambridge University Press.

WILLIS, P. (1977) *Learning to Labour*, London, Saxon House.

WILKINS, J. E. and VELICER, W. F. (1980) 'A Semantic Differential Investigation of Children's Attitudes Toward Three Stigmatized Groups', *Psychology in the Schools*, 17, pp. 364–71.

WOODS, P. (1983) *Sociology and the School*, London, Routledge and Kegan Paul.

Index

access, 94
active learning, 6
actors in residence, 76
advocacy, 62
Ainscow, M., 28
Aldrich, R., 175
alienation, 9, 10, 182
Allen, C., 114
anti-racism, 21, 45, 127
anti-sexism, 21, 45
Apple, M. W., 19
Armisted, N., 33
asylums, 22, 23
attitudes: ambivalent 28–30; negative, 105, 106; positive, 105, 106; pupils, 31–33 (see also pupils): to disability, 105, 106 (see also teachers)
autobiography, 148, 149
autonomy, 7, 8, 18, 38
awareness, 76, 117, 168

Baker, J. L., 34
Baker, K., 176
Balch, P., 10
Ball, S., 12, 147
Banks, J. A., 8, 11
Bardsley, P., 127
Barton, L., 30
Bayley, M. J., 27
Beasley, K., 114
Bell, R. E., 33
Bennett, C., 19
Better Services for the Mentally Handicapped (1971), 26
Bines, H., 36, 37
Biott, C., 44

Bogdan, R., 108
Booth, T., 36
Brigham, J. C., 46, 162
Broadfoot, P., 176, 181
Bruininks, R. A., 31
Budoff, M., 31
Burgess, R., 45
Burton, T. A., 31

Carpenter, R., 28
Carr, W., 13
Carrington, B., 5
change, 11–13
child-centred approach, 7, 69–80, 163
Clarricoates, K., 33
Clough, P., 43
Cohen, E. G., 6
Cohen, P., 127
Coleshill Project, 28
collaborative group work, 37, 38, 62, 179
community, 18, 66, 108, 162, 169; care, 26, 27; involvement, 66, 71
competitive individualism, 10, 37
computer activity, 136, 137
conflict, 14
contradictions, 148
counter-productive, 169
criterion-referenced, 180
critical reflection, 6, 38, 164
cross curricular, 42, 173, 176, 178
cultural deprivation, 182
cultural meanings, 31 (see also pupils)

Dale, R., 18, 40
dance, 85

dangerous classes, 23, 24
deficit model, 7
degeneracy theory, 24
Demuth, S., 6
determinism, 29, 30
deviance, 35
didacticism, 6, 10, 46, 173
differentiation, 32, 178
disability, 5, 30, 34
disapplication, 179
discourse, 21
'dossers', 31
Downie, R. S., 29
Down's children, 28
drama, 62, 77, 85
Dunn, L. M., 31

Education Act (1970), 26
Education Act (1981), 26, 179
education for all, 11, 172
Education Reform Act, 173, 175–82
Efron, H. V., 34
Efron, R. E., 34
Egerton Commission (1889), 24
empathy, 29, 171
Entwistle, H., 7
equality, 5, 36, 41, 175, 181
ethnography, 31
eugenics movements, 24
evaluation, 45, 161–173
Evans, B., 32, 33
Everhart, R., 32
experiential learning, 6

Fabian, 25
feebleminded, 24
Fine, M. J., 34
formal culture, 171
formative assessment, 180
Forster's Education Act (1870), 24
Fromm, E., 16

GCSE, 56, 146
gender, 32, 33, 37, 92, 130, 132, 135–6, 170
Gipps, C., 178
'good education', 5
Goodman, H., 33, 105
Gottlieb, J., 31, 34
graded assessment, 181
Grant, N., 33
Green, A., 35

Hamilton, D., 161
Hammersley, M., 13, 147
Hargreaves, A., 10
Hargreaves, D., 9, 35, 176, 182
Harré, R., 16
Hatton, E. J., 18
Hegarty, S., 34
hidden curriculum, 9, 17, 35, 41
Hirshoren, A., 31
historical determination, 8
Holt, M., 11, 12
Horne, M. D., 32, 34
Hoyle, E., 160
humanitarianism, 5, 21–5, 26, 28, 29, 30, 35
humanities, 82–5, 164

idiots, 22, 23, 26
Idiots Act (1886), 23
imbeciles, 24
individual differences, 179
individualization, 37, 179
integration (see special needs)
intensification, 19
interests, 22, 30 (see also teachers and pupils)
inter-group contact, 46, 55–68, 162–3
interview study, 128–143
Itard, 22

James, M., 106, 161
Jeffcoate, R., 6
Jones, R. L., 31

Kehoe, J., 6
Klein, G., 6
Kleinig, J., 9, 15
Krachai, J., 41
Kutner, B., 31

labelling, 9, 26, 34, 35, 45, 47, 51, 63
Labour Party, 151
Lair, C. V., 34
Leighton, A., 29
liberal education, 40
Lower Attaining Pupils Project (LAPP), 40, 173
lunacy, 23
Lynch, J., 6, 8, 44, 122

MacIntyre, A. C., 7, 8, 14
Makaton, 85

Manpower Services Commission, (MSC), 40, 176
Marsh, P., 16
McCormick, R., 106, 161
Measor, L., 31
Meighan, R., 177
MENCAP, 28, 42, 43, 100
Mental Deficiency Act (1913), 25
mental handicap, 21–37; attitudes towards, 23, 28–30, 34; and deviance, 47; and labelling, 9, 25 (see also labelling)
Mental Health Foundation, 100
micro-politics, 13, 19, 45, 46
Miles, M., 106
mixed ability, 145, 146, 173, 179
moderate learning difficulties, 145
module, 62–6; in humanities, 81–8
modularization, 40, 41, 173
Moon, B., 181
Moore, J., 34
moral agents, 6, 12, 30, 38
moral community, 5, 7, 10
moral conflict, 171
moral judgement, 106 (see also teachers)
moral reasoning, 8, 38, 115
moral sensitivity, 9–10, 45
moral treatment, 23
Mortimore, P., 181
multicultural, 21, 45

National Assessment System, 167, 178, 180–1
National Association for the Care and Control of the Feebleminded, 24
National Curriculum, 167, 173, 175, 176, 178
National Curriculum Council, 179
negotiation, 94–5
Newman, F. M., 6
new vocationalism, 40, 177
Nias, J., 148
Nicholson, B., 176
Nixon, J., 40, 45
norm-referenced, 41
novitiates, 15
Nuttall, D., 182

objectivity, 99
Oliver, M., 27
ownership (see teachers)

Page, A., 6

paradigmatic concerns (see teachers)
Parlett, M., 161
Paulsen, K., 10
'pecking order', 181
personal and social education, 42, 145, 177
physical disability, 28, 34
Pring, R., 182
Pocklington, K., 34
Pollard, A., 40
Poppleton, P., 15, 160
practice, education as, 13
pragmatic concerns (see teachers)
prejudice: and education, 5–10; and the Education Reform Act, 175–82
pre-specified objectives, 161
progressive, 14, 166, 173, 175, 176, 178
pupils: alienation, 9; attitudes to handicap, 170; attitudes to school, 138; boys' perceptions, 170; conformists, 31; conservatism, 37; cultural meanings, 127–43, 162; deviant, 31, 35; 'dossers', 31; experiences and images of handicap, 73–4, 108–10, 130–1, 133–4; feelings about mental handicap, 111; girls' perceptions, 170; ideological concerns, 16; integration, 111–14, 138, 139; interests, 16–18; judgements, 6, 8, 38; knowledge of mental handicap, 110; language, 74, 140, 141; as moral agent, 6, 38; as moral critic, 17; picking on, 74; progress, 105–26; resistance, 17; responses to project, 80; stereotypes, 31; as strategic actor, 17; swots, 31; views on project, 79

questionnaire study, 106–26
Quicke, J. C., 6, 9, 32, 46, 127, 147, 170

race, 37, 182
racial prejudice, 6, 11
racism, 6
Rawls, J., 30
Records of Achievement, 40, 181
reform, 5, 11, 15, 17, 21, 22, 25
reproduction, 182
resistance, 127
respect for persons, 9, 16, 29, 47, 175, 182
Revised Code, 24
'ripple effect', 78
Riseborough, G., 15, 160

Robertson, W., 44
role of researcher, 89–104
Rose, C. D., 33, 105
Rosser, E., 16
Roth, J., 33
Rudduck, J., 6, 42, 45
Rutter, R. A., 6
Ryan, J., 23

Salmon, P., 37
Sandberg, L. D., 32
Sauser, W. I., 34
School Focused Secondment, (SFS) 56, 142, 145
Schwab, J. J., 12
Scull, A., 23, 26
Seguin, 22
severe learning difficulties, 28, 31, 32, 34, 36, 148
Sharp, R., 35
Shearer, A., 25
Sheffield Curriculum Initiative, (SCI), 39
Short, G., 5
Simmons, K., 32, 33
Siperstein, G. N., 31
Social Darwinism, 24
sociality, 37, 179
social justice, 5
special needs: integration, 26, 27, 32, 34, 35–8, 42, 178, 179; support services, 27; (see also whole school approaches)
standardized assessment tasks (SATS), 180
Stenhouse, L., 11
Stephan, W. G., 6, 46, 162
stereotypes, 34, 35, 108, 146, 173 (see pupils)
strategies, teaching and learning, 6–9, 46–54
stratification, 177
Sutherland, G., 24
Swann, W., 27, 178
'swots', 31
systems model, 12

Task Group on Assessment and Testing (TGAT), 180
Tattum, D., 17
Taylor, S. J., 108
'teacher assessment', 180, 181, 182

teachers: career, 19; commitment, 13, 14, 145–60, 174; and handicap, 44; ideology, 13, 14; interests, 13–16; judgements, 45; knowledge of mental handicap, 44; as moral agents, 12; motivation, 162, 166; novitiates, 15; ownership, 5, 12, 16, 18, 41, 72, 148, 162, 165, 166, 169, 181; paradigmatic concerns, 147; perceptions, 34–5, political beliefs, 151; pragmatic concerns, 147; religious beliefs, 152; special school, 65, 66; veterans, 15; views on integration, 150, 157; worries, 157, 158
teaching about mental handicap in secondary schools, 8, 162, 173
teaching strategies, 6–8, 41, 46–54, 163, 164, 177
teaching styles, 40
team work, 169
Technical and Vocational Education Initiative (TVEI), 40, 173, 176, 177
theatre in education, 62
Thomas, D., 32, 105
Thomas, F., 23
Thomas, K., 6
Tomlinson, S., 22, 24, 30
tradition, 7, 8, 21
traditional curriculum, 10, 17, 175
Tringo, J. L., 34
Turner, G., 31
TVEI-related In-service Training (TRIST), 40, 173
Tweddle, D., 28
Twitchen, J., 6
typifications, 35

value dilemma, 6, 171
values-driven, 15, 148, 167
Velicer, W. F., 32
Verma, G., 11
vertical grouping, 180
veterans, 15 (see teachers)
video, 62
virtues, 10
Voeltz, L. M., 31, 32

warehousing, 27
Warnock Report (1978), 26, 179
Wedell, K., 178
Weir, S., 28

Welcome Home Jelly Bean, 44, 67, 72, 136
'whole school' policies, 5, 8, 11, 12, 27, 36, 37, 38, 155, 179
Wilcox, B., 42, 45
Wild, R., 11
Wilkins, J. E., 32

Williamson, D., 32, 105
Willis, P., 31
Woods, P., 31, 32
workhouse, 23
working class, 10, 25, 182
'Working Together – Education and Training' (1986), 176